Bhāratīya Mānas Śāstra

INDICA

Bhāratīya Mānas Śāstra

PROF. MALA KAPADIA

INDICA

IA

Published by Indica

ISBN 978-1-97045-202-0

Bhāratīya Mānas Śāstra is dedicated to

- the Guru Paramparā
- all who have contributed to creating this knowledge
- Smt. Indumati Tai Katdare, without whose inspiration these pages would have remained mere scribbled notes
- INDICA, for introducing the Indic Psychology Courses, and
- all my learners, who have encouraged me to continue this journey

Contents

Foreword *9*
Preface *13*
Introduction – Bhūmikā *15*

Chapter 01 Involution & Cosmology 25

Chapter 02 Mānas – The Important Link to Wellbeing and Happiness 57

Chapter 03 Hṛdaya – The Centre of Our Existence 83

Chapter 04 Beyond Traits, Types, and Temperament – Svabhāva 113

Chapter 05 Citta and Citta Vṛttis, Yama and Niyama 135

Chapter 06 Science of Aesthetics and Psychology 155

Chapter 07 Future Frontiers of Bhāratīya Mānas Śāstra 181

Appendix 1 .... *185*
Appendix 2 .... *196*
Appendix 3 .... *223*
Appendix 4 .... *247*

Foreword

The 21st century is marked by unprecedented transformations in all spheres of human life. Rapid technological advancement, shifting social values, and reimagined political orders have not only changed the way we live but also how we think. As cultures evolve and encounter one another more intensively, long-held assumptions about human nature, society, and well-being are being re-examined. One of the domains where this reflection has become particularly urgent is psychology, the modern science about the nature of human beings.

Psychology, as it developed in the West, was deeply shaped by specific historical, cultural, philosophical and theological contexts. It emerged from European intellectual traditions and took root globally through institutions established during colonial expansion. As a result, most of the psychological theories today continue to reflect the experience of singular cultural lineage. While modern psychology has grown into a vast, multidisciplinary field that includes experimental, behavioral, developmental, cognitive, and evolutionary branches, the question remains: how universal are its foundational concepts?

This is not an idle or academic query. Around the world, we observe growing mental health crises, social unrest, and existential dissatisfaction. Despite the scientific sophistication of contemporary psychology, it often struggles to address the deeply rooted issues individuals and communities face. One reason may lie in its limited cultural grounding. When a discipline seeks to understand human beings but draws its core assumptions from one culture's experience, it risks not only overlooking other ways of being, feeling, and knowing but also appears inadequate to solve human problems across cultures.

It is in this context that Bhāratīya Mānasaśāstra, or Indian psychology, assumes urgent relevance. Indian traditions have, for millennia, engaged in a profound inquiry into the nature of the human being. Texts from Sāṃkhya, Vedānta, Yoga, Āyurveda, and other śāstras reflect elaborate models of the mind, emotion, behavior, and well-being. These systems were not merely speculative. They were practical, experiential, and designed to help individuals navigate the complexities of life toward a state of ānanda, a permanent state of living in happiness and flourishing.

In recent decades, a small but growing number of scholars, practitioners, and educators have begun to revisit these traditions seriously. Rather than romanticizing them or treating them as artifacts of the past, they are asking how these reflections from diverse Indian traditions can contribute to a deeper and more culturally rooted, yet universally applicable understanding of human psychology today.

Dr. Mala Kapadia's work, Bhāratīya Mānasaśāstra, is a significant and thoughtful step in this direction. It does not claim to be a comprehensive system, nor does it pretend to offer final answers. What it does is open a much-needed space for conversation. This book invites readers to consider what it means to reflect on manas, buddhi, ahaṃkāra, and citta, not merely as Sanskrit terms but as living ideas with explanatory power.

One of the strengths of Dr. Kapadia's approach is her careful attention to translation and interpretation. Rather than forcing equivalence between Indian and Western concepts, for instance, mapping manas directly onto "mind" or ahaṃkāra onto "ego", she acknowledges the incommensurability that exists. These Indian categories are part of a different way of experience and making sense of the world, one in which the pursuit of adhyātma, is central to understanding human life.

In Indian culture, terms like prakṛti, uṣṇa, śīta, kapha, and pitta are still used by everyday people to describe moods, constitutions, and tendencies. In therapeutic settings, expressions like cittaśuddhi or manakleśa arise organically. Yet, when professionals trained only in Western psychology encounter such vocabulary, they may lack the conceptual framework to engage meaningfully with these experiences. The result is a gap, not of science or evidence, but of language, culture, and framework.

The purpose of Bhāratīya Mānasaśāstra is not to discard modern psychology, but to complement and enrich it. In doing so, it challenges us to rethink our assumptions. Is the psyche a universal idea? Can we meaningfully discuss psychological well-being without acknowledging cultural differences in cognition, perception, emotion, and selfhood? What happens when we ignore the deeply integrated nature of mind, body, and consciousness, as Indian traditions have long affirmed?

To answer these questions, this book draws from multiple śāstric streams such as Sāṃkhya for its ontology, Vedānta for its metaphysics, Āyurveda for its physiological and psychological typologies, and Yoga for its sādhanā-based approach to transformation. These systems are not isolated silos. Rather, they are intertwined in the Indian tradition, forming a holistic and dynamic understanding of the human being. Concepts like triguṇa and tridoṣa help explain the diversity of psychological tendencies, while faculties such as jñānendriya and karmendriya highlight the interaction between perception and action.

Equally important is the discussion of hṛdaya. In Western science, the heart is often seen as a physical organ. In Indian traditions, hṛdaya plays a crucial role as the seat of consciousness, intuition, and moral discernment. Such differences go beyond translation. They reflect fundamentally different ways of knowing and being.

Dr. Kapadia does not reduce these ideas into neat psychological tools. She resists the urge to create psychometric scales or simplistic experimental designs. Her approach is one of patient and principled enquiry. She attempts to articulate a conceptual language that can connect the Indian and the Western ideas, without compromising either. She brings to this task her training, her professional experience, and her lived relationship with the traditions she draws from.

The questions this book raises are as important as the answers it offers. Is manas equivalent to mind? Can ahaṃkāra be understood through the lens of ego? What does it mean to speak of adhyātmavidyā as a science?

How can we train future psychologists who are attuned to cultural difference, not just as context, but as content?

We must not dismiss these reflections as nostalgic or patriotic appropriations. Knowledge systems are part of our shared human heritage. Just as Indian mathematics, linguistics, and medicine have made enduring contributions to global knowledge, so too can Indian conceptions of the self, the mind, and the path to flourishing. These are not "Indian" in a narrow nationalistic sense. They are Indian in origin, but potentially universal in relevance.

This foreword is not a declaration of finality. It is an invitation. The work of articulating a culturally grounded, theoretically rigorous, and practically useful Indian psychology has only just begun. That effort must be collective. Scholars of philosophy, linguistics, neuroscience, education, and medicine must join the conversation. So must practitioners, teachers, caregivers, and all those who care about the well-being of people, not in abstraction, but in their lived, embodied, cultural contexts.

The goal is not simply to revive Bhāratīya Mānasaśāstra for India's sake. It is to ask how we can draw upon this deep well of thought to enrich our understanding of human life, wherever it is lived. In a world seeking more integrative, meaningful, and compassionate approaches to mental health and well-being, this tradition has much to offer.

Let us read this work with the openness it deserves. Let us question it critically, engage, and build upon it. And let us recognise that in this effort, we are not merely reclaiming the past. We are shaping the future of psychology and our reflection of human well-being flourishing itself.

Prof. M. S. Chaitra
Director & Senior Fellow
Foundation for Study of Indian Culture
Bengaluru

Preface

Oṁ Gurubhyo Namaḥ

I bow down to the Guru Paramparā and the Bhāratīya Jñāna Paramparā, as this work is only a drop in the vast ocean of wisdom.

Why I was one of the chosen ones to integrate Psychology and Āyurveda-Yoga, I still have no answers. However, the journey has been very fulfilling, though the path was difficult.

The curriculum of Psychology at a College in Mumbai, where I studied, was a colonial construct, devoid of the culture-specific and rich wisdom of Bhārat. After graduation, I had decided never to study Psychology again. This was in 1979. However, my journey through M.A. & Ph.D. in regional literature gave me a better understanding of Psychology. In 1995, Daniel Goleman's book *Emotional Intelligence* became popular. On reading *Families of Emotions* within the book, I was reminded of Nāṭya Śāstra and thought of writing a book on Emotional Intelligence with Indic perspectives. *Heart Skills: Emotional Intelligence for Life and Work* was published in 2003 and later in 2009.

During my research on Emotional intelligence, Āyurveda and Yoga opened up their vast canvas of knowledge and wisdom. A Diploma in Āyurveda and Yoga from Tilak Maharashtra Vidyapeeth helped me to dive into the ocean to discover pearls that are now chapters in this book.

I started writing in 2022, and INDICA introduced a course on the same theme. However, for various personal reasons, the final version of the book is ready only now, in 2025. Indumati Tai has been a great inspiration for me to complete this book. Her trust in me kept me going through the research and writing.

Today the world is suffering from a pandemic of ill health at both the physical and psychological levels. Bhāratīya Jñāna Paramparā had made us *Viśva Guru,* enabling us to participate in the evolution of humanity and contribute to universal well-being and happiness. Our intention has always been: *Sarve Bhavantu Sukhinaḥ, Sarve Santu Nirāmayāḥ*.

May this book guide and inspire younger generations to take this work forward.

Astu

Introduction – Bhūmikā

We, as humanity, have searched for happiness, health, and meaning for millennia. My own search for a deeper understanding of what Life is and who I am has led to research, reflection, and the synthesis of various disciplines. This work is the result of my journey from ignorance to the light of knowledge. It is difficult to capture the entire journey and how the dots connected to reveal the larger picture; however, explaining the *why*, *what,* and *how* of this work will create a foundation. There are many who have walked this path before me. Their work, along with personal interactions with some contemporaries, has helped immensely in the synthesis of this book. I was introduced to Indian Psychology as Integral Yoga through the works of Sri Aurobindo and The Mother at a very early age in school, by my Sanskrit teacher Jayashree Bhat. This created the desire to go deeper, and I chose Psychology as my major subject in graduation, only to be disillusioned by the American textbook-based curriculum. The path to understanding human psyche led me to study literature, and later, Human Resources and Management. The quest continued through deeper explorations of Āyurveda and Yoga, as they seemed to be sciences that integrate the wisdom of Life. Today, when I look back, all the dots connect, leading to this work. The *why* of my search led not only to a paradigm shift but also a U-turn – back to the ancient wisdom of my own land, Bhārat (India) and the vast ocean of knowledge.

The word **Bhāratīya** denotes not just a geographical boundary, but also a psycho-spiritual, cultural, and civilisational space where knowledge was created and have survived through the passage of Time. In India, the current educational design is disconnected from this ethos; hence this work is an attempt to revisit and reclaim the wisdom of this land.

Mānas is commonly understood as "mind"; however, mānas is much more than mind. It is the link between body and consciousness, the inner faculty of knowing that connects the Self with the outer world though the senses (*indriyas*).

Śāstra is not just "science". It is a collection of knowledge that is scientific, artistic, experiential, intuitive, verifiable, philosophical, and even poetical. Śāstra provides *pramāṇa* – a proof or valid means of knowledge – for whatever we seek. While Mānas Śāstra may be loosely understood as "Psychology", the field of Psychology in the Western tradition and the Bhāratīyatradition differ in approach, context, application, and curriculum design. This work can serve as a foundation for reimagining Psychology curricula and can expand the understanding of each theme within the discipline. Bhāratīya Mānas Śāstra (BMC) is interdisciplinary, multidisciplinary, and even transdisciplinary. To understand mānas, one begins with cosmology, physics, biology, environmental sciences, ethics and values, food and nutrition, medicine, sociology, and philosophy. Ultimately, one realises that *mānas* is only a miniscule part of who we truly are and, in this realisation, transcends the limited understanding of self. BMS is inclusive and holistic.

Why BMS?

Bhāratīya Mānas Śāstra is a largely unexplored world of wisdom. In Bhārat, there was never a separate branch of "Psychology". The inner quest to understand the Self and the Universe resulted in experiential knowledge, expressed poetically and philosophically since Vedic Times. The ancient (*prācīna*) knowledge creators were known as *ṛṣis* or seers. They used their own intuitive laboratories of Life to generate knowledge. The *ṛṣis* envisioned humanity's interconnectedness with the universe, and accordingly created paths and practices that would allow us to live healthily and happily. They worked on what we today might call "inner engineering and development".

In contrast, the way humanity has lived since the Industrial Revolution is contrary to that Vision and worldview. Disconnected from *ṛta* – the cosmic order and roots of Nature – humanity is caught up in a way of life that has created outer development but left an inner void, with crumbling health and happiness. Understanding the bigger picture, realising how we are as interconnected with each other and with the universe, and adopting a philosophical approach to life based on interdependence are urgent needs for humanity – especially now, at the threshold of possible annihilation. This Śāstra is the *soft power* of Bharat, making Her a Thought Leader for confused humanity. BMS is a science every individual must learn – to understand the Self, others, and the environment.

How?

This work brings together ancient wisdom from the Yajur Veda, Atharva Veda, Nāṭya Śāstra, Āyurveda, and Patañjali's Yoga Sūtras. These śāstras contain profound insights into what it means to be human – how we should live, how to understand our anatomy and psychology, and how to cultivate health and happiness. This approach is holistic, not a shallow or myopic pursuit of individual happiness. In this vision, health and happiness are integrated through *śarīra* (body), *mānas* (mind), *hṛdaya* (heart), and *cetanā* (consciousness). To understand svasthya (health and being established in the Self) is to create healthy individuals, societies, and nations. When teachers, managers, leaders, and parents are rooted in *svasthya* – aware of their role, of others, and of their civilisational roots, while being interdisciplinary and multidisciplinary, they can nurture true human potential.

What?

The content for Bhāratīya Mānas Śāstra in this work is primarily drawn from the Vedas, Āyurveda, Nāṭya Śāstra, and Patañjali Yoga Sūtras. These are woven together with insights from modern psychology, quantum physics, and psychoneuroimmunology – demonstrating both continuity and complementarity between ancient and contemporary knowledge systems.

Psychology – Modern and Bhāratīya

Psychology, in the sense of reflection upon the nature and activities of the mind, is a very ancient discipline.[1] The word *psyche* denotes both consciousness and mind, yet what "mind" truly is remains a puzzle for modern psychology. In contemporary discourse, "modern" is often equated with being advanced, while "ancient" is dismissed as outdated. This work challenges that view, showing how the wisdom of psyche in India emerged from an eternal quest and remains deeply relevant today. In ancient India, psychology was never a separate discipline. It was embedded within philosophy, with an approach that was at once empirical, pragmatic, and synthetic. The Atharva Veda, from which Āyurveda originated, was profoundly psychogenic, presenting an integrated understanding of body, mind, and pañca-kośa (the five sheaths of being). Over time, Yoga and Āyurveda developed as distinct branches of knowledge. While Āyurveda increasingly emphasized the physical body and treatment, spiritual and metaphysical aspects Āyurveda moved into the background. The historical shift explains why there is debate in scholarly circles on whether psychology truly belongs within Āyurveda.

Every major system of Indian philosophy treated the subject of psychology in its own way, though none developed it as an independent discipline. Their purpose was different: the goal was not to produce a self-contained psychological theory but to understand human nature, mind, and processes as part of a larger vision of life and liberation. And this interest naturally engendered in the course of time numerous contributions which should now be styled as psychological.[2]

1 G. Murphy. *An Historical Introduction to Modern Psychology*, (Routledge & Kegan Paul,1956), p. X

2 S. K. Ramchandra Rao. *Studies in Indian Psychology* (All India Institute of Mental Health, Bangalore, 1958) p.5.

'Philosophical inquiries are enormously important in the history of psychology.[3] Indeed, there is not a single system of Indian philosophy that does not address the nature of the mind. Yet, the very word "mind" carries a confusing and limiting understanding, particularly in the West where there is no consensus on its nature. In this work, we therefore use the term Mānas – which conveys an integrated and nuanced meaning, as do many other Sanskrit terms – to define and understand what is commonly referred to as "mind."

Indian psychology has been interdisciplinary in the sense that it has its roots in Vedic Philosophy, Āyurveda, and Yoga – the well-being sciences. Common themes in Āyurveda and Yoga are: Sva-stha and Sva-Rūpa. *Sva* is self and Self – where the small 's' self is our physical existence, which is conceivable through our senses, while the 'S' Self is the Higher Energy Self, or what is commonly known as Spirit in the Western world. 'Who am I?' is the question of understanding self and Self both. Āyurveda speaks of being rooted in Self, or 'Sva-stha', while Yoga expands on the theory and practices of how to integrate self with 'Rūpa' or the original Self. Both these Śāstras are paths to self-discovery, self-management, and self-transcendence.

Secondly, both deal with Vipāka as a construct – vipāka is the final digested product of sensory inputs including food, thoughts, and emotions. Our daily routine creates digested inputs that nourish us, while undigested ones become toxic, called *Ama* in Āyurveda. This *Ama* becomes the main reason not only for physical diseases, but also mental misconceptions, emotional distortions, and overall health issues. Yoga goes one step deeper and says that all the sensory imprints are the vipāka of whatever we ingest. They are the below-iceberg *Saṃskāras* that not only generate above-iceberg visible habits and patterns, but are carried forward into future lifetimes. Hence, through Yogic practices, these imprints can be dissolved, and what we now call in modern

3 R. S. Peters. *Brett's History of Psychology (Abridged)*, (1962), p. 33

language, our "discs" can be reformatted. Understanding the role of *saṁskāra* in our present self, reformatting them through practices, and knowing how modern Psychoneuroimmunology refers to *saṁskāra* in creating well-being is a new area of research. The role of *Saṃskāras*, the subtle life impressions in guiding our behaviour and thought-emotion patterns, relates to this subtle biology of what a human being is made up of. *Saṃskāras* play a significant role in our decisions in life, and hence practices to access and purify them are an integral part of Yoga. Yoga, as the foundation of Yama and Niyama, and as practices of prānayama, āsana, dhyana, and dharana for refining the body-mind continuum, is a co-science with Āyurveda in BMS. We can relate this to Intergenerational Trauma healing. The study of *Saṁskāra* is a unique contribution of Bhāratīya Mānas Śāstra.

Life or Āyu is defined very well in Āyurveda, which forms the foundation of BMS. To understand Life is critical and the foundation of all our other sciences. Today we see consultants describing lack of engagement at the workplace, in academia, and in life in general. This lack of engagement can be overcome by understanding what Āyu or Life is. Chapter 1 deals with this concept in more detail. There are four types of Āyu or life that are lived depending on how well one relates to the Self as Macrocosm. Engagement is also a function of balance and self-discipline that generates Prāna, Tejas, and Ojas within us. These three are important aspects of engagement and are discussed at length in later chapters. The West has defined happiness in life as instant gratification of desires, consumerism, and outer technological advancement. In contrast, BMS defines life in a very holistic way, with inner engineering practices to create happiness that is sustainable and life-enhancing.

Another difference between the West and East is the role of the Heart and Cakras. The Yogic and even Āyurvedic Anatomy integrates the subtlest energy bodies and the energy centres, apart from the one visible to our eyes. Chinese, Tibetan, and other ancient healers have known of these subtle extensions of our physical bodies, which today are being captured by sophisticated instruments. How did the ancient seers have such scientific acumen? The Heart or Heart Cakra, to be precise, has been the centre of our existence and higher possibilities. The heart, also as an organ, is not just one that pumps blood and has heartbeats; it is the centre of Prāṇavaha and Manovaha strotas and hence plays a significant role through the Nāḍīs. The Heart is the seat of Citta, or consciousness, Antaḥkaraṇa, or the four faculties of consciousness, subtle nāḍīs – the term "nervous system" does not describe it fully and all the major arteries of the body, along with the seat of Prāna – the life force. Carl Jung and Candace Pert have both referred to the Heart Cakra in their respective works of Psychology and Psychoneuroimmunology.

The scope of this work is kept within the wisdom and insights from Āyurveda and Yoga, with the only exception being the integration of Nāṭya Śāstra to understand emotions. Emotional Intelligence has become an in-depth area of research and training in the West, while in India, though having our own science of Aesthetics that deals with emotions, we have yet to revive and integrate our wisdom into modern constructs like Positive Psychology, Flourishing, or Emotional Intelligence. In Vedic times, positive emotions and the pursuit of transcendence from negative emotions formed a thread of knowledge. Western Psychology has only recently awakened to the shift from pathology to Positive Psychology and Well-being. Martin Seligman is considered the father of this shift. However, the ṛṣis in India knew Joy as the foundation of Life and Creation. There are rituals and practices aligned to invoke these positive emotions in the human self. Vedic literature, of course, has many hymns; the Atharva Veda has chapters on enthusiasm and the strength of positive emotions, and the Taittirīya Upaniṣad has an entire chapter on *Ānanda Valli* – the hierarchy of joy and happiness.

To summarise, this work on BMS is a compilation of wisdom and insights from ancient (*prācīna*) works of our scientists, known as ṛṣis, which is *sanātana* – eternal and universal. The unique contributions of BMS are in these areas:

1. BMS begins with involution and expands on our participation in the evolution of ourselves and the Universe. BMS works on the principle that the Universe is not mechanical and finite, but pulsating with Life Energy – infinite, ever expanding, and full of unmanifest possibilities.
2. BMS is interdisciplinary, multidisciplinary, and transdisciplinary.
3. The matter-energy continuum is well examined and explained. Ātma, Cetanā, and Consciousness as energy aspects, and our visible body or Śarīra as the matter aspect, can be reviewed. The psychosomatic connection and continuity were well known to Bhāratīya ṛṣis.
4. Psyche, or Mānas, is well-understood in BMS, while Western Psychology is still struggling to integrate the knowledge of Mānas in the understanding of Self. The composition of Mānas, its functions, and its relationship with our senses and higher intelligence or Buddhi is the core of BMS.
5. Saṁskāras, or life impressions, need to be studied to understand how we see the world, how we learn, what choices we make, what traumas we store, and how we can erase the saṁskāras by reformatting ourselves.
6. The brain is seen as the centre of human existence and decision-making in the West, while BMS sees the heart as the centre of human existence and the seat of consciousness, connecting the human with the Universe. The heart-space is where transcendence happens – the highest need described by psychologist Carl Jung.
7. *Dharma*, or sustainable universal principles, is the foundation of BMS. To be able to live a happy and healthy life with integrity and authenticity, we need to understand and integrate *Dharma* into everyday life. Āyurveda describes *Hita* and *Sukha Āyu*. One can see the correlation with the UN's Sustainability Goals and understand why these goals are not able to manifest positive results

without the inclusion of *Dharma*. The *Puruṣārtha Framework* explains how Dharma is the guiding force for our life.

8. The modern discoveries of Psychoneuroimmunology about psychosomatic illness and psychosomatic wellness were already known and are described in BMS.
9. Positive Psychology, which deals with optimism, hope, flourishing, and transcendence, is only a recent entry in the Western Psychology, while these have long been the foundation of BMS.
10. Last, and most important, are lifestyle, character, and life skills – all are integral parts of BMS. Character, or Śīla, is the foundation of individual and collective health.

This work intends to share in detail all the above themes. It is complementary to any Psychology textbook and has the potential to become a strong resource for faculty development, aligned with the New Education Policy (NEP) 2020.

Many areas still need to be explored, researched, expanded, and applied. This work, I hope, opens new paths to self-discovery and transformation.

CHAPTER 01

Involution & Cosmology

In this chapter we cover these themes:

- Why study Cosmology to understand human Psychology?
- Involution to understand who we are – the journey from unmanifest to manifest
- Weave Physics and Āyurveda insights to know the self
- Pañca Mahābhūta, Triguṇa, and our psyche – Svabhāva and Svadharma Framework
- The Four Puruṣārtha Framework for Flourishing

Introduction

Bhāratīya Mānas Śāstra begins with the Beginning. The evolution of Cosmos and Consciousness has been the foundation for understanding the human being. To understand 'Who we are' has been the oldest quest of humanity. One may wonder, why cosmology? What does psychology have to do with cosmology? This is the difference between the epistemologies of different cultures. While most of the 'modern' disciplines are anthropocentric place the human being at the centre of their epistemology, India and many other indigenous cultures see the entire creation and human beings as interconnected and in continuum with each other. In fact, in Indian Philosophy, the Cosmos and individuals are One and made up of the same essence. Āyurveda, the science of life and living, begins with the Indian philosophical view of cosmology to explain human existence. Everything is living and evolving. The Universe is not mechanistic. This context makes cosmology from Sāṅkhya Philosophy, adopted in Āyurveda, a meta-theory of a meta-view of who we are.

This wisdom from Vedic times is now being validated by modern physics. What we know today as quantum physics offers a very different understanding of the Cosmos compared to earlier paradigms. The uniqueness of Indic wisdom lies in the fact that even after many millennia, the knowledge is authentic and does not require paradigm shifts.

The classical understanding and modern research in physics have continued to refine our understanding; at many levels, however, new revelations have led scientists to question the premises of their predecessors. Fritjof Capra writes, "In it (*Physics and Philosophy*) Heisenberg gives a vivid account of the experience of a small group of physicists — Niels Bohr, Erwin Schrödinger, Wolfgang Pauli, and others — who were the first to explore physical phenomena involving atoms and subatomic particles, which brought them in contact with a strange and unexpected world. In their struggle to grasp this new reality, those scientists became painfully aware that their basic concepts, their language, and their whole way of thinking were inadequate to describe atomic phenomena. Their problems were not merely intellectual, but amounted to an intense emotional and, one could say, even existential crisis."[4] The beginning of this chapter is with physics, specifically the quantum theory of energy fields, as this is where science and philosophy (or spirituality) are coming closer to each other. This is where the *Bhāratīya* quest from Vedic times being reaffirmed by scientists in the field of physics. Capra continues to describe how the new understanding created "a profound change of worldviews, or paradigms, that is now happening in all the sciences and throughout society – a change from the mechanistic worldview of Descartes and Newton to a holistic and ecological view."[5] However, what is surprising is that the new paradigms

---

4 Capra F. (2017, April 7-9). *Mystics and Scientists in the Twenty-First Century: Science and Spirituality Revisited.* 40th Anniversary Mystics and Scientists Conference, Horsley Park, Surrey.

5 ibid

of holistic and ecological views are yet to be reflected in the allied sciences of humanities, specifically psychology.

Involution & Cosmology

The holistic and ecological view that Capra refers to is the foundation of Āyurveda. The matter and energy correspond to *Padārtha* and *Cetanā* or *Ātma* in Bhāratīya Darśana. *Sṛṣṭi Utpatti* or Cosmology from Sāṅkhya is accepted as a premise in Āyurveda. This is extremely important in understanding psyche and mind (*mānas*) in psychology, as our *mānas* is manifested from the *Sṛṣṭi*. The term is derived from the dhātu *Srji Visarge* (सृज्यतेऽन्येन इति सृष्टिः), meaning that which is created, produced, or manifested. According to this definition, that which brings out the hidden factors from within is called *Sṛṣṭi*. Just as a grain comes from a seed, the Universe too is manifested.[6] *Sṛṣṭi* is manifested from the primordial nature known as *Mūla Prakṛti* or *Avyakta*. In Āyurveda, Ācārya Caraka uses the terms *Ātma*, *Vibhu* and *Kṣetrajña* for *Avyakta*.[7] *Ātma* will be explored in detail later. *Vibhu* means omnipresent, omnipotent, and omniscient – present everywhere at the same time, with unlimited potential and knowing everything. *Kṣetrajña* means Supreme Knowledge Holder. This becomes a fascinating realisation of who we are in the deepest and highest possible way.

Mūla Prakṛti is energy and gets manifested as matter. This energy has three fundamental qualities known as Guṇas: *Sattva, Rajas,* and *Tamas*. According to Kāśyapa Saṃhitā, *Sattva's* nature is light (*Prakāśa*), which illuminates and gives knowledge. *Rajas's* nature is movement and generates action. *Tamas* controls both by restraining overindulgence.[8] The three *Guṇas* descend during the involution and

---

6 Narsimhacharyulu, K. V. L. (2017). *Padartha Vijnana* (7th ed). Chaukhamba Krishnadas Academy, Varanasi, India, p. 381

7 Charaka Saṃhitā. Acharya Vidyadhar Shukla and Prof. Ravi Dutt Tripathi (Eds.). (2000), Chaukhamba Sanskrit Pratishthan, Delhi, India, p. 686

8 Desai, Vaidya Ranjitrai. (2010). *Ayurveda Kriya Shareer*. Shri Baidyanath Ayurved Bhavan Limited, Nagpur, India, p. 85.

are inherent in the cosmos. *Avyakta* is the causative factor for the creation of all sentient beings and is without a cause itself, as per Suśruta. Āyurveda has accepted Sāṅkhya's chronology that 24 *tattvas* evolved from *Avyakta*.[9] *Avyakta* is the cause (*kāraṇa*) of all the 24 *tattvas*, though itself causeless. Mūla Prakṛti is known as Avyakta since it cannot be perceived with our senses; we can only perceive its manifestations. *Sattva*, *Rajas*, and *Tamas* are embedded within everything in the cosmos. The manifestations of *Mahat* or *Buddhi*, *Ahaṃkāra*, *Pañca Tanmātras*, 10 *Indriyas*, *Pañca Mahābhūta*, and *Mānas* evolve from various combinations of *Sattva, Rajas,* and *Tamas,* creating the *svabhāva*. *Bhāva* in *Svabhāva* refers to the being from the perspective of its accomplished state, while *Sva* is Self.

Avyakta, the *Mūla Prakṛti* or the Primordial Energy, is that from which the *Bhūta Prakṛti* and all other manifestations have emerged.[10] *Bhūta* is derived from the root *Bhū*, meaning "to be", and expresses the idea of growth, development, and prosperity – the dynamic aspect of being. *Bhū* refers to a being from the perspective of the process of creation: being produced, taking birth, becoming, and getting enriched. *Bhāva*, in contrast, refers to the being from the perspective of its accomplished state. Thus, while *Bhū* refers to the process of becoming, *Bhāva* refers to the realization of being. [11] This is where *Mahābhūta* become our *Svabhāva* based on their own nature and the combination within our self.

---

9 Sharma, Anantram. (n.d.). *Sushrut Samhita*, Su. Sha. 1/3–4. Chaukhamba Sur Bharati Prakashan, Varanasi, India.

10 Ibid.

11 Mishra, Rishi Kumar. (2000). *Before the Beginning & After the End.* Rupa & Co., India.

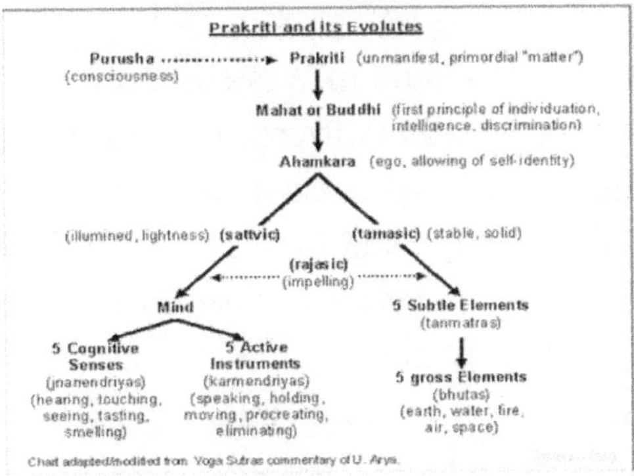

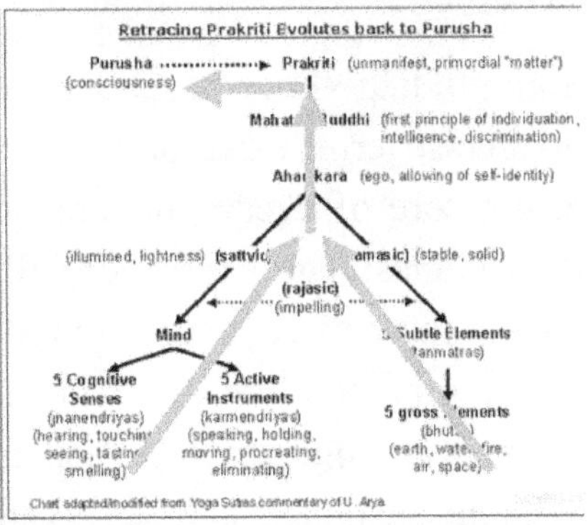

Avyakta (Unmanifest) and Quantum Physics[12]

This chapter begins with Indic wisdom; however, modern physicists are increasingly reaffirming ancient knowledge. The difference is only a matter of language. In this section, both ancient Indic thought and Western physics merge and overlap.

Physicists now recognise that the Universe is a dynamic web of inseparable energy patterns. Fundamental physical laws cannot be understood by reducing reality into isolated parts. David Bohm, in *The Implicate Order*, wrote of an "implicate enfolded order" which exists in an unmanifest state and is the foundation upon which all manifest reality rests. He calls this manifest reality "the explicate unfolded order."[13] This resonates with the wisdom of Sāṅkhya philosophy. *Avyakta* – the Unmanifest – holds the blueprint of the manifested reality. All that emerges from the Unmanifest is the explicate unfolded order.

12 Bhushan, Sanjay. *Towards an Integrative and Causal Epistemology of Consciousness*. ResearchGate, June 2012.

13 Brennan, Barbara Ann. *Hands of Light: A Guide to Healing Through the Human Energy Field*. Bantam Books, June 1988, p. 25.

Triguṇa

Some Indian views of reality can be understood in Western terms. Yet no precise terms exist for the primal forces at work in creation – the triad at the core of every phenomenon. These all-pervasive forces are the three Guṇas: Sattva (essence), Rajas (activity), and Tamas (inertia). The idea of these three essential modes of Nature was developed by ancient Indian thinkers. Its truth is not immediately obvious, for it arose from long psychological experimentation and profound internal experience. Without sustained self-observation and intuitive perception of these Nature-forces, it is difficult to grasp them accurately or apply them effectively.[14] *Mūla Prakṛti*, the primary existence, is a state of complete balance or equilibrium. This Prakṛti is without gender, identification, or form – without any defining qualities. It is undifferentiated, beyond human sensory perception. In this stage of unity, existence assumes only the purest and lightest frequencies – all is Sattva. For this state of wholeness, Sattva continually generates Space from itself. This generation of Space marks the first step in the creation cycle. At first, Space pours forth freely, like water flowing in the ocean. But once manifestation begins, the pull is inexorably downward.

As currents of Space are generated, obstructions arise when the flow eddies back on itself. This obstruction is Tamas. It is Tamas that becomes the prime cause of creation, for without resistance, sāttvic frequencies would never descend from subtle to gross. The presence of Tamas breaks the uniform flow of Space, forming an independent circuit. This circuit – formed from the frequencies of root Prakṛti – is called the golden egg (*Hiraṇyagarbha* in Sanskrit).

So long as Prakṛti is inert and motionless, nothing exists but pure Sattva. The generation of Space introduces motion and activity. Creation unfolds such that once action begins, energy inevitably flows from

14 Sri Aurobindo. (2001). A Greater Psychology. Pondicherry, India: Sri Aurobindo International Centre of Education, Sri Aurobindo Ashram, p. 108.

high to low, from subtle to gross. The Guṇas may be visualised as three coloured strands braided together. Sometimes one colour dominates on the surface, sometimes another. Yet observing the whole cord reveals that dominance is an illusion: all three are always present, only one may temporarily conceal the others. They are not three separate entities but three forms of one existence. The Guṇas neither disturb nor contradict one another; they act in coherence, evolving together, present in everything in varying proportions.

Sattva is light – in density and brightness. Rajas excites and moves. Tamas is heavy and obstructs.

Mānas (the mind) is Sattva in its purest form. However, Rajas and Tamas create different manifestations of Mānas, which may be healthy and balanced or unhealthy and disturbed. Āyurveda describes all mental pathology as an imbalance of Rajas and Tamas. The aim of healing is to restore the Sattva of the Mānas and allow Sattva to guide and regulate Rajas and Tamas. We explore this further in the appendix on *Sattvavajaya Cikitsā*.

Mahat Tattva (Buddhi)

The first Tattva from Avyakta (*Ātma-Mūla Prakṛti*) is Mahat or Buddhi. Mahat means vast, infinite, meta, expanded. Buddhi is intelligence, inner knowing. Since Mūla Prakṛti is *Triguṇātmaka* – consisting of Sattva, Rajas, and Tamas – every subsequent Tattva also carries these three Guṇas inherently. Everything in the *Sṛṣṭi* (Cosmos) is infused with Buddhi, inherent intelligence. Yet our limited perspective confines "intelligence" only to the human brain. In truth, insects, plants, animals, and birds – all are infused with intelligence in varying degrees.

In the *Purāṇas*, Buddhi is also called Brahmā, the Creator.[15] The Universe is known as *Brahmāṇḍa* – the cosmic egg that holds Brahmā.

15 Vaidya Ranjitrai Desai, Ayurveda Kriya Shareer, published in 2010, Shri Baidyanath Ayurved Bhavan Limited, Nagpur, India, page 87.

The term Brahmā is often misunderstood. Here, Brahmā is not a deity but the unified field of energy – the creative power that expands and descends. It exists within every being. Brahmā is higher intelligence, Buddhi itself. Knowledge of Brahmā (*Brahma Jñāna*) is the highest wisdom, leading to enlightenment (*Bodhi Tattva*). Even the highest joy is called *Brahmānanda.* In India, even unlettered but enlightened individuals had this insight. The poet-saint Dadu Dayal writes, "There is no greater sin than contraction of our Brahmā Cetanā." The nature of Brahmā is to expand and to include. When we restrict its movement, we became trapped in a xenophobic existence, cut off from the Universal Intelligence.

The seed contains the information or blueprint of its growth. Once sprouted, the inherent intelligence guides its development. This principle holds true for everything in the Cosmos, as Intelligence–Information is embedded in the Energy-Matter matrix and exists in subtle form. Buddhi is a combination of instincts and intelligence working together.

Modern science is now rediscovering this truth, long embedded within each one of us and the Universe. Energy and information are the same. Everything that exists has energy, energy is filled with information, and this stored info-energy constitutes our cellular memories.[16] Modern medical science and physics have taken many years to arrive at this conclusion. Newtonian mechanistic thinking dominated their worldview and self-view for centuries. Nobel Prize-winning physicist David Bohm summarises this M (Matter) = E (Energy) = I (Information), noting that a limitless amount of information is enfolded into the structure of the Universe, and we are a manifestation of that energy.[17] The insight from this statement aligns with our Cosmology Theory – energy is Avyakta, information is Mahat or Buddhi, and matter is our body-mind and the

---

16 Pearsall, P. P. (1999). *The heart's code: Tapping the wisdom and power of our heart energy*. Harmony.

17 Pearsall, P. P. (1999). *The heart's code: Tapping the wisdom and power of our heart energy* (p. 52). Harmony.

perceived Universe. Our Ṛṣis *knew* this Truth through their connection to Higher Intelligence. Modern science, however, remains fragmented, and such 'philosophy' still lies outside the mainstream curriculum of biology, psychology, or medical sciences. Energy medicine, an emerging field of healing, has begun to understand and integrate the wisdom as foundational knowledge. Everything that is alive pulsates with energy, and all energy contains information.[18]

The Vedas often use metaphors and stories to share such coded knowledge. For example, the son of Brahmā is Dharma.[19] Brahmā created the Sṛṣṭi, and the Nature of Sṛṣṭi, along with its sustainable principles, are coded as Dharma. Later, we reconnect with Dharma while exploring the framework of Puruṣārthas.

Prakṛti and Vikṛti

After Mahat, we must understand the concepts of Prakṛti and Vikṛti from the perspectives of Yoga and Āyurveda. The twenty-four tattvas are divided into eight Prakṛtis and sixteen Vikṛtis. Mūla Prakṛti, Mahat, Ahaṅkāra, and the five Tanmātras – Śabda, Sparśa, Rūpa, Rasa, and Gandha – are known collectively as the Aṣṭa (eight) Prakṛtis. The sixteen Vikṛtis consist of the five Mahābhūtas—Ākāśa, Vāyu, Agni, Āp, and Pṛthvī – along with the eleven Indriyas: five Jñānendriyas (ears, skin, eyes, tongue, and nose); five Karmendriyas (speech, hands, legs, reproductive organs, and organs of excretion); and the eleventh, Mānas. The tattva from which another tattva evolves is called Prakṛti, while the one that evolves from it is called Vikṛti. Mūla Prakṛti is regarded as the only true Prakṛti, whereas the remaining seven of the Aṣṭa Prakṛtis function both as Prakṛti and as Vikṛti; they evolve from Prakṛti and also serve as causes for subsequent tattvas. In contrast, when a tattva does

18 Myss, C. (2011). *Anatomy of the spirit: The seven stages of power & healing.* Penguin Random House Australia.

19 Katdare, I. (Ed.). (n.d.). *Bharteeya Shiksha Granthmala* (Vol. 2, p. 20). Punarutthan Prakashan Seva Trust.

not give rise to another, such as the five Mahābhūtas and the eleven Indriyas, it is known only as Vikṛti. Sage Kapila, in Sāṅkhya philosophy, clarified the Prakṛti–Vikṛti concepts to aid in understanding both the subtle and the gross dimensions of existence. Vikṛti is Vyakta (manifest) and therefore perceivable in its existence and actions, while Prakṛti is Avyakta (unmanifest), Vibhu (all-pervading), and omnipresent.[20] Modern science also reflects similar concerns. The timeless human question, "How did life evolve on Earth?", has led to various theories. Early proposals of spontaneous generation gave way to the principle of omne vivum ex ovo ("every living thing arises from a pre-existing living thing"), and ultimately to the modern theory of biopoiesis.[21]

Ahaṅkāra and Beyond

The second tattva is Ahaṅkāra – the principle of individuation and inherent function within all manifestation. This is often mistranslated as ego in English. In reality, Ahaṅkāra refers not to vanity or self-centredness but to the unique identity that differentiates forms while retaining their essence. For example, if we compare Mūla Prakṛti to gold, then the ornaments made from gold each carry their own name, form, and function – yet their essence remains gold. To shape the ornaments, additions and modifications are required, just as Ahaṅkāra conditions and differentiates the pure essence.

Ahaṅkāra is of three types:

- Vaikārika (Sāttvic)
- Taijasa (Rājasic)
- Bhūtādika (Tāmasic)

From Tāmasic Ahaṅkāra, with the support and activation of Rājasic Ahaṅkāra, the five Tanmātras evolved. Sattva – foremost among the

---

20 Omanand Teerth, Shri Swami. (2013). *Patanjal Yog Pradeep* (pp. 103–104). Gorakhpur: Gita Press.

21 Rastogi, S. (2010). Building bridges between Ayurveda and modern science. *International Journal of Ayurveda Research, 1*(1), 41–46.

Triguṇas – symbolises illumination and creative intelligence. Rajas represents dynamic activity and movement. Tamas signifies inertia and latent potential, which transforms only under the influence of Sattva and Rajas.'[22] These subtle principles precede the five Mahābhūtas. The Pañca Mahābhūtas themselves emerge from the Pañca Tanmātras through the process of Pañcīkaraṇa (mutual interpenetration and combination).

This cosmological framework in Āyurveda serves as a map of both creation and involution. The body–mind continuum we experience is not merely gross matter but a condensation of subtle energy and intelligence, encoded as information within the Self. Conditioned thinking makes us identify only with the gross, visible level of existence. Yet, beneath it lies an energy matrix, innate intelligence, and the process of involution. These must be integrated to truly understand not only the Universe as Macrocosm but also ourselves as Microcosm.

Cetanā and Acetanā

After Ahaṅkāra, creation (*Sṛṣṭi*) is divided into two categories – Cetanā and Acetanā – based on the quality of Ahaṅkāra.[23] Everything in the cosmos either possesses Indriyas (senses) or does not. Entities with Indriyas are called Cetanā, while those without are called Acetanā. The Viśeṣa Dharma (unique property) of Cetanā is knowledge or Chaitanya. This knowledge arises from Sattva Guṇa; hence the Indriyas evolved from Sāttvic Ahaṅkāra. To express this knowledge in outward action, Rajas is required, while Tamas functions to balance and check Rajas.

---

22 Rastogi, S. (2010). Building bridges between Ayurveda and modern science. *International Journal of Ayurveda Research.*

23 Desai, Vaidya Ranjitrai. *Ayurveda Kriya Shareer*. Shri Baidyanath Ayurved Bhavan Limited, 2010, Nagpur, India, p. 88.

The Indriyas are of three kinds:

- Five Jñānendriyas (senses of knowledge): ears, skin, eyes, tongue, and nose
- Five Karmendriyas (senses of action): speech, hands, legs, reproductive organs, and organs of excretion
- Mānas (mind): which connects both

However, the Indriyas do not merely reflect the gross-level functioning of the body–mind complex; they also possess subtle aspects related to the Ātma. Mānas serves as the bridge connecting the Indriyas to the Ātma. The only true Cetanā Dravya is the Ātma. Mānas and the Indriyas cannot function independently of the Ātma. Although the Indriyas constantly move outward in connection with Mānas, they can be trained to turn inward.

When aligned with Ātma, they can even access extra-sensory perceptions beyond ordinary bodily awareness. Much of what occurs within and around us lies beyond the reach of the gross Indriyas. Why is it important for Psychology to understand Cetanā and Acetanā? Consider the analogy of a laptop: the hardware represents Acetanā – lifeless on its own until software (Mānas) is installed and powered by electricity (Consciousness). Similarly, our body is hardware, Mānas is software, and Consciousness is the power that animates life.

Pañca Tanmātra and Pañca Mahābhūta

While all eleven Indriyas evolve from Sāttvic Ahaṅkāra, the five Tanmātras and five Mahābhūtas evolve from Tāmasic Ahaṅkāra.

Each Tanmātra has a specific Dharma (function):

- Śabda (sound)
- Sparśa (touch)
- Rūpa (form)
- Rasa (taste)
- Gandha (smell)

These correspond directly to their respective sensory functions. Tanmātras also correspond to Mahābhūtas:

- Ākāśa → Sound/Śabda
- Vāyu → Touch/Sparśa
- Agni → Form/Rūpa
- Āp → Taste/Rasa
- Pṛthvī → Smell/Gandha

The Tanmātras possess only their specific quality, while the Mahābhūtas accumulate the qualities of the preceding ones. For example:

- Ākāśa has only sound
- Vāyu has touch and sound
- Agni has form, sound, and touch
- Āp has taste, sound, touch, and form
- Pṛthvī has smell along with all earlier Tanmātras

The sense organs act as points of sensitivity receiving these inputs: ears receive sound, skin receives touch, eyes perceive form, tongue senses taste, and nose detects smell. Each organ is sensitive only to its respective capacity.

The Holographic World

Modern science supports the idea that the five Tanmātras are progenitors of their visible counterparts. Basic formative particles (electrons, protons, and neutrons – analogous to Tanmātras) combine in different proportions to form atoms, elements, and compounds. Āyurveda states: *"Sarvaṁ dravyaṁ hi Pañcābhautikam"* – every substance in the universe is composed of five basic elements. This demonstrates a conceptual similarity between modern science and Āyurveda regarding substance generation.[24] Ācārya Suśruta emphasised that the Five Elements are holographic –

24 Rastogi, S. "Building Bridges between Ayurveda and Modern Science." *International Journal of Ayurveda Research*, vol. 1, no. 1, Jan–Mar 2010.

intertwined, mutually influential, and concomitant.[25] The universe is holographic, and so is our brain and Mānas. As mini-universes, we reflect the same pattern as the cosmos. The holographic principle states that every fragment contains the whole, capable of reconstructing the totality. Vedic wisdom expresses this as: "Yathā piṇḍe tathā brahmāṇḍe" – as is the microcosm (piṇḍa), so is the macrocosm (brahmāṇḍa).

Dr. Karl Pribram, a renounced brain researcher, proposed that the brain structures sensory perception (sight, hearing, taste, smell and touch) holographically. According to him, the brain abstracts from a holographic domain beyond time and space.[26] This explains why Jīvātma is said to transcend lifetimes, carrying a continuity of experience. This also challenges earlier Western notions of left-brain/right-brain dominance and brings Einstein's relativity of time-space into psychology.

Each Mahābhūta is associated with one or more dominant Guṇas:

- Ākāśa → Sattva-dominated
- Vāyu → Rajas-dominated
- Agni → Sattva–Rajas dominated
- Āp → Sattva–Tamas dominated
- Pṛthvī → Tamas-dominated

The Pañca Mahābhūta–Triguṇa matrix forms not only the blueprint of the cosmos but also the blueprint of the individual. Bhāratīya Psychology, therefore, does not merely examine the mind as the tip of the iceberg but situates it within a cosmological framework of involution that extends down to the Mānas itself. According to Suśruta Saṃhitā (3.1.19)[27], the relationship between Mahābhūtas and Guṇas can be classified accordingly.

25 Kannan, Vidyanidhi K. S. *Ayurvediya Padarth Vijnanam: The Theoretical Foundations of Ayurveda*. FRLHT, Bengaluru, India, 2011, p. 50.

26 Ibid., pp. 25–26.

27 Kannan, V. K. S. (2011). *Ayurvediya Padarth Vijnanam: The Theoretical Foundations of Ayurveda*. FRLHT, Bengaluru, India, p. 187.

	Bhūta	Guṇa	Symbolic Representation
1	Ākāśa	Sattva Bahula	S
2	Vāyu	Rajas Bahula	R
3	Agni	Sattva-Rajas Bahula	SR
4	Aap	Sattva- Tamas Bahula	ST
5	Pṛthvī	Tamas Bahula	T

Anatomy – Gross & Subtle

The metaphysical tenet of the Upaniṣads, *Yat piṇḍe tat Brahmāṇḍe*[28]; states that the self is a reflection of the *Self*. Just as the Universe is ever-expanding, manifesting, and full of possibilities, so too is the self. The epistemology of Āyurveda rests upon the relationship between microcosm and macrocosm, constituted of the five Mahābhūta, the three dynamic principles of doṣa, the seven dhātu, and other unique concepts.[29] The earlier description of *involution* provided a detailed account of the macrocosm–microcosm continuum.

Āyurveda accepts the fundamental principle of a unified field of consciousness, while also developing an applied philosophy of life. This Energy manifests as body, mānas, senses, and individual consciousness in the form of human beings. Each of us is a miniature replica of the Universe, and our life expresses the expansion or constriction of this Energy. Our worldview, self-view, health, thoughts, choices in relationships, and careers are all reflections of these Energy expressions. Psychology and Physics converge here: we are not a static product but an ever-evolving process with infinite possibilities. "A human being," wrote Einstein, "is a part of the whole, called by us "Universe,' a part limited in time and space. He experiences himself, his thoughts, and

28 Vasishtha, S. (2009). *Nadi Tatva Darshanam.* Ramlal Kapoor Trust, Sonipat, Haryana, India, p. 71.

29 Patwardhan, B. "Bridging Ayurveda with Evidence-Based Scientific Approaches in Medicine." *EPMA Journal*, vol. 5, no. 1, 2014, p. 19.

feelings as something separated from the rest – a kind of optical delusion of his consciousness. This delusion is a kind of prison for us, restricting us to our personal desires and to affection for a few persons nearest to us. Our task must be to free ourselves from this prison by widening our circle of compassion to embrace all living creatures and the whole nature in its beauty. Nobody is able to achieve this completely, but the striving for such achievement is in itself a part of the liberation and a foundation for inner security."[30] What Bhāratīya thought calls *Maya*, Einstein refers to as an "optical delusion." The only difference is that this delusion, according to Indian thought, is created not by consciousness but by the mind or Mānas. The unified energy field and the human energy field merge into a continuum extending from the subtle to the gross body. Ātma and Jīvātma lie along this spectrum, connected to the body through *mānas*.

At the body–mānas level, this wisdom unfolds into a unique anatomy of both body and mind, deeply interconnected with the cosmos. Yoga explains this anatomy through the pañca kośa model:

- Annamaya Kośa – the gross, visible body
- Prāṇamaya Kośa – the vital energy field
- Manomaya Kośa – the mental sheath
- Vijñānamaya Kośa – the wisdom sheath
- Ānandamaya Kośa – the sheath of bliss

The concept of Pañca Kośa originates in the Taittirīya Upaniṣad of the Yajurveda. These Upaniṣads explored the nature of self and its relationship with the universe, and the pañca kośa is among the earliest conceptualizations of the human being.

A natural question arises: if all humans are made of the same fundamental principles, how do we explain the immense diversity of existence? Why

---

30 *The Einstein Papers: A Man of Many Parts. The New York Times*, 29 March 1972. https://www.nytimes.com/1972/03/29/archives/the-einstein-papers-a-man-of-many-parts-the-einstein-papers-man-of.html

do we differ in appearance, thought, emotion, health, and disease? Āyurveda addresses this through the concept of prakṛti – each person is unique, much like fingerprints, due to the play of the individual soul (jīvātma) expressed through combinations of the five Mahābhūta and the three Guṇa. Thus, we are all living stories. The self is the central character, and the concept of jīvātma helps us recognise and understand the uniqueness of our own unfolding narrative.

Jīvātma

An individual being is known as *Jīva*. When the universal Consciousness (*Ātma*) expresses itself through an individual, it is called *Jīvātma*. We may think of Jīvātma as a character wishing to live out its unique story. The fundamental difference between a living entity and a dead one lies in the presence or absence of this *Jīva* or Life Force. Ācārya Caraka and Ācārya Suśruta described the characteristic features of Jīvātma in human anatomy. At a superficial level, these functions are often attributed to the brain. However, upon deeper exploration, it becomes evident that they arise from a subtle Life Force – Mahā Prāṇa. If the brain alone were responsible, such functions would not cease at death. The defining difference between the living and the dead is the presence of this Energy, called Jīvātma.

Though the idea of Jīvātma may appear philosophical or culture-specific, Āyurveda explains it in an experiential manner through observable signs that anyone can relate to:

प्राणापानौ निमेषाध्या जीवनं मनसो गतिः ।
इन्द्रियान्तरसंचारः प्रेरणं धारणं च यत् ॥

देशान्तरगतिः स्वप्ने पञ्चत्वग्रहणं तथा ।
दृष्टस्य दक्षिणेनाक्ष्णा सव्येनावगमस्तथा ॥1.सु.शा. १.१७ pg. 9.10.

इच्छा द्वेषः सुखं दुःखं प्रयत्नश्चेतना धृतिः ।
बुद्धिः स्मृतिरहङ्कारो लिङ्गानि परमात्मनः ॥-च० शा० १/७०-७२[31]

1. Inspiration and expiration (ucchvāsa-niḥśvāsa) – Respiration belongs only to the living. When broken down as "re-spiration," it reflects the process of re-spiriting – each inhalation inspires life; each exhalation expires it.
2. Blinking of the eyes (akṣi-nimeṣa) – Even the simple act of blinking requires the presence of Life Force.
3. Life itself (jīvanam) – Existence is sustained through Jīvātma.
4. Mental perception (manaso gatiḥ) – Just as we see with physical eyes, the mind has its inner eyes. Visualizing distant places or imagining people becomes possible through Jīvātma.
5. Shifting between senses (indriyāntara-saṃcāra) – The ability of mānas to move awareness from one sense organ to another is powered by Jīvātma.
6. Mobility and stability of mind (preraṇa-dhāraṇa) – Both action and restraint in thought arise through Jīvātma.
7. Dream travel (deśāntara-gatiḥ svapne) – In dreams, humans universally experience journeys across space and even time.
8. Anticipation of death (pañcatva-grahaṇam) – The intuitive awareness of one's approaching end belongs to Jīvātma.
9. Coordination of vision (dṛṣṭasya dakṣiṇenākṣṇā savyenāvagamaḥ) – The merging of two distinct visual inputs from left and right eyes into one unified perception occurs through Jīvātma, not merely the brain.
10. Psychological functions – Desire, aversion, pleasure, pain, effort, consciousness, stability, intellect, memory, and ego all arise when Jīvātma interacts with mānas, enabling the drama of human life.

31 Dr. K. V. Narasimhacharyulu. *Padarth Vijnana*. 7th Edition. Varanasi: Chowkhamba Krishnadas Academy; 2017. p. 90.

All these signs are markers of the living, absent in the dead. Hence, they are regarded as proof of the existence of Jīvātma. When Jīvātma departs, the body becomes lifeless, reduced only to its five Mahābhūta. This is why a corpse is said to have returned to the state of pañca-mahābhūta.

Pañca Mahā Bhūta and our Svabhāva (Nature)

Understanding Psychology requires a macro perspective to arrive at a micro understanding of the Self. In Western Psychology, personality or self has evolved from humour theories to traits and temperament models. While these provide partial truths, they do not offer a holistic understanding of the self. Though we are all made of the same fundamental elements, what makes us different and unique? The uniqueness arises from the Jīvātma, the individual Ātma participating in the processes of Involution and Evolution. Differences emerge from the Pañca Mahā Bhūta, which can be understood on two levels.

First Level – Innate Mahābhūtas

At conception, Ākāśa forms first, followed by the other four Mahābhūtas that constitute the embryo. The Jīvātma enters the foetus to create a distinct individual form.

Second Level – Guṇa Dominance in Mahābhūtas

Each Mahābhūta exhibits dominance of one or more Guṇa:

- Ākāśa: Sattva dominant
- Vāyu: Rajas dominant
- Agni: Sattva and Rajas dominant
- Āp: Sattva and Tamas dominant
- Pṛthvī: Tamas dominant

The Guṇa imparts a unique Dharma or inherent nature to each Mahābhūta. Understanding our Prakṛti reveals not only our nature (Svabhāva) but also our Svadharma – the inner order or sustainable pattern that maintains higher-order balance. Dharma operates at individual, social, and cosmic levels. Every celestial body, from the solar system to galaxies, follows this order, highlighting the universal principle of Dharma as the "right way of living" or sustaining existence.

First Level – Individual Differences due to Mahābhūtas

The Mahābhūtas form our body-mind continuum and shape our psychological profile or mānas orientation, akin to Carl Jung's concept of preferences. Below is a brief overview:

- **Ākāśa (Space):** Corresponds to bodily spaces such as nostrils, mouth, respiratory and gastrointestinal tracts, abdomen, thorax, lymphatic system, tissues, and cells. Modern science notes that atoms are over 99% empty space, making humans essentially fields of void. Ākāśa corresponds to sound, with ears as the sense organ. At the Svabhāva level, Ākāśa imparts expansiveness and profundity, producing individuals who are philosophical, spiritual, detached, knowledgeable, and wise.
- **Vāyu (Movement):** Governs muscular activity, heart and lung pulsation, stomach and intestinal movements, cellular motion, and the nervous system. Vāyu corresponds to touch, with skin as the sense organ. Psychologically, Vāyu produces creativity, innovative thinking, strong communication, and a propensity for dreaming and ideation.
- **Agni (Fire/Transformation):** Controls metabolism, digestion, enzymes, retinal function, and body temperature. Agni corresponds to sight, with eyes as the sense organ. At the Svabhāva level, Agni manifests as intelligence, vision, transformation, expansion, achievement orientation, and aspiration.
- **Āp (Water):** Āp is the life-sustaining force that maintains electrolyte balance and manifests in blood, digestive secretions, mucus membranes, plasma, and intracellular fluid. It corresponds to the sense of taste, with the tongue as its organ. As commonly said, "the taste changes with water," reflecting this connection. At the level of svabhāva, Āp imparts creativity, nurturance,

empathy, calmness, adaptability, and the ability to find a path of least resistance.

- **Pṛthvī (Earth):** Pṛthvī provides solidity and stability, represented in bones, nails, cartilage, teeth, tendons, skin, and hair. It corresponds to the sense of smell, with the nose as its organ. Psychologically, Pṛthvī imparts stability, composure, and contentment.

We are all made up of the Pañca Mahābhūta, and their combination is determined at conception. This combination shapes our svabhāva – our inherent nature. Each Mahābhūta also has its own Svadharma, the factors that sustain and nurture it versus those that deplete it. More on this will be discussed in Chapter 4.

Second Level – Individual Differences due to Triguṇa

Each Mahābhūta is associated with the Triguṇa (Sattva, Rajas, Tamas), as discussed earlier. While the Mahābhūta combination that forms our Prakṛti remains largely stable throughout life, it can become imbalanced, creating a Vikṛti. In contrast, the Triguṇas are dynamic and can be transformed.

- Sattva can be cultivated to guide and regulate Rajas and Tamas in our svabhāva.
- Changes in Triguṇa dominance influence our Citta Vṛttis, the outer expressions or fluctuations of the mind (mānas).

In Yoga, the mānas operates in five states based on Citta Vṛtti, which will be explored in Chapter 5, along with Saṃskāras.

Positive Psychology, Well-being & Worldview

At the heart of human existence is the need for meaning and contribution to something beyond one's immediate actions. This is the essence of logotherapy, designed by Viktor Frankl. [32] Our cosmology connects

32 Good Therapy. (n.d.). Retrieved from https://www.goodtherapy.org

us as humans to a larger understanding of who we are. The Pañca Mahābhūtas – the same elements that constitute the cosmos – form our physical body, influence our mānas, and are themselves affected by the time of day, diet, lifestyle, and seasonal changes, resulting in either a balanced or imbalanced state of health. Way back in 1968, in the preface to the second edition of *Towards a Psychology of Being*, Abraham H. Maslow mentions, "I consider Humanistic, Third Force Psychology to be transitional, a preparation for a still 'higher' Fourth Psychology, transpersonal, trans human, centred in the cosmos rather than in human needs & interest, going beyond humanness, identity, self-actualization, and the like." [33] This "Psychology centred in the cosmos" aligns closely with what we know from Āyurveda. A balanced state of Mahābhūta and Triguṇa produces self-actualising and self-transcending individuals, who are not stuck in deficit-driven needs but are inspired by growth and higher purpose, as Maslow described.

In his work on Motivation and Personality,[34] he states very clearly, "Holism is obviously true- after all, the cosmos is one and interrelated; any society is one and interrelated; any person is one and interrelated, etc. and yet the holistic outlook has a hard time being implemented and being used as it should be, as a way of looking at the world."

Modern psychology has introduced constructs such as health, wellness, well-being, and positive psychology – all paradigms that have evolved over time. Bhāratīya Psychology takes inspiration from classical texts in Āyurveda and Yoga, offering insights that are remarkably relevant in a modern context. Abraham Maslow (1962) was one of the first in the field of psychology to describe "wellbeing," with his characteristics of a self-actualized person. The description of self-actualisation foreshadows the PERMA model (Seligman, 2011), which outlines

---

33 Maslow, A. H. (1968). *Towards a psychology of being*. New York, NY: D. Van Nostrand Company.

34 Maslow, A. H. (1970). *Motivation and personality* (2nd ed., Preface ix). New York, NY: Harper & Row.

the characteristics of a flourishing individual and Wellbeing Theory (WBT). In 1998, Dr. Martin Seligman used his inaugural address as the incoming president of the American Psychological Association (APA) to shift the focus from mental illness and pathology to studying what is good and positive in life. From this point, theories and research began examining positive psychology interventions to define, quantify, and create wellbeing (Rusk & Waters, 2015). However, the dichotomy of body and mind remains unresolved. Consciousness, mind or Mānas, Antaḥkaraṇa, Hṛdaya (heart), gut, and related systems are still being rediscovered by modern psychology. Though Seligman mentioned the shift to Positive Psychology in 1998, even as recently as 2017, the APA's Health Psychology division had not fully recognized the continuum of body and mind. Mental health, as of 2017, was still not considered an integral part of Health Psychology, as reflected in the editorial:

"Division 38 celebrated its 38th anniversary in 2016. The Society for Health Psychology has been the leading organization for health psychologists ever since there has been an organized field of health psychology, and *Health Psychology* has been at the forefront of the field for almost as long... With due respect to holistic conceptions of human health, the field of health psychology is fundamentally concerned with *physical* health, not with mental health."[35]

Bhāratīya Psychology has evolved from a comprehensive understanding of the cosmos, emphasizing the interconnectedness not only of body and mind but also of humans with the cosmos, nature, and all living beings. This holistic integration is reflected in Āyurveda, where psychology and health are viewed as positive, interconnected constructs. The foundation of this framework is a worldview that encompasses the four types of Āyu, or life, possible for human beings.

35 Freedland, K. E. (2017). A New Era for Health Psychology. *Health Psychology*, 36(1), 1–4. Editorial. Washington University School of Medicine, USA.

Hita and Sukha Āyu

Āyurveda views an individual as interconnected with the human and ecological environment. Social milieu also affects individual health. Disconnection from community and nature, especially in the Post-Industrial Era, has contributed to the emergence of new illnesses. The WHO recognizes depression and other mental health issues as nearly epidemic. Maslow and Mittelman discussed the cultural and social etiologies of psychopathology and social disintegration.[36] This is also discussed in Atharva Veda. Atharva Veda (Whitney, Bloomfield, Satavalekar, & R. C. Sharma) addresses social integration at multiple levels:

- Family: AV II/30/1–5, III/30/1–7, VII/38/1–5
- Friends and small groups: AV VI/42/1–3, VI/64/1–3, VI/73/1–3, VI/94/1–3, VI/102/1–3, VII/52/1–2
- Nation and country: AV I/15/1–4, III/8/1–6

In these mantras, Mānas (mind) is repeatedly emphasized because social integration depends upon proper functioning of the mind.[37]

Āyurveda recognises interconnectedness at a deeper level, describing life in terms of welfare-oriented (Hita), self-centred (Ahita), happy (Sukha), and unhappy (Duḥkha) existence, including their promoters, non-promoters, span, and nature. Connectedness at the social and community level, and rootedness in nature, promotes welfare-oriented lives, whereas their opposites foster self-centred and xenophobic tendencies.

---

36 Maslow, A. H., & Mittelman, M. (1951). Principles of Abnormal Psychology (p. 375). New York: Harper & Row.

37 Singh, H. G. (1977). *Psychotherapy in India* (p. 40). Agra: National Psychological Corporation.

हिताहितं सुखं दुःखमायुस्तस्य हिताहितम् ।
मानं च तच्च यत्रोक्तमायुर्वेदः स उच्यते ।।
च.सू.1/41

Now what is a welfare-oriented and happy life? What leads to a self-centred and unhappy life? Hita is beneficial, welfare-promoting, and blessed. The root of the word Hita connects it to well-being and love.[38] A life guided by the well-being of everyone around, out of love for all entities – animate or inanimate – becomes sustainable.

"A life of a person is said to be good who is a well-wisher of all creatures. S/He does not long for other people's goods, speaks the truth, is peace-loving, acts with deliberation, and is not negligent. S/He is devoted to the three ends: viz., virtue, wealth, and enjoyment. S/He does not allow any one of these ends – virtue, wealth, and enjoyment – to conflict with the others."

These are the three psychological drivers, known as Puruṣārthas – Dharma, Artha, and Kāma. 'Virtue' is used here for easy understanding but is not the precise interpretation of Dharma. Throughout this work, we will explore the deeper meaning of Dharma and how it drives Rta (cosmic order). S/He is reverential toward those people who're worthy of respect, scholarly, scientific, and humble. S/He spends time in the company of the wise and elders.

S/He has well-curbed passion, desire, anger, envy, pride, and conceit. S/He is constantly engaged in charitable acts, devoted to austerity, knowledge, and tranquillity, and endowed with spiritual insights, memory, and understanding. S/He is single-minded, contemplating the good in this world and the next. That is which is the opposite nature

38 Bhagwat GoMandal, (1987) part 9, page 9199, second edition, Praveen Prakashan, India

to this is called as not good or Ahitāyu.'[39] Hitāyu is life philosophy or worldview which is in harmony with the society and environment. This precedes the Sukhāyu, life of happiness. For Āyurvedic Rishis, wellness and well-being of the environment came before personal happiness. Today, positive psychology is talking about social well-being. "Keyes (1998) conceived of a five-component model of social well-being: social integration, social contribution, social coherence, social actualization, and social acceptance. These five elements, taken together, indicate whether and to what degree individuals are overcoming social challenges and are functioning well in their social world (alongside neighbours, co-workers, and fellow world citizens)."[40] Noteworthy is the reference of Atharva Veda by H. G. Singh in his work Psychotherapy in India. He elaborates on process of 'Samaññāyani' in Atharva Veda which is about social integration and harmony. In Atharva Veda, there are given devices to create harmony in three broad social groups – family, friends and smaller groups and the nation.[41]

Today, the pursuit of happiness has ironically led to widespread dissatisfaction, to the extent that happiness courses are now taught at universities, and Ministries of Happiness have been established at national levels. The HAPPINESS Course at Harvard, for example, has been one of the most popular courses in recent years. Its description emphasises "a fulfilling and flourishing life," reflecting the rise of positive psychology, which focusses on what makes people feel good, rather than on the pathologies that cause suffering.

The field of psychology originally focused on pathology and has undergone decades of paradigm shifts to evolve into the Positive

---

39 Bhagwat Pranav, http://ayurgoa.com/article/āyurvedic-concept-of-life

40 Gallagher et al. (2009, p. 1027), The Science of Wellbeing and Positive Psychology, *Wellbeing, Recovery and Mental Health*, ed. Mike Slade, Lindsay Oades and Aaron Jarden. Published by Cambridge University Press, 2017

41 Dr. H.G Singh, Psychotherapy In India (From Vedic To Modern Times), 1977, National Psychological Corporation, Agra, India pg. 40

Psychology movement we see today. Health psychology, in particular, emerged as a response to problems created by the Industrial Revolution. What is often overlooked, however, is the alienation of humans from nature and community, and the well-being of the larger ecosystem as a factor in illness. When humans are reduced to mere cogs in the industrial machine, stripped of dignity and individuality, health becomes the first casualty. Sadly, this perspective is rarely addressed in literature on psychology, management, or health psychology.

Another way of life is Sukhāyu. In Sanskrit, 'Khā' means space, and 'Su' denotes auspiciousness. Auspicious space creates Sukha, commonly translated as happiness. This space operates on multiple levels: externally, in the environment in which one lives, and internally, within the body, mind, and heart. Happiness arises from maintaining harmony and flow in these spaces.

Happiness is the result of maintaining all these spaces – a body, mind, and heart – clutter-free, allowing the Prāna, or Life-force, to flow freely and sustain life. Any blockage in the body, mind, or heart restricts the flow of energy. Happiness resides in such unobstructed spaces. Unfortunately, in the West, and especially since the Industrial Era, happiness is often misconstrued as the accumulation of external, materialistic possessions. Greed and jealousy have been camouflaged as Achievement Motivation. Interestingly, the consequences of Achievement Motivation without Dharma are increasingly recognized by scholars such as Lyle Spencer. At an Emotional Intelligence Conference, he emphasised that Achievement Motivation carries within it the seed of self-destruction if not guided by Dharma.

Our society suffers from "affluenza." Gilbert Paul describes this aptly, quoting Oliver James: "We are suffering from 'affluenza' – an addiction to affluence and a desire for 'more and more.' John Naish makes essentially the same point, noting that our brains evolved to cope with scarcity, not abundance. We are born seekers and wanters because, for millions of years, that was our environment. Our lifestyles are physically, mentally, and spiritually exhausting us – and we know it. We are trapped in a culture driven by the 'business model' and profit, rather than a human-centred 'psychology model' or welfare-based model. In this drive for profit and efficiency, we lose contact with each other and the things that nourish, support, and nurture us."[42]

This clearly demonstrates that the current culture is Ahitāyu and Duḥkhāyu – devoid of true well-being and happiness.

How does Āyurveda describe Sukhāyu? "The life of such a person is called happy when s/he is not afflicted with physical or mental ailments, and is endowed with youth, strength, vigour, virility, reputation, endeavour, and boldness in applying his/her abilities. S/He is actuated in deeds by the combined urges of knowledge, science, the senses, and sense objects. S/He possesses diverse and delightful amenities accruing from great wealth, all of which prosper through effort, allowing planning at will." (More on Sukha is discussed in the chapter on Heart.)

A life contrary to this is called Duḥkhāyu or Asukhāyu – unhappy life.

Āyurveda offers a broad and integrated perspective, encompassing not only physical and psychological health, but also social and spiritual well-being, making it a true social medicine. Modern lifestyles, however, are increasingly stressful and aligned with Duḥkhāyu or Ahitāyu. Āyurveda advocates the opposite. While this may seem philosophical, it gives Āyurveda a unique edge over other medical sciences, as it addresses not only the body but also the mind (Mānas) and consciousness (Ātma) – which is its true strength.[43]

Puruṣārtha Framework, Wellbeing and Meaningful Life

Western Psychology's latest paradigm shift to positive psychology, flourishing, and the PERMA model highlights the centrality of

---

42 Gilbert, P. (2009). *The compassionate mind.* Constable & Robinson.

43 Bhagwat, P. (n.d.). *Āyurvedic concept of life.* Retrieved from http://ayurgoa.com/article/āyurvedic-concept-of-life

meaningfulness as a core aspect of well-being. The Japanese term *Ikigai* has gained popularity, meaning "purpose of life" or "reason for being." *Ikigai* emphasises that a meaningful life is often longer, healthier, and happier.

Bhāratīya Psychology has long integrated well-being, happiness, and meaningfulness as essential for a healthy life. One framework that provides a comprehensive and integrated understanding is the Puruṣārtha Framework, which predates *Ikigai* by centuries. "Puruṣa" refers to a human being, and "Artha" refers to meaning and purpose. The framework comprises four aspects of human life – Dharma, Artha, Kāma, and Mokṣa. The sequence of these aspects is critical; Dharma leads the other three. The Puruṣārtha Framework acts as a map for life, guiding us through four significant goals: Dharma (sustainability), Artha (meaning and prosperity), Kāma (desires and pleasure), and Mokṣa (outgrowing patterns and habits).

In many Western interpretations, Artha is often equated solely with economics or wealth, and some non-Indian interpretations of the Puruṣārtha Framework even reorder it, placing Artha first. This mindset has dominated global thought since the Industrial Revolution.

Dharma: Dharma is commonly mistranslated as "Religion," but the Sanskrit word comes from the root *dhṛ*, meaning "to uphold" or "to sustain." A key aspect of Dharma is that it sustains, nourishes, and integrates. Being polysemic, the word has multiple related meanings, each relevant in context. Swami Chinmayanand ji explains that Dharma is the essence that upholds, nourishes, sustains, and integrates the universe. Just as sweetness is the dharma of sugar, values uphold one's character, nourish life, sustain joy, give meaning, and integrate society. Hence, values themselves are Dharma.

Until recently, values were often excluded from psychology and taught separately as ethics. Only with the modern definition of human flourishing have character and virtues been recognised as part of well-being and happiness. Dharma is a much larger construct, serving as an inner compass or true north.

Dharma exists at multiple levels – individual, social, and Cosmic. "Dharayati iti Dharma" means "that which sustains is Dharma." In the Puruṣārtha Framework, Dharma comes first because it serves as the compass guiding Artha and Kāma. At an individual level, following Dharma ensures alignment with one's roles and responsibilities. In different stages of life, Svadharma adapts according to one's duties and context. Psychology can help individuals recognise their Dharma and restore balance if deviations occur.

Social order is also upheld by Dharma, ensuring the wellbeing and progress of the community. Dharma is grounded in *ṛta*, the cosmic order, or natural balance of the universe. When interrelated systems fall into disequilibrium, such as in open systems like nature, simple corrective measures are insufficient. Sometimes, a shift in worldview is necessary to restore balance.

Artha: The Sanskrit language is fascinating because a single word can hold layered meanings. Although often reduced to material wealth, "Artha" also signifies "meaning" and "purpose." It encompasses everything that provides direction, security, and stability in life. Artha is what grounds human existence and enables navigation through life's fluctuations. As a socio-economic goal, it advocates prosperity and stability through lawful and ethical (dharmic) means[44].

Every human being seeks resources and meaning to achieve life goals. However, since the Industrial Revolution, wealth and profit have been positioned as the backbone of economies, overshadowing ethical and holistic considerations. Economics has taken center stage in the social sciences, and unchecked consumerism and materialism have grown from pursuits disconnected from Dharma.

---

44 Ananthlakshmi, et al. *Panchkosha Pathway*. Anaadi Foundation, India, 2024, p. 17.

McClelland's notion of achievement motivation explains one dimension of human drive, but in the Dharmic context, Artha integrates interconnectedness, community wellbeing, and ecological sensitivity. In Martin Seligman's PERMA model, "M" for Meaning and "A" for Accomplishment[45] are both encompassed within Artha in the Puruṣārtha framework.

Kāma: Kāma refers to desire, love, and the pursuit of pleasure. It includes both sensual enjoyment and the aesthetic appreciation of life. Kāma reflects the intrinsic human need for emotional fulfilment through relationships, the arts, and cultural expression. At one level, it aligns with the Positive Emotions and Relationships dimensions in the PERMA model. At another, it resonates with Maslow's expanded hierarchy of needs, which recognizes Aesthetic Need as a fundamental human need.[46]

In the Dharmic framework, Kāma is always pursued within the guiding boundaries of Dharma and Artha. It can be expressed in diverse ways, from everyday acts like decorating one's home to higher pursuits such as theatre, literature, and the arts. This ensures a balanced and meaningful life.

Modern lifestyles, however, often distort Kāma. Entertainment today is frequently tied to foul language, substance use, casual sex, and violence, stripped of Dharma and Sattva. Relationships too often appear transactional or contractual, generating anxiety rather than joy. Later chapters discuss emotions and wellbeing from the perspectives of Nāṭya Śāstra and Saundarya Śāstra. Swami Chinmayananda ji explains that scriptures guiding Dharma are Dharma Śāstras, which can also be understood as a "Science of Desire Management." They outline how to manage and sublimate desires by providing a dinācārya (daily routine) and jīvan caryā (life plan).

45 Seligman, Martin. *Flourish*. Nicholas Brealey Publishing, Great Britain, 2011, p. 16.

46 Ward, D., & Lasen, M. (2009). *An overview of needs theories behind consumerism. Journal of Applied Economic Sciences, 4*(1(7)), 137-155.

Mokṣa: Mokṣa, usually translated as "liberation" or "enlightenment," refers to freedom from the cycle of birth and rebirth. It can also be understood as the process of outgrowing whatever binds, limits, or enslaves us. This includes habits, social conditioning, and instinctual compulsions. Mokṣa is liberation through transcendence, enabling the reduction of suffering and the realisation of higher states of being. Etymologically, Moha Kshya- dissolution of attachment is Mokṣa.

In Maslow's hierarchy, self-transcendence is the highest human need, though rarely addressed in mainstream Western psychology or management literature. The Puruṣārtha framework, however, positions Mokṣa as the ultimate human pursuit, attainable through self-realization. Recognising the true nature of being human reveals our current state as a milestone in evolution rather than its endpoint, thereby dissolving the Anthropocene mindset of domination over nature.

Overall, the Puruṣārtha framework offers a holistic, 360-degree perspective on life. Dharma expands the concept of self, informs development and social integration, supports deep ecology, and enriches the psychological sciences. Further research is needed to integrate this ancient framework systematically into Bhāratīya Mānas Śāstra.

Mānas – The Important Link to Wellbeing and Happiness

In this chapter, we cover these themes:

- Importance of Mānas in Flourishing
- What is Mānas?
- Location of Mānas & Manovaha Srotas
- Functions of Mānas
- Psychoneuroimmunology and Mānas
- Mānas and Indriya

Introduction

Psychology in Sanskrit is known as Mānas Śāstra or Mano Vijñāna. A human being is called Manuṣya in Sanskrit, meaning the master of the Mānas. Vijñāna refers to *Viśeṣa* – specialised knowledge or insight. From Vedic times, Mānas has been recognised as a central aspect of our existence. Our thoughts, emotions, and guiding forces behind behaviour, relationships, and all actions arise from Mānas. Therefore, cultivating a clean, well-connected Mānas is essential for individual and collective wellbeing.

All Indian philosophies emphasise the development of higher Mānas. Societies that nurture refined and enlightened minds are blessed with prosperity, health, and happiness. Mānas governs our activities at both personal and social levels. It is a soft power, a true superpower. A society dominated by contaminated or lower minds may accumulate wealth but remain deprived of true prosperity. The word "mind" is a limited translation of Mānas. Western psychology often divides the mind into conscious, subconscious, and unconscious layers (Sigmund Freud). However, the holistic nature and higher aspects of Mānas – described in Yogic and Āyurvedic texts – remain largely unexplored in the West. Our Ṛṣis had insights into these subtler dimensions, offering a detailed scientific understanding of Mānas.

Importance of Mānas

In Yoga, Mānas is one of the four parts of Antaḥkaraṇa, instrument of inner processes, along with Buddhi, Citta and Ahaṅkāra.[47] In Āyurveda, Mānas acts as the crucial link between Jīva (individual), Ātman (Consciousness), and the body through the Indriyas (senses). Without Mānas, the Ātman cannot function in the external world. It is Mānas that either binds us or creates freedom. If we consider Mānas as the software for our life, then understanding its programming, keeping it free from contamination, installing antivirus, and regularly cleaning it becomes essential. One of the oldest prayers from the Yajurveda emphasises the need for Mānas to be filled with Śiva Saṅkalpam.

In Sanskrit, Śiva has multiple shades of meaning: Supreme Energy, auspiciousness, and the source of Kalyāṇa (well-being) for all. Saṅkalpa means intention or desire. This prayer not only describes Mānas but also guides how it should be filled with auspiciousness.

In the previous chapter, we discussed Hita Āyu, where Hita denotes well-being of every being. Such a worldview and attitude toward life emerge only when we are connected with Śiva, representing Loka Kalyāṇa (universal welfare). There is an illustrative story from ancient literature about King Dakṣa and his yajña. He invites everyone, except his son-in-law, Śiva. Feeling insulted, his daughter Sati jumps into the fire of the yajña. When Śiva learns of Sati's death, He comes with His Gaṇa and destroys the yajña. This story holds a deeper meaning: Dakṣa, with all

---

47 Omananda Tīrtha, Swami. (2013). *Patañjala Yoga Pradīpa.* Gorakhpur: Gita Press.

his materialistic pomp, without Śiva, represents modern materialistic and consumerist society devoid of consideration for well-being. Hence, having a Mānaṣ filled with Śiva is critical for achieving individual and societal flourishing.

Yajurveda Chapter 34, Mantra 1-6

(यजुर्वेद अध्याय 34 मंत्र 1-6)

यज्जाग्र॑तो दू॒रमु॒दैति॒ दैवं॒ तदु॑ सु॒प्तस्य॒ तथै॒वैति॑ ।
दू॒र॒ङ्ग॒मं ज्योति॑षां॒ ज्योति॒रेकं॒ तन्मे॒ मनः॑ शि॒वस॑ङ्कल्पमस्तु ॥ १॥

Meaning: The Mānas that can travel vast distances in both conscious and dream states illuminates the senses, serving as the medium for the individual soul. May our Mānas be filled with Śiva Saṅkalpa – auspicious thoughts and intentions.

येन॒ कर्मा॑ण्य॒पसो॑ मनी॒षिणो॑ य॒ज्ञे कृ॒ण्वन्ति॑ वि॒दथे॑षु॒ धीराः॑ ।
यद॑पू॒र्वं य॒क्षम॒न्तः प्र॒जानां॒ तन्मे॒ मनः॑ शि॒वस॑ङ्कल्पमस्तु ॥ २॥

Meaning: The Mānas enables scholars to acquire knowledge, perform Yajña, and engage in virtuous deeds. The Mānas that resides in every human being, supporting sustainable engagement in life, may this Mānas be filled with auspicious thoughts and intentions.

यत्प्र॒ज्ञान॑मु॒त चेतो॒ धृति॑श्च॒ यज्ज्योति॑र॒न्तर॒मृतं॑ प्र॒जासु॑ ।
यस्मा॒न्नऽऋ॒ते किं च॒न कर्म॑ क्रि॒यते॒ तन्मे॒ मनः॑ शि॒वस॑ङ्कल्पमस्तु ॥ ३॥

Meaning: The Mānas which is imbued with wisdom, consciousness, and sustainable intelligence, residing within the Antaḥkaraṇa of each individual with eternal Light, without which no action is possible, may that Mānas be filled with auspicious thoughts and intentions.

येने॒दं भू॒तं भुव॑नं भवि॒ष्यत्परि॑गृहीतम॒मृते॑न॒ सर्व॑म् ।
येन॑ य॒ज्ञस्ता॒यते॑ स॒प्तहो॑ता॒ तन्मे॒ मनः॑ शि॒वस॑ङ्कल्पमस्तु ॥ ४॥

Meaning: The Eternal Mānas, which has the capacity to access knowledge beyond Time, and by whose guidance the Seven Hota perform the Yajña, may that Mānas be filled with auspicious thoughts and intentions.

यस्मि॒न्नृचः॒ साम॒ यजू॑ꣳषि॒ यस्मि॒न् प्रति॑ष्ठिता रथना॒भावि॑वा॒राः ।
यस्मिं॑श्चि॒त्तꣳ सर्व॒मोतं॑ प्र॒जाना॒ं तन्मे॒ मन॑ः शि॒वस॑ङ्कल्पमस्तु ॥ ५॥

Meaning: The Mānas which holds the Vedic knowledge, the Mantras of Sāma Veda and Yajurveda, like the spokes of a chariot wheel, may this Mānas, which preserves all knowledge, be filled with auspicious thoughts and well-being for all.

सु॒षा॒र॒थिरश्वा॑निव॒ यन्म॑नु॒ष्या॒न्नेनी॒यते॒ऽभीशु॑भिर्वा॒जिन॑ इव ।
हृ॒त्प्रति॑ष्ठं॒ यद॑जि॒रं जवि॑ष्ठं॒ तन्मे॒ मन॑ः शि॒वस॑ङ्कल्पमस्तु ॥ ६॥

Meaning: Just as an expert charioteer holds the reins of horses skilfully to reach the goal, the Mānas, ageless, agile, and residing in the heart, guides us toward our life goals. May this Mānas be filled with auspicious thoughts.

This ancient prayer from the Yajurveda depicts the true meaning of *mānas*. What neuroscientists and cardio-energetics are rediscovering about the nature of mind today, is known to the ṛṣis millennia ago. The crisis of mental health we face today can be better understood when we realise that *mānas* must remain in a state of śubha-saṅkalpa (right intention). *Mānas* has the capacity to elevate us, allowing our evolutionary potential to manifest, but it can also entangle us in habitual patterns that pull us downward. The Vedas, and their extensions such as Āyurveda and Yoga, regard mental health as a positive construct, offering rituals and practices that sustain positive states of mind.

What is Mānas?

Western science is still grappling with the distinction between the "mind" and the "brain." These terms are often used interchangeably, with the mind frequently reduced to nothing more than a function of the brain. Traditionally, psychology and biology have treated the brain as the physical substrate and the mind as the conscious output of neural activity. Yet, even within modern science, this view is shifting. Neuroscientists such as Candace Pert have provided important insights, suggesting that the mind cannot be fully explained as brain function alone. Similarly, Dan Siegel, professor of psychiatry at UCLA and author of *Mind: A Journey to the Heart of Being Human*[48], argues that the mind cannot be confined to what lies inside the skull—or even within the body. He defines the mind as the seat of consciousness, the very essence of our being. Without it, we cannot be considered meaningfully alive. This evolving perspective opens a dialogue between modern research and Āyurvedic wisdom, where Mānas is not merely a by-product of the brain but an integral principle connecting body, senses, and consciousness.

Mānas is also referred to as sattva and is considered the subtle organ of antaḥkaraṇa. It is counted among the 24 tattvas, evolving from ahaṅkāra. Because it connects both the organs of cognition (jñānendriyas) and the organs of action (karmendriyas), it is described as the "11th sense organ." Without mānas, none of the senses can operate. Only when the Ātman – the central source of consciousness – activates mānas do the senses become fully functional.

Mānas governs cognition and attention. In its absence, one may be physically present yet mentally elsewhere – an experience familiar to all. This demonstrates that mānas can "wander" beyond the self while the body and senses remain intact. The very fact that perception varies with the presence or absence of mānas indicates that it is a distinct principle, not reducible to the brain alone. Subtle and intelligent, mānas has the capacity to extend outward, while always retaining the ability to return to the self (Caraka Saṃhitā 1.18).[49]

48 Goldhill, O. (2016, December 24). *The mind is more than just the brain.* The Regents of the University of California.

49 Shreevathsa, D., & Dwivedi, R. (2011). *Manas Prakruti.* Varanasi: Chaukhambha Visvabharati, p. 7.

In Āyurveda, Mānas is described as a form of Dravya – literally, "that which flows." Darshan Shankar explains this with clarity, emphasizing that dravya in the Ayurvedic framework carries a specialized meaning. It denotes nine "fundamental generic states" of existence that constitute the universe. These states are not fixed; rather, they undergo continuous transformation while maintaining distinct and recognizable identities. They are presented in an ascending order, moving from gross to increasingly subtle levels of reality – beginning with solid, liquid, gaseous, and plasma states, then advancing to ether-like, mental state, time, and direction, and culminating in the unmanifest principle, Ātman. Outside the technical discourse of Āyurveda, however, the term dravya is often used more simply to indicate any substance derived from these nine foundational states.[50]

Mānas, being classified as dravya, cannot be assigned a precise physical location. Instead, it is identified and understood through its actions and functions rather than any fixed anatomical seat. Furthermore, Mānas is regarded as nitya dravya—eternal in nature. It remains in constant connection with the individual Ātman, carrying impressions (saṃskāras) and memories accumulated across time. As discussed earlier in Chapter 1, Ātman forms the foundation of consciousness. This continuity of Mānas recalls the words of Claude Lelouch's French film Ins and Outs, which begins with the line: "There are only three or four stories in the world that keep repeating themselves as if they never happened before." Mānas is the principle that weaves these recurring narratives, shaping experiences so that each individual perceives their journey as unique and personal.

At the microcosmic level, individual Mānas (Anu Mānas) mirrors the cosmic Mānas (Vibhu). Its functions encompass self-awareness, the sense of identity ("I–Me"), learning, preferences and aversions,

50 Kanna, V. K. S. (2011). *Ayurvediya Padarth Vijnanam: The theoretical foundations of Ayurveda* (p. 52). Bengaluru, India: I-AIM-FRLHT.

experiences of pleasure and pain, memory, recognition, self-control, restraint, sensation, perception, cognition, judgment, emotions, and volition. We come to know Mānas only through these functions. Even in sleep, when the body rests, Mānas remains active, generating the world of dreams. So subtle is its nature that it cannot be seen or measured directly, yet its operations shape the very distinctiveness of human experience. Modern sciences have often reduced Mānas to a byproduct of brain activity, whereas Āyurveda and allied traditions consistently regard it as a distinct and independent entity. In later sections, we will explore how contemporary research in psychoneuroimmunology and mind–body medicine is beginning to rediscover and validate this ancient insight.

Mānas is an internal, subtle Indriya – atomic (Anu) in nature and singular in existence. It is highly agile and is the reason for our continuity across lifetimes. As the Caraka Saṃhitā states: "अणुत्वमथ चैकत्वं द्वौ गुणौ मनसः स्मृतौ।" (च. शा. 1:19)[51]. (Atomic in nature and singular in form are the two inherent qualities of Mānas.) When the Jīvātma departs from the body, Mānas accompanies it. Modern science, too, is slowly rediscovering this principle of continuity through emerging studies on healing, consciousness, and memory. Psychologists like Brian Weiss have brought renewed attention to the idea of existence beyond a single lifetime. For this reason, Mānas is regarded as Nitya Dravya – an eternal substance. Even if one does not fully accept the notion of continuity beyond death, the relevance of Mānas remains universal, since our day-to-day lives are a direct manifestation of its functioning. In common speech, we often say, "I am in two minds." This captures the very nature of Mānas – restlessly agile, moving swifter than light, as mentioned in the *Yajurveda*. Though singular in existence, Mānas engages with different sense organs one at a time. Its agility (*Chanchalatva*) creates the illusion of many minds working simultaneously. Just as a burning

51 Shukla, A. V., & Tripathi, R. D. (2000). *Charak Samhita* (p. 677). Delhi, India: Chaukhamba Sanskrit Pratishthan.

stick moved rapidly in circles appears as a ring of fire, or how modern cinema creates seamless continuity through rapidly moving frames, Mānas produces the impression of multiplicity. Yet, when slowed and stilled, the movements of Mānas can be distinctly perceived. It has the rare capacity for self-reflection, inward turning, restraint, and transcendence. Buddhi (intelligence) begins to function only when the pendulum-like oscillations of Mānas between past and future are calmed. In the cosmological order of creation, Mānas arises when Sattva of Ahaṅkāra becomes vitiated, containing within it all three Guṇas – Sattva, Rajas, and Tamas. Its natural tendency is outward, towards multiplicity and distraction; but when directed inward, Mānas can re-establish its link with Buddhi and access higher intelligence for effective, conscious living. Ayurveda explains this sequence succinctly: "Tataḥ para Buddhi" – Buddhi follows Mānas. Most people, however, remain caught in the fluctuations of Mānas. A common misconception equates Mānas only with emotions and Buddhi with the logical brain. In truth, Mānas is far more complex and notoriously difficult to govern. Śaṅkarācārya offered a striking metaphor:

"मर्कटस्य सुरापनम् मध्ये वृश्चिक दंशनम्
तनमध्ये भूतसंचारो यद्वा तद्वा भविष्यति।"[52]

A monkey, drunk on liquor, bitten by a scorpion, and possessed by a ghost – such is the nature of the mind.

Restless, unstable, and mischievous, Mānas cannot be suppressed by force. It must instead be trained, tamed, and ultimately transcended.

Location of Mānas and Manovaha Strotas

Because Mānas is a subtle internal sense organ (*ati-indriya* – beyond perception through ordinary senses), it is difficult to assign it a precise

52 Anonymous. (n.d.). *Subhāṣita* ["Markatasya surāpānam..."]. In *Subhāṣita-kośa* (traditional Sanskrit verse collection).

anatomical seat. Even Indic seers and scholars of Āyurveda have not reached a consensus on its exact location.

Most scholars consider Mānas to reside in the *hṛdaya* (heart):

आत्मा च सगुणश्चेतः चिन्त्यं च हृदि सांश्रितम्। (Ca. Sa. Su. 30/4)

However, the meaning of *hṛdaya* (heart) and *śiraḥ* (head/brain) has undergone shifts in interpretation over time, leading to differing perspectives. The physical heart is visibly affected by the vibrations and actions of the Mānas, which explains the frequent association between the two. Yet, as a subtle organ operating at the energetic level, Mānas is more plausibly correlated with the *Anāhata Cakra* rather than the gross physical heart.

Suśruta, quoting Kṛtavīrya, describes the *hṛdaya* as the seat of both intellect and mind:

हृदयमिति कृतवीय बुधेर्मनश्च स्थानत्वात्। (Su. Sa. 3/32)

Similarly, Vāgbhaṭa in the *Aṣṭāṅga Hṛdaya* states that the *hṛdaya* is the seat of *sattva* and related faculties, locating it "between the breasts," which again aligns with the subtle center of the Anāhata Cakra rather than the anatomical organ:

सत्वादिधाम हृदयं स्तनोरः कोष्टमध्यगम्। (A.H. Sa. 4th Ch.)

Bhela, however, presents a different view. He places the seat of Mānas between the *śiras* (head) and *tālu* (palate), attributing to it the power of all *indriyas*. He explains that *citta* resides in the *hṛdaya*, acting as the causal factor for *buddhi* (intellect) and the basis of all mental functions. Thus, Mānas and Citta, both internal causal faculties, are intimately connected and function in alignment:

शिरस्तालान्तर्गतं सवैन्द्रियपरं मनः तंत्रस्थ तद्धि विषयानिद्रियाणां रसादकान् समीपस्थान् विजानाति त्रीन् भावांश्च नियच्छति तन्मनः प्रभवं चापि सवेन्द्रियमयं बलम्। कारणं सर्वबुदीनां चित्तं हृदयसंश्रितम्। क्रियाणां चेतरासां च चित्तं सर्वत्र कारणम्॥ (Bhela. Sa. Chi. 8)

This raises a critical question: if Mānas has a fixed location, how do we experience its influence throughout the entire body? Āyurveda resolves this paradox by describing Mānas as a form of Dravya – a subtle energy-substance capable of pervading and flowing through the organism. While this energetic language may sound esoteric to a Western scientific audience, modern research, particularly the pioneering work of Candace Pert, often called the "grandmother of psychoneuroimmunology (PNI)", has begun to reframe these insights in contemporary terms.

Being a form of flowing energy, Mānas requires specific channels for its movement. Modern anatomy has identified several gross pathways – the windpipe, food pipe, blood vessels, respiratory and lymphatic tracts, and the nervous system. Yet it has not been able to detect the subtle channels (*srotas*) that carry Prāṇa and Mānas. The channels that specifically carry Mānas are termed Manovaha Srotas (*vaha* = to carry, *srotas* = channels).

In the *Srotovimāna Adhyāya*, Ācārya Caraka does not explicitly mention Manovaha Srotas, but Chakrapani, in his authoritative commentary, clarifies that these channels are spread throughout the body, with their primary seat in the hṛdaya (heart). The ten dhamanīs, a subtle nervous system, loosely translated, arising from the heart are identified as Manovaha Srotas:

मनोवहानि स्त्रोतांसि पृथनोक्तानि तथापि मनसः

केवलं चेतनावत् शरीरमयनभूतम् इत्यथिधानात् सर्वशरीरस्त्रोतासि गृह्यन्ते।
विशेषेण तु हृदयाश्रितत्वान्मनः सस्तदाश्रित दश धमन्यो मनोवहा अभिधीयन्ते॥

(Chakrapani on Ca. Vi. 5/7)

A living being is defined by the presence of Mānas flowing through these channels, for Mānas signifies cetanā (consciousness) through its inseparable connection with Ātman. It is Mānas that activates the senses. At the time of death, Mānas gradually withdraws from the sense organs in preparation to depart with Ātman, leading the senses to fail one by one. This profound insight of the Ṛṣis demonstrates their subtle understanding of the life process.

According to Āyurveda, the Manovaha Srotas are not confined to a single organ or region but extend throughout the body, making them the most all-encompassing network of channels. Mānas quite literally influences, and is influenced by, every tissue and cell. Thus, there exists a reciprocal relationship between Mānas and the body: while Mānas affects physical health, the body's state equally conditions the quality of Mānas. Every experience we undergo has the potential either to restore balance or to disturb it – simultaneously at the mental and physical levels. Only in recent decades has modern medicine begun to rediscover this psychosomatic vision of health, a wisdom that Āyurveda has articulated and preserved for millennia.

Psychoneuroimmunology and Mānas

Since the early 1980s, the interdisciplinary field of psychoneuroimmunology (PNI) has played a key role in establishing a biological basis for the ancient insight that the mind influences both health and disease. Dr. Candace Pert's research was groundbreaking in providing scientific evidence for a biochemical basis of awareness and consciousness, affirming that the mind and body function as one. Her work emphasised that emotions and feelings act as the bridge linking these two dimensions. She explained: "The chemicals that are running our body and our brain are the same chemicals that are involved in emotion. And that says to me that we'd better pay more attention to emotions with respect to health."[53]

Pert was among the few scientists who had the courage to integrate Āyurveda and Yoga insights into biomedical research and to openly

53 Pert, C. (n.d.). *Candace Pert, PhD: Explorer of the Brain, Bodymind & Beyond.* Retrieved from https://www.candacepert.com/

acknowledge their relevance. She proposed that: "We might refer to the whole system as a psychosomatic information network, linking 'psyche,' which comprises all that is of an ostensibly nonmaterial nature, such as mind, emotion, and soul, to 'soma,' which is the material world of molecules, cells, and organs. Mind and body, psyche and soma."

In addition, Pert challenged the prevailing Cartesian and Newtonian models that had long dominated Western science. She pointed to how indigenous traditions across cultures have honored the mind–body–environment connection for centuries. Āyurveda, an ancient system of medicine dating back 3,000–6,000 years, has consistently correlated specific mental and emotional states with corresponding physical organs and diseases. Its goal is not merely to treat symptoms but to restore balance across mind, body, and spirit so that healing arises organically. Even Aristotle acknowledged this interconnection, yet Western eventually embraced the opposite view – that the mind and body were separate domains.[54] Pert's perspective invites a re-evaluation of this split. Notably, she also emphasised Heart Cakra meditation on her own platform, advocating it as a tool for psychosomatic wellness. For psychology, these insights suggest a paradigm shift: moving beyond body–brain concepts of the self to embrace a more integrative model. Incorporating PNI's findings into psychological theory and practice opens new avenues for understanding consciousness, health, and human flourishing.

Functions of Mānas

चिन्त्यं विचार्यमूह्यं च ध्येयं सङ्कल्प्यमेव च
यत्किञ्चिन्मनसो ज्ञेयं तत् सर्वं ह्यर्थसञ्ज्ञकम् ॥ (Ch. Sa. 1:20)[55]

The functions of Mānas are profoundly significant, inspired by the Jīvātma – our individual soul. Mānas drives the senses and

---

54 ibid

55 Shukla, Vidyadhar & Tripathi, Ravi Dutt. (2000). *Charak Samhita*. Chaukhamba Sanskrit Pratishthan, Delhi, India, p. 677.

simultaneously possesses the capacity for self-control (svasya nigraha). The five core functions of Mānas – Cintya, Vicārya, Ūhya, Dhyeya, and Saṅkalpa (CVUDS) – govern our mental and cognitive processes. While modern medical science often attributes these functions solely to the brain, Āyurveda emphasises that the brain is merely the hardware, whereas Mānas functions as the software.

Cintya is the most basic and continuous function of Mānas, representing the stream of thoughts in the mind – the process we commonly call thinking. Largely unconscious, this process can become overwhelming, leading to overthinking or mental turbulence. However, when engaged consciously, Cintya can be productive. By observing our thought patterns, we can identify recurring themes. Between each thought exists a small pause – an interval where Mānas transitions from one point to another. Cultivating awareness during this pause transforms mere worry (Chinta) into deliberate reflection (Cintana). Vicārya occurs when rational and logical analysis is applied. If the pause in Cintya is missed, Vicārya may not manifest, as thoughts can become chaotic. Vicārya involves evaluating consequences, weighing pros and cons, and deliberating critically on potential actions, playing a decisive role in decision-making.

Ūhya is the imaginative projection of possibilities and hypotheses, arising after deliberation, enabling comprehension beyond immediate reasoning. Dhyeya represents the concentration and fixation of the fluctuating mind on a goal or knowledge, embodying an intention with firm commitment. Saṅkalpa, or Conviction, is the will, volition, or resolve to achieve Dhyeya. It is a definitive intention formed in the heart, profoundly influencing intellect and decision-making. This framework of Mānas functions is highly effective for self-understanding and in counselling others. By observing self-talk or others' expressions, one can discern the functional level of Mānas. Most often, we operate at Cintya, and even when accessing other functions, we tend to return to it. In Cintya, the mind is caught in a whirlpool of thoughts, making direction or solutions difficult to discern. Disciplines such as Yoga, Prānayama, and the 3 SRB practices (detailed in the Appendix) cultivate the pause necessary for Vicārya and Ūhya to function effectively.

Unfortunately, Western interpretations have appropriated Āyurvedic wisdom, often repackaging it under modern labels. As Dr. Bhaswati notes: "The understanding of the indriya (five senses) as a bridge between the mānas (mind) and sharira (body) was known in āyurveda and transformed to practical rituals in all Bhāratīya traditions, and is now called 5-sense therapy. While conservative and outdated physicians are laughing at āyurvedic concepts of smell and flavour, neuroscientists have discovered olfaction and taste have more robust aspects in the wiring of the brain. These require understanding of smell and flavour as multi-sensory intertwined experiences of the mind and light, sound, and chemicals. Āyurveda called them indriya then and still calls them indriya now. The wisdom remains consistent 5000 years later."[56]

Mānas directs itself outward via the five senses, each possessing its own intelligence. Eyes perceive forms, the tongue perceives taste, and each sense is constrained by the Pañca Mahābhūta associated with it. Without Mānas, the sense organs cannot function. This process is described in Āyurveda as Pañcīkaraṇa. Touch is unique, as it pervades the entire body through the skin while also carrying deeper symbolic significance, such as "touching the heart." Touch affects both physical and psychological realms. Carakā Saṃhitā's Pañcā Pañcaaka describes all five Jñānendriya (sense organs) in terms of their Mahābhūta Dravya, bodily location (adhiṣṭhāna), Tanmātra or artha, and intelligence (buddhi), highlighting the intricate connection between senses, Mānas, and cognition (buddhi).[57]

---

56 Everyday Ayurveda, Dr. Bhaswati Bhattacharya, The South Asian Times, Dec. 2021

57 Acharya YT. Charaka Samhita of Agnivesha, 5th Ed, Varanasi: Choukhambha Prakashana, 2007, 290.

Sl. No.	Sense-Indriya	Mahābhūta-Dravya	Place in body-Adhiṣṭhāna	Tanmātra-Artha	Intelligence-Buddhi
1.	Shrotra	Ākāśaa	Ear-Karna	Śabda	Shrotra
2.	Tvak	Vāyu	Skin-Tvak	Sparśa	Tvacya
3.	Cakṣuḥ	Agni	Eyes-Akṣiṇī	Rūpa	Cakṣuḥśa
4.	Rasanā	Jal	Tongue-Jihvā	Rasa	Rasanā
5.	Ghrāṇa	Pṛthvī	Nose-Nāsikā	Gandha	Ghrāṇaja

Mānas and the Indriyas (senses) share a profound and dynamic relationship. The natural tendency of Mānas is to flow outward, with each sense organ drawn to its corresponding object – eyes to forms, tongue to tastes, and so on. However, Mānas also possesses the capacity for self-reflection and judgment. When it exercises self-restraint (svasya nigraha in Sanskrit), Mānas can pause, evaluate its activity, and make deliberate, conscious decisions. In Āyurveda, this process of self-restraint and informed decision-making is supported by the faculties of Buddhi (intelligence), Dhṛti (steadfastness), and Smṛti (memory). The realm of Buddhi emerges only when the restless chatter of lower Mānas is silenced, allowing one to transcend ordinary Mānas functions. Together, Buddhi, Dhṛti, and Smṛti constitute 'Prajñā' – the higher wisdom within us. This wisdom is often obscured by the ceaseless fluctuations of Mānas. Āyurveda identifies diseases arising from the misuse or neglect of this intelligence as Prajñāparādha – transgressions of wisdom.[58]

इन्द्रियाभिग्रहः कर्म मनसः स्वस्य निग्रहः ।
ऊहो विचारश्च ततः परं बुद्धिः प्रवर्तते' ॥ २१ ॥
(Cha.Shar. 1/21[59])

Only when Mānas engages with the Indriyas do the Indriyas function effectively. Without the involvement of Mānas, the senses lack strength and direction. Mānas can operate in two ways: it may flow outward,

58 Shri Taranath Bhattacharya. Shabda stoma Mahanidhi. 3rd Ed, Varanasi: Chowkamba Samskrita Series Office, 1967, 343.

59 Acharya Vidyadhar Shukla and Prof.Ravi Dutt Tripathi, Charak Samhita, 2000, Chaukhamba Sanskrit, Pratishthan, Delhi, India, Page 678

accompanying a sense organ toward objects of desire, or it may turn inward, withdrawing from external stimuli. Understanding this distinction makes the question, "Who am I?", pivotal. If we identify solely with the outward movement of Mānas, we oscillate between likes and dislikes, happiness and unhappiness, high and low energy. But when we recognize Mānas as an instrument and ourselves as the Jīvātma wielding it, we can observe, control, and direct our actions. This inward withdrawal is practiced as Pratyāhāra, leading to Tataḥ Paraḥ Buddhi – the emergence of Buddhi once the restless chatter of Mānas ceases.

In summary, Mānas connects the individual soul (Jīvātma) with the world. It has dual possibilities: outward flow toward external objects via the indriyas, and inward flow for mastery over desires, preventing engagement with non-beneficial (ahitkara) objects. Outward flow naturally dominates, and most of us are carried along without pausing. Only when mānas takes a pause can Buddhi function, enabling informed, effective decision-making. Buddhi is described in Āyurveda with multiple facets: Dhī, Mati, Medhā, Dhṛti, and Smṛti. Together with Dhṛti and Smṛti, it forms Prajñā. Deviation or failure of Prajñā – Dhīdhṛtismṛtivibhrasṭa karma – leads to Prajñāparādha, the root cause of all illnesses (Caraka, Śarīrasthāna 1/102). Therefore, the sole reason for disease is the lapse or misalignment of Prajñā, which encompasses Dhī, Dhṛti, and Smṛti.

Prajñā – Dhī, Dhṛti, Smṛti

According to Chakrapani[60], Prajñā represents knowledge, comprising three faculties: Dhī, Dhṛti, and Smṛti. Prajñā signifies the ability to know, understand, discern, distinguish, be acquainted with, discover, perceive, learn, and exercise wisdom, intelligence, discrimination, and judgment. It is the intellectual and discrimination of the mind that identifies the

60 Singh R.H Trikramjiyadav ji, editor, (Ist edition), Ayurveda Deepika teeka sharirsthan, katidhapurushiyaya shariradhyaya, Chapter 1, verse 1/98. Page 296, chaukhambha surbhartiprakashan: reprint 2013

right and Amarkośa[61] defines "Dhī" as to perceive and to reflect. Vivekā is a special attribute of Dhī.

While animal instincts are survival dominant and limited to fight, flight or freeze reactions, humans have the Dhī or Vivekā to go beyond these animal instincts. Dhī works at two levels, perception from memory and perception from senses and logic. The sensory perception only gives an input which is neutral. It is the mānas which has Smṛti gives a label of like or dislike to the input. Then there is Vivekā, which decides whether it is right or wrong, beneficial, or harmful. The function of **Dhī** is to create a realistic perception- as it is. What is momentary and what is eternal, what is Hita- wholesome or beneficiary, and what is Ahita-unwholesome or not beneficiary is decided by Dhī. Therefore, Dhī is called NishchayĀtmaka- one that takes decision. The nature of Dhī is righteousness. It sees things rightly. The main function of Dhī is firmness, contentment, and resolution. Functions of buddhi or Dhī are:

1. Ālocana – Perception
2. Manana – Contemplate
3. Abhimāna– Pride
4. Avadhāraṇā - Determination.

Dhṛti is the intelligence that holds the knowledge of Dhī and is able to control the mānas from getting carried away by the senses. Dhṛti is the holder and sustains the knowledge. Without dhṛti, the Dhī remains at theoretical knowledge, and does not get applied. One of the functions of Mānas is to control itself- svasya nigraha. This happens with dhṛti. विषयप्रवण सत्त्व धृतिभ्रंशान्न शक्यते । नियन्तुमहितादर्थात् धृतिः हि नियमात्मिका ॥ (च. शा. १ - १००)[62] Dhṛti stops the mānas from flowing outward. Self-control, will power, concentration and power of restraint are due to

61 Saraswat Bhawna, Sabharwal, P., Gaur, M. B., & Pandey, Y. (2018). A rational Ayurvedic approach to Smriti in purview of modern science. *International Ayurvedic Medical Journal, 6*(12).

62 Shukla, V., & Tripathi, R. D. (2000). *Charak Samhita* (p. 693). Delhi, India: Chaukhamba Sanskrit Pratishthan.

Dhṛti. Such people are called Dheer- one with lots of dhṛti. Dhī is the power of decision, dhṛti is the power of niyama or discipline. Dhṛti is the function of Sattva. Keeping distractions and temptations at bay, staying focussed, not getting overly affected by external environment, and having equanimity are the qualities of person with higher Sattva. Will power and resilience are driven by dhṛti and connected with the strength of mānas known as Mano bala.[63]

Smṛti is a very interesting aspect of intelligence. Smṛti literally means to remember. While the Western brain dominant thinking believes that we are learning 'new'. The concept of Smṛti is that all the knowledge that exists, all that we have learnt earlier, is only 'remembered', unveiled from within.[64] The knowledge of Āyurveda was 'remembered' by Brahmā, the Creative Energy of Creation. Our entire education processes will change when enough research is done in this aspect of Smṛti and integrated in the philosophy of education. One way of looking at Smṛti as memory is at a more mundane level, Smṛti is remembering what is learnt from childhood till now. The Evolutionary Psychology, a branch of Psychology studies, has been researching the evolutionary memory aspect within the brain.[65] The evolutionary psychologists are rediscovering the wisdom that 'we are out of the stone age, but the stone age is not out of us.' Hence many of the reactions that we have for the present moment could be outdated as they were the learnt reactions to stone age. This aspect needs to be integrated in Psychology curriculum.

---

63 Thakar, V. J. (n.d.). *Man ane Manovikar* (pp. 22, 35). Gujarat, India: Gujarat Ayurveda University.

64 Ibid, pg. 22

65 Nicholson, N. (1998, July–August). How hardwired is human behaviour? *Harvard Business Review.*

Mānas and Indriya

We have seen earlier the relationship of mānas with Indriya or sense organs and how the natural attraction of mānas works when coming in contact with the arthas or object of attraction. Prajñā or higher intelligence can play a role of decision maker in managing this outward flow of mānas. We also now understand that Prajñā can play a role only when mānas is transcended. Hence mānas is the key to our intelligence or lack of it. When the relationship of Indriya with the artha or object is balanced, or in harmony, this is known as Sātmya in Āyurveda. However, we all have experienced that mānas is difficult to control and does create imbalance or disharmony. This is known as Asātmyendriyārtha in Āyurveda. This imbalance is one of the causes of illness – physical or mental. The Sātmya or balance are essential for health. We have seen earlier the matrix of senses, organs, and their functions.

Let us look at three levels in which imbalances may happen.

Our contact with the outer world through the sense organs can be in imbalance due to excess, lack or contra indication. These are known as Ati, hīna or ayoga or mithyā in Sanskrit. Ati is Excessive contact of sense organ with its object, Hīna is Less contact of sense organ with its object, Mithyā is Incorrect contact of sense organ with its object. We all are living life, which is imbalanced, where nourishment to each sense is not happening. A simple example is of touch. How often do small children get nourishment to skin through touch? A mother giving a bath, a grandparent hugging and cuddling, a father carrying them. As we grow, our relationships become distant, and most adults are touch deprived. Hīna Yoga of touch. Touch deprivation could be one of the reasons for mental health issues in adolescents and adults. On a physical level, most people are deprived of Sun Light, and hence have Vitamin D deficiency.

Our modern lifestyle is full of these examples and a good insight into why we see so much of deviation in health at physical and psychological level. Modern lifestyle seems like a collective amnesia of health and health creating routines. Āyurveda expands our sense of self with the circadian rhythms and has great details on how we need to align with the cycle of Sun and Moon, seasons and time. Whenever we live against these alignments, we live a life that is Asātmyendriya. We observe them at body, mānas and speech level, food and sleep, exercises and daily routines. Some of the examples are:

Sound: Excessive sound, such as loud machines, music, fireworks, fights, or movies in an auditorium, is Atiyoga (overuse of sound). Too much silence or isolation from sound is Ayoga (deficiency). Strong criticism, harsh words, and shouting represent Mithyā Yoga (improper use of sound). Sound is linked to Ākāśa (Ether). Spending time under open skies and in open spaces improves our ability to listen, cultivates openness in the Mānas, and fosters Ākāśa Vṛtti – detachment and spaciousness in the mind.

Touch: Extreme sensations – like very hot or cold sunlight, air, or water – are Atiyoga of touch. Lack of touch, sunlight, air, or water is Ayoga of touch. Improper practices, such as alternating hot and cold touch immediately, bathing post-exercise or cooking, or unhygienic contact, are Mithyā Yoga of touch. Touch occurs both at the skin level and the emotional level of Mānas. Some people are highly sensitive and "touchy," while others seem unaffected – illustrating the mind–heart interconnection.

Vision/Seeing: Working in overly bright light, staring at screens for long hours, or exposure to excessive artificial light is Atiyoga of vision. Very dim or dark conditions are Ayoga. Viewing extremely close or distant objects, or frightening and disgusting images, constitutes Mithyā Yoga. Modern lifestyles with constant artificial light disrupt natural cycles, melatonin production, and sleep patterns. Lack of sunlight is Hīna Yoga, while excess artificial light, especially post-sunset, is Atiyoga.

Taste: The tongue, like touch, has dual functions: taste and speech. Overindulgence in specific tastes (sweet, salty, etc.) is Atiyoga of taste, while deprivation is Ayoga, and consuming unpleasant or harmful foods is Mithyā Yoga. Taste (Rasa) affects both the body and Mānas. Speech, also governed by the tongue, is essential for expression, though research on its subtle functions is still evolving.

Smell: Excessive environmental odors, such as in chemical factories or waste sites, are Atiyoga of smell. Absence of smell is Ayoga, and foul, strong, unnatural, or poisonous odors are Mithyā Yoga. Artificial perfumes are generally Mithyā Yoga, whereas natural aromas promote a healthy Mānas. Smell and taste are primordial senses, crucial for survival, as seen in both reptiles and newborns, who recognize their mother primarily through scent.

Karma/Action:

The principle of Ati, Ayoga, or Mithyā Yoga applies not only to the senses but also to speech, Mānas, and physical activity.

- Atiyoga: Overuse – speaking excessively, overthinking, constant mental chatter, excessive exercise or physical labor.
- Ayoga: Deficiency – sedentary lifestyle, suppression of natural urges (urination, sneezing), lack of engagement.
- Mithyā Yoga: Improper action – gossip, harsh or disrespectful speech, unethical behavior, living in fear, grief, anger, greed, ego, jealousy.

Understanding these patterns helps cultivate self-awareness and self-management, aligning actions of body, speech, and mind with natural rhythms and higher intelligence.[66]

These are very good starting points to identify any health issue at physical or mental level. Mānas plays an important role here and hence Mano bala

66 Shukla, V., & Tripathi, R. D. (2000). Charak Samhita (Sutrasthana 11.39, p. 174). Chaukhamba Sanskrit Pratishthan.

or will power and resiliency of mānas are critical to understand. Just as physical bala or strength depends on the nourishment and exercising of the body, the mānas bala also depends on nourishment and exercising of the mānas.

Mānas Bala: Strength and Resilience of the Mind

Identifying physical or mental health issues often begins with observing Mānas, as the mind plays a central role in overall well-being. Just as physical strength (Bala) depends on nourishment and exercise of the body, the strength of Mānas (Manobala) depends on its own nourishment and disciplined practice.

Bala & Nourishment of Mānas

Traditionally, Bala is associated with the body – enhanced through exercise, diet, and guidance from trainers. The younger generation widely embraces gym culture, investing time, energy, and money in physical fitness. However, holistic wellness also requires strengthening the Mānas and Ātma.

Āyurveda classifies Manobala into three categories based on Sattva:

1. Pravara Sattva (Strong Willpower / Uttam Bala)
    - Individuals with strong Mānas are called Sattva Sāra and possess Pravara Sattva.
    - They may be thin, small, or physically weak, yet their mental resilience enables them to endure pain, illness, accidents, and life's challenges.
    - Traits include self-discipline, good memory, gratitude, compassion, holistic thinking, and acting beyond self-interest.
    - Dr. Bhaswati notes: "Resilience training is actually Manobala. The mind-gut connection, often called 'The Second Brain,' was originally understood as Āhāra science. Lifestyle medicine is essentially Āhāra-vihāra (food and

activity), Pathya (suitable diet), and Hita (wholesome actions) in Āyurveda."

- High resiliency or Adversity Quotient is rooted in Pravara Sattva. This strength is both mental and physiological, tied to gut health. Cultivating Sattva through proper Āhāra, Vihāra, Pathya, and Hita enhances Manobala. Optimism, cognitive ability, and mental resilience are closely linked to Sattva.

2. Madhyama Sattva (Medium Willpower / Moderate Bala)

   - Individuals with medium Mānas experience distress more easily and struggle to endure pain or adversity.
   - With encouragement, support, or counseling, they can cope better.
   - They often rely on external guidance or motivation but can improve Manobala with proper nurturing.

3. Avara Sattva (Weak Willpower / Low Bala)

   - Individuals with weak Mānas are easily frightened, pessimistic, and problem-focused rather than solution-oriented.
   - They may exaggerate pain or illness, lose hope, experience heart palpitations, or even faint under fear.
   - Counselling or motivation is often challenging.
   - They are prone to fear, sadness, depression, anxiety, and self-centredness, showing that physical fitness alone cannot guarantee mental strength.

Cultivating Manobala

Strengthening Mānas requires cultivation of Sattva, which can be achieved through:

- Proper diet (Āhāra)
- Physical activity and outdoor time (Vihāra)
- Choosing wholesome and beneficial practices (Pathya and Hita)

By nurturing Sattva, one enhances Manobala, willpower, and resilience – key factors in mental health and holistic wellness. Future assessments of Manobala can aid both healthy individuals and those facing mental health challenges.

Triguṇātmaka & Pañcabhautic

Since Mānas has evolved from Ahaṅkāra, which is Triguṇātmaka, Mānas itself is also Triguṇātmaka. Āyurveda, when defining constitution, segregates Body and Mind into Tridoṣa and Triguṇa respectively, which somewhat limits the integrality of Āyurveda. Triguṇa is all-pervading and forms the basis of the Pañca Mahābhūta, the latter combining in Tridoṣa of Vāta, Pitta, and Kapha. Thus, body constitution and mānas form a continuum, with Tridoṣa and Triguṇa creating a matrix. The main difference is that Tridoṣa determines Prakṛti, which is fixed at birth and remains relatively constant throughout life, whereas Triguṇa is flexible and changeable. Many typologies of mental constitution based on Triguṇa create the illusion that this typology permanently defines our svabhāva (personality). In reality, Triguṇa can change despite an initial template influenced by mother's diet and lifestyle during pregnancy, upbringing, social interactions, food habits, and spiritual sādhana.

From Sri Aurobindo's perspective, Triguṇa reflects the starting point of one's life journey and is not fixed: "The dominant Guṇas are not the essential soul-type of the embodied being but only the index of the formation he has made for this life or during his present existence and at a given moment of his evolution in Time."[67]

It is insightful to observe how mānas functions under the influence of various Triguṇa combinations. The Guṇa dominant at birth and shaping the psyche during life defines personality or svabhāva as Sāttvic, Rājasic, or Tāmasic (SRT). Sattva domination helps utilize Rajas and

67 Sri Aurobindo, *A Greater Psychology*, 2001, Sri Aurobindo International Centre of Education, Sri Aurobindo Ashram, Pondicherry, India, p. 115

Tamas beneficially, as Sattva carries Kalyāṇa Ansh – the energy of purity. Individuals may exhibit traits guided by anger, gratitude, action, peace, or laziness, reflecting various shades of Rajas and Tamas. No one exists solely in one Guṇa; all individuals display a dynamic interplay of the three Guṇas.

CHAPTER 03

Hṛdaya – The Centre of Our Existence

In this chapter, we cover these themes:

- The heart in everyday language
- Modern and ancient understanding of the heart – a full circle
- Carl Jung, the Upanisads and the Anāhata Cakra (Heart Cakra)
- Etymology of Hṛdaya (Heart)
- Rhythm of the Hṛdaya & modern resonance research
- Psychosomatic wellness and the heart
- Health-promoting and compromising behaviours
- Svasthya Vṛtta and Ācāra Rasāyana

Introduction

In everyday language, the heart occupies a central place. Even children, when introducing themselves, instinctively place a hand on their heart. Our expressions reflect this deep connection: "Heart of the matter" for the core of an issue, "Heart-to-heart conversation" for deep communication, "Cross your heart" when promising truth, "Heartwarming" or "Heartfelt" for emotional impact, "Heartbroken" when trust is violated, "Follow your heart" for passion and purpose, "Half-hearted" for lack of engagement, and "Heart of gold" or "Heart of stone" to describe character. Expressions like "Change of heart", "Take heart", and "Pour your heart out" highlight the heart's role in courage, compassion, and emotional authenticity.

Imagine replacing 'heart' with 'brain' in these phrases: "Brain-to-brain conversation", "Mind of the matter", or "Bottom of my mind". These simply do not resonate. It is the heart where love, trust, compassion, gratitude, and authentic human experience reside.

Psychologist Carl Jung describes the Heart Cakra as a space for transformation and transcendence, where the lower and higher aspects of self-meet – a theme explored in detail later. While the term "brainwashed" is common, "heartwashed" is not. This highlights the profound intelligence inherent in the heart, which modern science is beginning to rediscover.

In this chapter, we explore the ancient and modern understanding of the heart:

- Insights from the Atharva Veda, classical Āyurveda texts, and Upaniṣads
- Carl Jung's perspective of the heart as an alchemical space
- Candace Pert's prescription of Heart Meditation in psychoneuroimmunology for psychosomatic wellness

We examine the heart at multiple levels:

- As a physical organ, vital for life
- As brain or mastikṣa in Āyurveda, with the heart-brain connection described in cardiology and neuroscience
- As a subtle Heart Cakra in Yogic physiology, experienced in love and the aesthetics of emotion

Poet Rainer Maria Rilke frequently refers to the Heart Space in his poetry. Meditating on this space allows one to experience the vastness of the Self – Dahara Ākāśa, the Ākāśa within. The Chāndogya Upaniṣad (Chapter 8) describes this inner expanse. As previously discussed, the Macrocosm and Microcosm are reflections of each other, inviting us to explore the Ākāśa Mahābhūta within.

In Indic Aesthetics, heart is the space where ability to experience the joy of emotions resides. When there are blocks here, the person loses the sensitivity to emotions. In Nāṭya Śāstra, this is referred as Hṛdaya

Granthi. Though this is explored later in the chapter on Nāṭyaśāstra and Emotions, we will touch upon the Granthi – knot or a block – briefly in this chapter too.

Modern and ancient understanding of Heart – A full circle

To facilitate understanding, it is helpful to start with modern research and then connect it to ancient insights about the heart. For those interested in exploring this further, the HeartMath Institute (https://heartmath.org) offers extensive research on the heart. Another valuable resource is Paul Pearsall's The Heart's Code: Tapping the Wisdom and Power of Our Heart Energy, which explores the heart as more than a pump. Pearsall describes the heart as a conductor of a cellular symphony, capable of loving, feeling, thinking, remembering, communicating with other hearts, regulating immunity, and storing information that continually pulses throughout the body.

Modern science is increasingly recognizing the heart (and, to some extent, the gut) as a form of "secondary brain," with a complex intelligence that interacts dynamically with the brain. This paradigm shift is reminiscent of Galileo's rediscovery of the Sun as the center of the solar system, challenging long-held assumptions. Traditionally, human anatomy and psychology have considered the brain as the central processor of all thoughts and emotions. However, research now highlights the heart's active role in cognition, emotion, and overall psychosomatic functioning. The concept of Cardiac Psychology was first proposed in 1996 by cardiologist Dr. Robert Allan and health psychologist Dr. Stephen Scheidt.[68] While promising, it is still an emerging field, evolving toward a broader science of Heart Psychology that integrates physiological, emotional, and cognitive dimensions.

---

68 Pearsall, P. P. (1998). *The heart's code: Tapping the wisdom and power of our heart energy* (p. 70). Broadway Books.

Etymology and Functions of Hṛdaya or Heart

According to the Śatapatha Brāhmaṇa and Bṛhadāraṇyaka Upaniṣad, the word Hṛdaya is formed from three dhātu (root verbs):

- Hru – Harati (to receive)
- Da – Dadati (to give or contribute)
- Ya – Yajati (to control or regulate), also understood as rhythmic self-generated activity (Gatau)[69]

Rhythm is essential for the right functioning of our physical and psychological health. HRV or Heart Rate Variability is researched a lot today. We reconnect with rhythm, HRV and psychology a little later in more detail. However, we need to acknowledge the special role of rhythm. Since all life is both biorhythmic and info-energetically rhythmic, and scientists know that rhythmic energy contains information, every oscillation of our heart represents the resonance of nature's code within us.[70] The heart functions as the metronome of the body's biorhythm, and health emerges when we are in rhythm internally, synchronised with other living systems, and aligned with our intrinsic beat[71]. This rhythmic synchronization is why, for example, a lullaby can so effectively soothe and calm a baby. The rhythm relaxes the heart. Rhythm helps resonance response to life's situations. We also have Appendix on 3 Step Rhythmic Breathing at the end of the chapters.

It is interesting to note that the heart performs exactly these three functions of giving blood, receiving blood and circulating blood by acting as a pump. The heart has sometimes been referred to as 'Sindhu' or ocean. Just as the culmination of rivers is the oceans so is heart,

---

69 Kumar, M., et al. (2022). Concept of Hṛdaya in Ayurveda. *World Journal of Pharmaceutical Research, 11*(11).

70 Pearsall, P. P. (1998). *The Heart's Code: Tapping the wisdom and power of our heart energy* (pp. 70, 222). Broadway Books.

71 Ibid. p. 222

the culmination of blood circulation. This signifies cyclic circulation.[72] The circulation is not just of blood, but also the nutrients as Āyurveda describes the Rasa Vaha strotas or channels originating from the Heart. So, it receives the nutrition of digested food and circulates to the body. Other important channels are the Mano Vaha strotas or channels of the mānas-mind also originate from the Heart and spread throughout the body. The rhythm of the Heart gets easily impacted by the emotions we experience. Mānas and Heart have very close relationship. Not poetically only or philosophically, but as Āyurveda texts and modern research reaffirm, the relationship is biological as well.

Shape of the Heart and Biomimicry

The Hṛdaya (heart) is poetically described as resembling an inverted lotus flower—opening when the person is awake and closing during sleep[73]. Anyone familiar with a lotus flower will notice its circadian rhythm, opening with sunrise and closing at sunset. In a modern context, the "closing of petals" should not be taken literally. Rather, it symbolises the heart's natural tendency to withdraw from the external world and turn inward after sunset. Traditional lifestyles supported this wisdom: evenings were for winding down external activities, allowing the heart and mind to relax. Today, modern routines often disrupt this natural rhythm. Evening gym sessions, late-night work, and high-intensity activities may overstimulate the body and heart, contributing to physical and psychological heart-related issues, as well as accidents like treadmill collapses among youth.

This observation aligns with biomimicry, a design science inspired by nature. Biomimicry is the practice of learning from and emulating nature's genius to solve challenges in human design. The term comes

---

72 Vinaya, P. N., & Prasad, J. S. R. A. (2015). The concept of blood circulation in ancient India with special reference to the heart as a pumping organ. *International Ayurvedic Medical Journal, 3*(2), 3.

73 Murthy, K. R. Shrikantha. (2023). *Susruta Samhita, Vol. 1, Sarir Sthana, 4.32* (p. 61). Varanasi, India: Chaukhamba Orientalia.

from Greek, meaning "to imitate life." Through biomimicry, we study how nature creates conditions conducive to life. However, while we have applied biomimicry to technology, architecture, and industry, we rarely apply these principles to ourselves, overlooking nature's guidance for our own rhythms and well-being.

Hṛdaya as Centre of Cetanā or Consciousness

Ācārya Caraka and Ācārya Suśruta both emphasised the importance of Hṛdaya. Hṛdaya is the Cetanā Sthana[74], the seat of consciousness, and therefore everything related to Prāna, Ojas, and Mānas is intimately connected with it. The *Carakā Saṃhitā* recognises the heart as the center of circulation and the vitalising Prāṇavaha Srotas: *Tava praṇavahānām srotasām hṛdayam mūlam mahāsrotasca.*[75]

Cetanā refers to consciousness. Hṛdaya is also the adhiṣṭhāna, or seat, of the three Guṇas – Sattva, Rajas, and Tamas.[76] The marma located in the thorax (ūras), between the two breasts (stanyormadhye) and near the esophageal orifice (Āmāśayadvāra), is identified as Hṛdaya[77] housing these three Guṇas. Ācārya Caraka elaborates further on the central role of Hṛdaya in sustaining life and consciousness.

The concept of the heart as the seat of the soul is also found in other ancient cultures. Aristotle regarded the heart as the seat of the soul, while Hippocrates and Plato emphasized the brain as the center of human essence. Despite these differences, all three agreed that life depends on an innate, subtle energy associated with the heart. Modern research and practice continue to support this view. Sara Paddison, Vice President of the Institute of HeartMath, notes: "Whatever your religion or cherished

74 Ibid, 4.31, page 60, 4.34, page 63

75 Kashinatha Sastry and Ghoraknath Chaturvedi. Charaka Samitha Vol.I. Chaukamba Bharati Academi.Varanasi.1984. Ch. Vi. 5.7

76 Ibid, 6.25, page 111

77 Das, T., et al. (2018). Analytical study of heart in Ayurveda. *International Journal of Research & Review, 5*(11). Retrieved from https://www.ijrrjournal.com

beliefs, the heart is the access point in the human system for experiencing God."[78] Likewise, individuals who have experienced life-changing events – through illness, accidents, out-of-body experiences (OBE), or near-death experiences (NDE) – have affirmed this truth. Pearsall Paul states in his Introduction, Heart's Code, "As a cancer and bone marrow transplant survivor…I have little doubt that the heart is the major energy centre of my body and a conveyor of a code that represents my soul."[79]

Heart as the Source of Ten Arteries

The heart is the origin of the main ten arteries (*Mahā Dhamanī*) that form a network throughout entire body.[80] Through these great arteries, Prāna, Rasa, and Mānas flow and interact with every part of the organism. The terms *Mahat* (great), *Arth* (serving all purpose), and *Hṛdaya* (heart) are considered synonymous in this context. The mānas flowing out from the Hṛdaya permeates the entire body. Descriptions of channels for the activities of the mind (*Manovaha Srotas*) are scattered across Āyurvedic classics and have not been fully elucidated. These channels are understood as pathways through which the mind and body interact, responsible for the flow of thoughts, emotions, and other psychological functions. The heart, being highly vascular, is surrounded by ten major dhamanī – spokes of a wheel – known as *Rasavaha Strotomula* (sites of origin for channels of nourishment). These channels are comparable to the Manovaha Srotas [Chakrapani on *Cha. Sa. Cikitsā Sthana 9/4*]. In this framework, Mānas functions as a medium between the heart and the brain, with the brain responsible for sensory and motor functions, while the heart governs the emotional aspects of the psyche. Modern

78 Paddison, S. (1992). *The hidden power of the heart* (p. 9). Boulder Creek, CA: Planetary Publications.

79 Pearsall, P. P. (1998). *The heart's code: Tapping the wisdom and power of our heart energy* (p. 4). New York, NY: Broadway Books.

80 Shukla, V., & Tripathi, R. D. (2000). *Charak Samhita* (Vol. 1, pp. 440–444, Sutrasthana 30.1–15). Delhi, India: Chaukhamba Sanskrit Pratishthan.

Psychoneuroimmunology (PNI) corroborates this understanding, as discussed later in this chapter.

Although Āyurveda does not extensively elaborate on Manovaha Srotas or the role of the ten Mahā Dhamanī, deeper insights emerge from Yoga and the study of the subtle body (*Sūkṣma Śarīra*) and nāḍīs. These ancient perspectives reconnect when we explore the Heart Chakra (Anāhata Cakra) in Yogic anatomy, highlighting the integrative wisdom of mind, body, and energy.

Heart, Mānas and Immunity

The Ojas, or the final nutritional essence that ensures immunity, also travels through the channels of the body. Ācārya Caraka emphasizes that the entire body, consciousness (*Ātma*), cognition of the five senses, *Saguṇa Cetas* (including desires, happiness, sorrow, etc.), Mānas, and all functions of the mind are dependent on the heart (*Caraka Saṃhitā, Su. Sth. 30.4*). In essence, all activities that sustain life are rooted in the heart. The heart holds central significance not only in physiology, as recognized by Western medical science through its role in circulation and respiration, but also in psychology. The intimate connection between heart and Mānas means that any negativity in the mind – stress, worry, or emotional imbalance – can directly affect the heart and Ojas, thereby impacting immunity. Earlier, we discussed the Triguṇa – Sattva, Rajas, and Tamas – within Mānas. Rajas and Tamas can become vitiated due to lifestyle, diet, thoughts, and emotions. When these qualities disturb the Manovaha Srotas, they can create blockages or imbalances. Over time, these disturbances affect brain function, cognitive processes[81], and overall immunity.

One significant cause of vitiation in Manovaha Srotas is excessive thinking or worry (*Aticintana*) [*Cha. Sa. Vimāna Sthana 5/13*]. Contemporary

---

81 Acharya Vidyadhar Shukla & Tripathi, R. D. (2022). *Charak Samhita* (Vol. 2, Chi. Sthana 10.59, p. 255; Revised ed.). Chaukhamba Sanskrit Pratishthan, Delhi, India.

research supports the interplay between the circulatory system and the psyche.[82] Rajas, for instance, manifests as anxiety or overthinking. German professor Ludwig Braun pioneered research into the psychological and emotional aspects of cardiac diseases, especially angina. He demonstrated a correlation between cardiac disease and 'Angst' – a constrictive, tightening, and crushing sensation that evokes dread, profoundly altering the patient's emotional outlook. Cardiac tissue possesses a specialized apparatus responsive to anxiety, richly supplied with nerve endings that react to emotional stress. This phenomenon, in which emotional states influence cardiac tissue, is termed cardiac psyche.[83]

Touch the Heart

The inner tactile sensation described in Āyurveda brings us full circle in understanding the connection between Mānas and the heart. People who are highly sensitive are often referred to as having "touchy hearts." Āyurveda provides a scientific explanation for this. The Sparśaendriya, or cognition of touch, is discussed in *Caraka Saṃhitā, Su. Sth. 30.7*, where it is noted that no true knowledge occurs without the touch reaching the heart. Later clarifications in *Śarīra Sthana* emphasise that both happiness and sorrow manifest in the Mānas Sparśa, or tactile perception of the mind. Touch is not only physical, occurring at the skin, but also psychological and emotional, as in the phrase "something touched the heart." This awareness is possible only in the Hṛdaya, where Mānas resides, reflecting the profound scientific understanding of the heart in Āyurveda.

Heart and Brain

In contrast, Western medicine and psychology often limit cognition, emotion, and awareness of happiness and sorrow to the brain. Most

---

82 Bhojani, M. K., Varma, S., & Deole, Y. S. (2023, October 12). Manovaha srotas. In G. Basisht (Ed.), *Charak Samhita New Edition* (1st ed., p. 286). CSRTSDC. https://doi.org/10.47468/CSNE.2023.e01.s09.157

83 Herz und Angst. (1932). *Archives of Internal Medicine*, 50(2), 350.

literature on Emotional Intelligence is brain-centric. While heart and mind are occasionally referenced, Western science lacks a framework for understanding Mānas and the heart. The medulla, the most primitive part of the brain, governs automatic survival reactions: fight, flight, or freeze. It reacts faster than the higher brain, which stores learned knowledge about Emotional Intelligence. Thus, even with extensive learning, survival threats – real or perceived – trigger the medulla's automatic response. Āyurveda's wisdom provides a way to regulate this: although we cannot directly control the medulla, we can influence one of its functions – the rhythm of breathing. Since the heart also has a rhythm influenced by the medulla, conscious attention to breathing can help modulate automatic reactions and maintain emotional balance when encountering stress or threat. As human beings, we are not limited to fight, flight, or freeze responses. We can self-regulate and initiate pro-social behaviours when we encounter challenges, disagreements and stressors.[84]

The heart and brain are deeply interconnected, influencing each other in multiple ways. Recent research shows that communication is bidirectional—and often more significantly from heart to brain. The heart communicates with the brain through four major conduits:

1. Neurologically – via transmission of nerve impulses
2. Biochemically – via hormones and neurotransmitters
3. Biophysically – via pressure waves
4. Energetically – through electromagnetic field interactions

Signals transmitted from the heart can profoundly influence brain activity and, consequently, performance. In this context, Mānas acts as a medium between the heart and brain: the brain manages sensory and motor functions, while the heart governs the emotional aspect of the psyche.[85]

---

84 McCraty, R. (n.d.). *Science of the heart* (Vol. 2). HeartMath Institute, USA.
85 Ibid.

The Three Hearts or Brains

Āyurveda has long recognized the wisdom of three critical centers in the human body, as described in *Caraka Saṃhitā, Siddhisthāna*: the heart, head, and Basti[86]. These three centers are in constant communication, coordinating cognition, emotion, and bodily functions. In modern terminology, they are often referred to as the Head Brain, Heart Brain, and Gut Brain – though the gut and Basti are not exactly synonymous. Notably, in Āyurveda, the brain itself can also be called Hṛdaya, highlighting the dynamic interaction between heart and brain in regulating both cognition and emotional experience.

A commentary on Caraka Saṃhitā explains:

- Head Hṛdaya – Śiraḥ Hṛdaya
- Heart Hṛdaya – Uraḥ Hṛdaya
- Gut Hṛdaya – Āmāśaya Hṛdaya[87]

The Sanskrit terminology reflects both location and function beautifully. The heart is called *Uraḥ Hṛdaya* due to its position near the breasts. It is intimately connected with Mānas, and Mānas with emotions, known in Sanskrit as Ūrmī, a word that also signifies a wave or ocean. The Āmāśaya Hṛdaya aligns closely with what modern science identifies as the "Second Brain" in the gut, a concept extensively studied by Dr. Michael Gershon, chairman of Anatomy and Cell Biology at New York–Presbyterian Hospital/Columbia University Medical Center. While Psychology often disregards gut feelings or intuition as scientific, practical experience – such as business leaders like Jack Welch writing *Straight from the Gut* – shows the gut's critical role in decision-making. Furthermore, the gut or Nābhi is linked with birth trauma and primal fears, an area explored in Primal Therapy by Arthur Janov, which

86 Acharya Vidyadhar Shukla & Tripathi, R. D. (2022). *Charak Samhita* (Vol. 2, Siddhisthana 9.1-4, p. 945). Chaukhamba Sanskrit Pratishthan, Delhi, India.

87 Acharya Vidyadhar Shukla & Tripathi, R. D. (2000). Charak Samhita (Ch. 30.1–15, p. 443). Chaukhamba Sanskrit Pratishthan, Delhi, India.

emphasises how early life experiences impact both psychological health and gut function.

Historical psychophysiology research also supports these connections. John and Beatrice Lacey, over two decades of study in the 1960s and '70s, observed that the heart communicates with the brain in ways that influence perception, emotion, and behaviour. More recently, Robert Cooper, co-author of *Executive EQ*, discussed at a 2005 conference the concept of Three Intelligences – head, heart, and gut – highlighting that intelligence is not solely located in the brain.

The integration of these three centers – head, heart, and gut – into a framework of Integrated Intelligence can profoundly reshape our understanding of human wellbeing, decision-making, and happiness. Recognizing and cultivating this integration within psychology and education promises a significant paradigm shift in both theory and practice.

Location of Hṛdaya

Isn't it fascinating that we have three "hearts" or Hṛdaya, also referred to as three brains, each profoundly impacting who we are and how we live? In this chapter, we focus on the Uraḥ Hṛdaya (physical heart) and its subtle counterpart, the Anāhata Cakra (Heart Chakra).

Physical Heart:

The physical heart is located on the left side of the body. Modern science primarily views the heart as a vital organ involved in blood circulation and respiration. However, classical texts such as the *Atharvaveda* (AV Kaṇḍa II.33.2 & III.25.6) also highlight its connection with Mānas and Citta. Similarly, Āyurvedic classics like *Caraka Saṃhitā* and *Suśruta Saṃhitā*[88] describe Srotas, the channels that allow flow of bodily liquids, emphasising the centrality of the heart in maintaining life and vitality.

---

88 Prasad, P. V. V. (2001). Human anatomy in Atharvaveda. *Bulletin of the Indian Institute of the History of Medicine, XXXI*, 1.

Energy-Level Heart – Anāhata Cakra and Hita Nāḍī:

While Āyurvedic anatomy focuses on the physical body, Yogic anatomy complements this view by exploring subtle bodies, energy channels (Nāḍīs), and energy centers (Chakras). One of the oldest treatises on Chakras, *Sat-Cakra Nirupan* by Shree Poornanand Yati (16th century, Bengal), describes 72,000 nāḍīs in the human body. Where these nāḍīs converge, lotus-like energy centers emerge, six of which are major Chakras. The Anāhata Cakra, or Heart Chakra, corresponds closely with the physical heart.

The Heart Chakra represents Ākāśa Mahābhūta (the element of space) and embodies spiritual intelligence—the pure space where the Divine resides (Ishwar, Devi Lalita Maha Tripura Sundari). In Sanskrit, it is called Anāhata, meaning "unstruck" or pure sound. Meditation on this heart space – Daharah Ākāśa, the inner sky – allows one to experience the vastness of the Self beyond identification with body, brain, and mind. This practice helps transcend cellular xenophobia – evolutionary memory that limits our perception – promoting compassion, gratitude, selflessness, forgiveness, universal love, and devotion.

The concept of recursion, or the mirroring of the cosmos within the body, is central to the Upaniṣads. The *Chāndogya Upaniṣad* (8.1.1 & 8.1.3) describes a lotus-shaped mansion within the heart, containing heaven and earth, sun and moon, fire and air, lightning and stars – essentially, the entire universe. What is contained within this inner ākāśa reflects the wholeness of existence.[89]

Modern research also reconnects with this concept of the energetic heart. Researchers suggest that terms like intuitive heart and spiritual heart refer to this energetic aspect, linked to our higher self or higher capacities – what physicist David Bohm describes as "our implicate order and undivided wholeness."[90]

---

89 Kak, S. (2000). *Garbha Upanishad.* In S. Kak, *The astronomical code of the Rigveda.* Munshiram Manoharlal, New Delhi.

90 McCraty, R. (n.d.). *Science of the heart* (Vol. 2). HeartMath Institute, USA.

Hita Nāḍī

The Anāhata Cakra is the origin point of many important Nāḍīs, and further research is needed to explore the correlation between the 72,000 nāḍīs and the ten Mahā Dhamanī of the physical heart. The *Bṛhadāraṇyaka Upaniṣad* refers to them as Hita Nāḍīs, because they promote Hita – well-being and welfare.[91]

हिता नाम नाड्यो द्वासप्ततिसहस्राणि हृदयात् पुरीततमभिप्रतिष्ठन्ते

(hitā nāma nāḍyo dvāsaptatisahasrāṇi hṛdayāt purītatamabhipratiṣṭhante)

– Bṛhadāraṇyaka Upaniṣad 2.1.19

It is noteworthy that the veins originating from the heart are called Hita Nāḍīs. In Āyurveda, Hita signifies welfare, wellbeing, suitability, and benefit. One classical description highlights its significance: "Hita nāḍī is of particular significance for just as a road connects two towns, this nāḍī is connected to the Sun, collecting energy. By concentrating on this nāḍī, one can achieve various powers, such as perceiving distant events, performing healing, and having visions of gods, saints, or past incarnations."[92] Future research in Yoga and Indic psychology can further explore Hita Nāḍī and its role in psychological and spiritual wellbeing.

Psychosomatic Wellness, Transcendence and Immunity

Candace Pert and Carl Jung have emphasized the significance of the Anāhata Cakra. Meditation or focus on the Heart Chakra fosters self-transcendence, expands identity, and reveals the interconnectedness of the universe, creating what Pert termed psychosomatic wellness. She, along with her husband Michael Ruff, explained the body as a psychosomatic information network, linking psyche (mind, emotion,

---

91 Siddhantalankar, V. S. (1979). *Ekadashopanishad* (Vol. 1, 3rd ed., p. 741). Vijaykrishna Lakhanpal, Delhi, India.

92 Kundalini Maha Yoga – Hita Nadi connects to the Sun. (n.d.). Retrieved from https://sunlightenment.com

soul) with soma (molecules, cells, organs). Their research shows that the mind and body are inseparable, with emotions serving as the bridge between consciousness and physiology.[93] Dr. Pert's research provides scientific evidence that a biochemical basis for awareness and consciousness exists, that the mind and body are indeed one, and that our emotions and feelings are the bridge that links the two.[94]

Modern immunology also aligns with these insights. In Āyurveda, Ojas, the essence of nutrition that sustains immunity, resides in the heart and is distributed via the ten major arteries. Dr. Richard Gerber highlights that the Heart Chakra is closely associated with the thymus, central to T-lymphocyte development, making the heart an energy core of healing in the mind-body system. Dr. Gerber writes, "One of the most important links between the heart cakra and a physical organ is seen in the association of the heart cakra with the thymus, a primary mediator of the development of immune cells called T lymphocytes."[95] Because it is the energy of the heart that helps to propel the neuropeptides throughout the body, cardio-energetics suggests that it makes sense to speak of the heart not just as another organ influenced by the neuropeptides but as the energy core of a healing mind composed of a brain/heart/body dynamic system.[96]

Dr. David McClelland (Boston University) emphasizes love as a body-mind state, noting that the power of love strengthens immunity more than the love for power.[97] He introduced the two powerful opposites – love for power and power of love. The immunity of the former is lesser than the latter. Hence, the emotion of love, residing in the heart is a very powerful immunity booster. More recently, it was discovered

---

93 Pert, C. (n.d.). Retrieved from http://candacepert.com

94 ibid

95 Gerber, R. (1988). *Vibrational medicine*. Santa Fe, NM: Bear and Company. p. 378.

96 Heart Code

97 McClelland, D. C. (1986). Some reflections on the two psychologies of love. *Journal of Personality, 54*, 334–353.

the heart also manufactures and secretes oxytocin, which can act as a neurotransmitter and commonly is referred to as the love or social bonding hormone.[98]

Wherever we place our focus, energy expands. Focusing on disease prolongs healing, while attention on wellness enhances it. Concentration on the Anāhata Cakra regulates heart rate variability (HRV), removes blocks (granthi) in the nāḍīs, and dissolves suppressed emotions. Importantly, these blocks first arise in the subtle body before manifesting in the physical body, a concept modern science is beginning to explore through the emerging field of cardio-energetics.

Sahṛdaya and Hṛdaya Granthi – Abhinavagupta

It is noteworthy how Indic Psychology integrates with interdisciplinary philosophy. The Hṛdaya Granthi is not merely a medical condition; it is a block that impedes joy, positive emotions, relationships, and the connecting of hearts. This insight is discussed by Abhinava Gupta, the Kashmiri scholar and philosopher, in his work on Nāṭyaśāstra, the science of aesthetics. Sahṛdayatā, or the connecting of hearts, forms the foundation of joy in life. One obstacle to this is the Hṛdaya Granthi.[99]

A Sahṛdaya should have a taste in poetry and a sensitive heart. According to Abhinava Gupta, a Sahṛdaya must possess the following qualities: rasikatva (taste), sahṛdayatva (aesthetic susceptibility), power of visualisation, intellectual depth, contemplative heart, psycho-physical fitness, and the capacity to identify with the aesthetic object.[100] The word Sahṛdaya, literally meaning "having a heart", denotes a person able to identify with the subject matter – the mirror of their heart polished by constant study and practice of literary art, responding sympathetically in

98 Pearsall, P. P. (1998). *The Heart's Code: Tapping the wisdom and power of our heart energy*. Broadway Books, New York. p. 7.

99 Sastri, P. P. (1940). *The philosophy of aesthetic pleasure*. Annamalai University. pp. 185–192.

100 IGNOU. (n.d.). Unit 4: Abhinavagupta's philosophy of Rasa. [Course notes].

their own heart.[101] The science of aesthetics positions literature, poetry, and theatre as tools for expanding consciousness.

In modern terms, this forms a foundational requirement for emotional intelligence. Hṛdaya Granthi obstructs emotional intelligence, and both constructs deserve deeper exploration in modern psychology, emotional intelligence studies, and healthcare as part of body-mind integration. Integrating Sahṛdayatva and Hṛdaya Granthi in psychotherapy may yield surprisingly positive outcomes.

Carl Jung- Alchemical Heart

Carl Jung integrated insights from the Upaniṣads regarding the Heart Chakra (Anāhata Cakra). However, mainstream psychology curricula do not include this understanding, and few Western scholars have advanced this work. Abraham Maslow emphasized the need for Transpersonal Psychology, and Jung viewed the Anāhata Cakra as a site of psychic transformation, akin to alchemy.

Through a Jungian lens, the heart becomes a womb where psychic opposites reside in tension, birthing an alchemical "third" – a new, unforeseen attitude or expansion of consciousness capable of integrating polarities such as matter and spirit, human and divine.[102] Jung's lectures on kuṇḍalinī yoga interpret the Sat-cakra-nirpana (16th-century Tantric Bengali text) as a psychological unfolding of individuation occurring in the heart, where both individuation and transcendence take place. A Greek inscription at the beginning of Jung's essay on Mercurius describes the god as "dweller in the heart". For Jung, as in alchemy, the heart is the seat of primacy (Mather, 2014).

101 Raksamani, K. (n.d.). The validity of the Rasa literary concept: An approach to the didactic tale of Phra Chaisurjya.

102 Odorisio, D. M. (2014). The alchemical heart: A Jungian approach to the heart center in the Upanishads and in Eastern Christian prayer. *International Journal of Transpersonal Studies, 33*(1), 27–38.

The Upaniṣads also locate divinity in the heart, framing it as a "metaphor for consciousness". The heart is "not only the abode of the Ātman, but also the instrument by which the Ātman is known."[103] To know the heart is to be transformed by what one discovers in the heart.

Jung teaches that bringing mind and heart together in prayer is a form of enlightenment, homecoming, and reintegration (pp. 74, 128). Attention descending into the heart unites the powers of soul and body in a single point (p. 94), resulting in a reintegration of one's spiritual organism (p. 157) and a transfiguration of body and soul. The fertile soil of the heart allows the cultivation of personal awareness of the transpersonal Self.[104]

The time is now for psychology practitioners and students to deepen their understanding of the Upaniṣadic heart and Jungian perspectives.

Rhythm of the Hṛdaya, HRV, Psychology & Modern Resonance Research

We have seen the importance of the heart's rhythm in the etymology of Hṛdaya. Along with rhythm, heart rate is also a critical factor, demonstrating how body and mānas are deeply interconnected. The neural communication pathways between the heart and brain are responsible for generating heart rate variability (HRV). The autonomic nervous system (ANS) controls the body's internal functions, including heart rate, gastrointestinal activity, and secretions of various glands. The ANS is a combination of sympathetic and parasympathetic (vagus) systems. In Yoga, this combination is represented by Piṅgalā and Iḍā nāḍīs. Various Prāṇāyāma practices help regulate HRV.

Āyurveda and Yoga view the body and mind as a continuum. Thus, HRV is not merely a physiological phenomenon; it also affects mental

---

103 Müller-Ortega, P. (1989). *The triadic heart of Śiva: Kaula tantricism of Abhinavagupta in the non-dual Shaivism of Kashmir*. Albany, NY: SUNY Press.

104 Odorisio, D. M. (2014). The alchemical heart: A Jungian approach to the heart center in the Upanishads and in Eastern Christian prayer. *International Journal of Transpersonal Studies, 33*(1), 27–38.

states and overall psychological health. The concept of heart coherence is far from new. Rhythmic breathing, alternate nostril breathing, and the controlled combination of inhalation, exhalation, and breath retention are all Yogic techniques that regulate HRV. A steady heart rhythm and regular rate are crucial for emotional balance, mental stability, and adaptability to life situations.

Modern research is validating this ancient wisdom. Heart rate variability reflects psychological resiliency and behavioural flexibility, indicating an individual's capacity for self-regulation and adaptation to changing social or environmental conditions. Numerous studies have linked vagally mediated HRV to self-regulatory capacity, emotional regulation, social interactions, sense of coherence, and personality traits such as self-directedness and coping styles.[105]

Self-regulation, or Indriya Jaya, is essential for a meaningful life. The modern world often promotes instant gratification and high sensory arousal, yet the heart "knows" this is suboptimal for health. HRV can be maintained only through conscious self-regulation. Mānas, which often seeks external gratification, also has the capacity to turn inward and self-regulate. The heart and mānas are intimately connected, influencing each other profoundly. Even if one cannot always manage a restless "monkey mānas", rhythmic breathing and HRV regulation enable the heart to modulate the mind. Āyurveda provides deep guidance on maintaining the heart and the ten great arteries (Dasha Dhamanī) in optimal health, ensuring both physical vitality and emotional equilibrium.

Important Care Guidance for Hṛdaya

In Caraka Saṃhitā, Ācārya Caraka emphasizes the centrality of the heart, the arteries originating from it, and their optimal health. What maintains their vitality? This is where our Śāstra provides guidance for holistic living. The text briefly mentions, in just three lines, how life philosophy,

---

105 McCraty, R. (n.d.). *Science of the Heart* (Vol. 2). HeartMath Institute, USA.

mindset, lifestyle, and diet contribute to the health and happiness of the heart. Āyurveda integrates manasā (mind), vācā (speech), and karmaṇā (actions). Mind represents thoughts and emotions, speech reflects communication, and actions reflect behaviour. Harmony among all three is essential. Any gap between thought, speech, and action creates internal disharmony, which directly affects the heart.

The sūtra begins by describing what protects the heart and the ten arteries.[106] Ojas – the essence of nutrition that supports immunity – travels from the heart through these arteries to reach every cell in the body. This is safeguarded by preventing disturbances in mānas, such as grief, anger, torment, or agitation. Āyurveda recognised the connection between mind and immunity long before modern Psychoneuroimmunology. A healthy, balanced mānas supports strong immunity, a profound truth noted in just half a line of a sūtra, easily missed by students studying for examinations only. To maintain Ojas and keep the arteries free of obstruction in a prasāda (balanced) state, one should follow a lifestyle (Āhāra), engage in appropriate physical activities (Vihāra), and cultivate positive mental states. Creating an environment of peace, harmony, and knowledge further supports heart health.

Ācārya then offers six key practices to enhance life force (Prāṇa), strengthen the body (Bala), maintain mental health (mānas), and cultivate overall happiness:

1. Ahiṁsā (non-violence): Best for increasing life force (Prāṇa). In the chapter on Citta and Citta Vṛttis, Ahiṁsā is discussed within Yama and Niyama.
2. Veerya (self-regulation): Living a disciplined life preserves energy and strengthens Bala. Overindulgence of the senses depletes vitality, so self-regulation is essential.

---

106 Shukla, A. V., & Tripathi, R. D. (2000). *Charak Samhita* (Ch. Su. 30.13–15, pp. 444–446). Delhi, India: Chaukhamba Sanskrit Pratishthan.

3. Knowledge: Expands mental and physical capabilities, supporting both cognitive and bodily evolution. Modern education often emphasizes career-oriented knowledge, whereas Ayurveda views knowledge as a tool for holistic growth.
4. Indriya Jaya (victory over the senses): Creates Nandana – a state of profound bliss. Sanskrit offers many nuanced terms for happiness; Nandana and Harṣaṇa represent higher levels of joy and contentment. Self-mastery over sensory impulses leads to health and life satisfaction.
5. Tattvabodha (self-transcendence): Awareness of our true nature brings joy and delight. While Maslow's hierarchy of needs places self-transcendence at the top, Ayurveda considers it foundational for a meaningful life, health, and happiness.
6. Brahmācārya: Walking on the path of Brahmā supports overall life well-being. This principle is explored further in the chapter on Citta.

Let us explore some health-promoting attitudes, behaviours, practices and mindsets, as explained in Āyurveda.

Health Psychology has shifted from a purely biomedical model to a biopsychosocial (BPS) model, which integrates health behaviour change. Health psychologists study how people adopt and maintain health behaviours, such as physical exercise, good nutrition, condom use, or dental hygiene. This model serves as a heuristic to understand the complex mechanisms behind motivation, temptation resistance, and long-term behaviour maintenance. It applies to both health-compromising and health-enhancing *behaviours* (462).[107]

Aligned with the goal of protecting and promoting the health of healthy individuals, Āyurveda's first section emphasises Health-Promoting Beliefs and Behaviours, known in Sanskrit as Svasthya Vṛtta.

---

107 Pawlik, K., & Rosenzweig, M. R. (Eds.). (2002). *The international handbook of psychology*. Sage Publications. (Chapter by Schwarzer, R., & Gutié Rrez-Doña, B.)

Svasthya Vṛtta comprises two words: Svasthya and Vṛtta. We have seen earlier that Svasthya refers to balance of body, mind, and consciousness, resulting in joy and complete wellness, well-being, and happiness. To achieve this state, one must understand the intricate relationships among body, mind, and consciousness, as well as the connection between the individual and the Universe. These insights form the foundation for health-promoting behaviours.

Health-enhancing behaviours and practices are described in Āyurveda as:

- Dināċārya (daily routine)
- Rātricaryā (night routine)
- Rutucaryā (seasonal adaptations)

However, practices alone do not guarantee good health. In many cases, mind precedes the body, and hence Āyurveda also prescribes practices of the mind, described as Sadvṛtta and Ācāra Rasāyana.

- Sadvṛtta: From Sanskrit "Sad" (good) and "Vṛtta" (way of action), meaning good conduct or virtuous actions.
- Ācāra Rasāyana: From Sanskrit "Ācāra" (behaviour, derived from root "Char" meaning to go about) and Rasāyana (chemical/alchemical rejuvenation), referring to behavioural practices that rejuvenate body and mind.

Modern medicine recognises similar concepts in circadian rhythms, which are internal biological clocks that regulate daily activities such as sleep, wakefulness, eating, and hormone secretion, as well as body temperature and metabolism. These rhythms are intimately tied to health, well-being, and the aging process. In humans, these biological clocks or circadian rhythms anticipate various activities throughout the day, from waking up to sleeping and eating. In addition, these clocks regulate hormone levels, body temperature, and metabolism.[108]

108 Rao, R. V. (2018). [Title of the article]. *Journal of Ayurveda and Integrative Medicine, 9*, 225–232.

Dinācārya: The Science of Beginning the Day

How we begin our day – and when we begin it – sets the tone, rhythm, and mood for the hours that follow. Āyurveda recommends starting the day at dawn, well before sunrise, during a period called Brahmā Muhūrta. Brahmā represents the Creative Energy of the Universe. This is a time when the mind is most receptive to higher consciousness and divine guidance. Free from the distractions of daily hustle, this is our sacred time for self-reflection and to gather creative energy for the day ahead. The air is fresh, abundant with Prāna (life-force). Positive Psychology also acknowledges the benefits of connecting with a higher energy or divine source, as it can provide guidance, courage, and abundance.

The hours between 4-6 a.m. are ideal for prayers, meditation, or spiritual practices, which set the tone for the day with positive thoughts, ideas, and vibrations. One Vedic practice is to touch the ground and seek forgiveness from Mother Earth for trampling Her, cultivating mindfulness, respect for the planet, and sustainable living consciousness.

Āyurveda provides detailed guidelines for morning self-care, including teeth, nose, and eye care, drinking lukewarm water to aid elimination, and bowel cleansing before exercise. Exercises are prescribed according to one's constitution (prakriti) and season. Modern practices often involve exercising at the wrong time, such as post-work evening gym sessions, leading to various health issues noted in Āyurvedic texts. Pre-bath oil massage (Abhyanga) is essential for calming the nervous system and promoting health. If full-body massage is not possible, at least massaging the head, ears, and feet for 10 minutes provides significant balancing and rejuvenating benefits. Bath rituals with natural herbs help stimulate the nerves and cultivate mindfulness. These practices can be inferred from Svasthya Vṛtta.

Āyurveda emphasizes alignment with nature and the circadian rhythm. Waking early, creating positive vibrations through prayers, cleaning the body, exercising, practicing breathing rituals, and following proper meal timings are all essential. Evening practices, described in Āyurveda as Rātricaryā, constitute a wise nightly routine to prepare the body and mind for rest.[109]

Modern medicine prescribes serotonin and melatonin externally, but following Dināсārya and Rātricaryā naturally regulates these neurochemicals. Melatonin peaks at night and is the precursor to serotonin, while serotonin levels are highest in the early morning, highlighting the importance of waking up at Brahmā Muhūrta.[110]

Rātricaryā: Nighttime Routine and Sleep Hygiene

Insomnia has become a major health concern in today's digital lifestyle. Many people follow routines that directly contradict the principles of Rātricaryā, leading to sleep deficits, disorders, and chronic fatigue. The wellness industry often promotes pharmaceutical solutions like melatonin and other sleep-inducing supplements. However, the root solution lies in correcting lifestyle and integrating Rātricaryā.

Dinner should be light, easily digestible, and consumed at least 2–3 hours before sleep. Applying oil to the feet, palms, and head can enhance relaxation and promote better sleep quality. Modern research shows melatonin secretion begins around 9 p.m., while Āyurveda notes the metabolic fire (agni) is active from 10 p.m. to 2 a.m. Therefore, after 9 p.m., food and heavy intake should be avoided. A brief period of meditation or reflection before bedtime helps release the stress and emotional baggage of the day. Melatonin is naturally produced by the pineal gland during daylight, but is activated by darkness at night. Unfortunately, modern lifestyles reduce exposure to natural darkness, with artificial lights from homes, TVs, and phones delaying melatonin activation and disrupting sleep cycles.

---

109 Bhattacharya, B. (2015). *Everyday Ayurveda*. Penguin Random House India. (pp. 15, 17)

110 ibid. p. 15

Ācāra **Rasāyana**

When our body-mind-action alignment is rooted in health-enhancing mental models, we create health at both individual and societal levels. Ācāra Rasāyana encompasses codes of conduct, guiding what a person should or should not do, and is an integral aspect of preventive medicine in Āyurveda. Āyurveda considers physiological, psychological, social, behavioural, dietary, and spiritual factors for optimal health. Ācāra Rasāyana strengthens mental control, enhances immunity, and promotes overall well-being.[111]

Ācāra Rasāyana works in three dimensions:

1. Enhancing personality and mental strength
2. Improving social relationships
3. Supporting physical health and psycho-neuro-immunity.[112]

Modern psychoneuroimmunology confirms the connection between thoughts, emotions, social relationships, and health, but this wisdom has long been articulated in Āyurveda. While Western medicine often emphasises pharmacology, Āyurveda prioritises mind and lifestyle correction. Such therapy is Adravyābhūta (non-material). Ācāra Rasāyana is a form of Adravyābhūta rejuvenation that develops mental health, strengthens immunity, and improves overall human function without pharmaceuticals.[113]

Traditional Behavioural Rasāyana:

Follow the rules of Sadvṛtta (ethical and moral conduct) for Nithya Rasāyana (daily, non-material rejuvenation):

- Truthfulness (Satyavādinam)
- Freedom from anger (Akrodha)

---

111 Shriwas, H. K., & Chandrakar, R. (2018). Conceptual study of achara rasayana in Ayurveda science. *European Journal of Pharmaceutical and Medical Research, 5*(7), 146–149.

112 ibid

113 ibid

- Non-indulgence in alcohol
- Nonviolence (Ahimsa)
- Calmness and emotional balance
- Sweet and mindful speech
- Regular meditation
- Cleanliness and personal hygiene
- Perseverance
- Charity and respect toward teachers, parents, and elders
- Loving and compassionate behaviour
- Balanced sleep and wakefulness
- Using ghee in diet regularly
- Time and place awareness
- Senses control and mindful social interactions
- Keeping the company of wise and virtuous people
- Positive attitude and self-controls[114]

This list can be translated into modern health practices. Āyurveda emphasizes character, rooted in ethics and morality, as the foundation of health. Religion, in this context, is less about temple visits or deity worship and more about spiritual mindset and faith in higher energy or consciousness.

One may wonder why ghee is emphasised in a primarily psychological framework. Āyurveda identifies gut health as the foundation of overall wellness, a concept modern science is rediscovering. Digestive issues like constipation, leaky gut, and irritable bowel syndrome are major health concerns. Healthy digestion is a pillar of good health. Ghee enhances digestive function, nourishes nearly all body tissues – especially the gastrointestinal tract – reduces inflammation, prevents leakage of undigested particles, and repairs the mucosal wall.[115]

Health-compromising behaviours and lifestyles are described in great detail in Āyurveda. Balance is central to health and well-being.

114 ibid

115 Dhaliwal, M. (2017). *A new year, a new you* [E-book].

Therefore, our lifestyle and diet are primary determinants of wellness, or the lack thereof. In Āyurveda, "diet" is not limited to the food we eat; it encompasses all inputs to the five senses – eyes, ears, touch, smell, and taste. A proper "diet" for all senses fosters well-being. Conversely, excess, deficiency, or improper sensory inputs lead to dis-ease, stress, or lifestyle-related disorders.

In Āyurvedic terminology:

- Excess is called Atiyoga (Ati = excess).
- Deficiency is called Ayoga (A = lacking).
- Improper or counter-productive input is called Mithyā Yoga (Mithyā = false, wrong, or counter-productive).

When these imbalances are linked to the five senses, it is termed Asātmyeindriyārtha Saṁyoga: a union with the senses that is harmful to the body. In modern terms, this corresponds to lifestyle-created disorders, which can often be corrected through health-enhancing behaviours.

When these imbalances are influenced by external environmental factors, Āyurveda calls it Pariṇāma, which in contemporary language we may relate to climate change. The World Health Organization (WHO) is now highlighting the impact of ecological changes on emotions and well-being.[116] Jeffry Pfeiffer[117] introduced the concept of the Knowing-Doing Gap, which explains how organisations often know what constitutes best practices but only a fraction (1/8th) actually implement them. In Āyurveda, this is known as Prajñāparādha: "Pragñā" means wisdom, and "Āparādha" means transgression or acting against wisdom. Prajñāparādha is a key cause of diminished well-being at both individual and collective levels.

---

116 Shukla, V., & Tripathi, R. D. (2002). *Charak Samhita* (Vol. 1, Sutra 1/54, p. 26, 2nd ed.). Chaukhamba Sanskrit Pratishthan.

117 Luthans, F. (2011). *Organizational behavior* (10th ed.). Tata McGraw-Hill.

Asātmyeindriyārtha Saṁyoga: Indulgences and Imbalances of the Senses

Excess or Atiyoga – Overuse of electronics such as computers, TV, and phones, excessive artificial lighting at workplaces, prolonged exposure to harsh sunlight, and extended periods of sitting or standing. Modern society has recognised the consequences of such excesses, leading to the rise of digital detox programs.

Lack or Ayoga – Deficiency of sensory inputs, such as insufficient physical touch, lack of appreciation, inadequate exposure to sunlight during the day, insufficient darkness during sleep, and limited access to open sky or outdoor spaces. Sunlight through the eyes stimulates the pineal gland to secrete serotonin, essential for calmness, happiness, and sustained motivation. Sunlight also aids melatonin production, while darkness triggers melatonin release, regulating biological rhythms like sleep and wake cycles.[118]

Counter-productive or Mithyā Yoga – Viruddha **Āhāra** (incompatible food combinations) and behaviors that disrupt natural rhythms. Āyurveda identifies toxic food combinations (Viruddha **Āhāra**) and warns against negative activities while eating, such as engaging in argument or stressful conversations, which impair digestion. Exercising at night or engaging in activities contrary to one's physical and mental peak times constitutes Mithyā Yoga, as it undermines health rather than enhancing it.

Prajñāparādha: Knowing-Doing Gap

Āyurveda emphasises specific functions of intelligence and mind, known as Dhi (intelligence), Dhṛti (the capacity to sustain intelligence), and Smṛti (memory of knowledge). When these faculties are impaired, poor decisions and reduced well-being occur, reflecting a failure to live a Hitāyu – a life aligned with individual and social welfare.

---

118 Church, M. (2007). *High life 24/7: Balance your body chemistry & feel uplifted.* Thought Leaders Ltd.

Examples include failing to honour natural bodily urges like hunger, thirst, and excretion, indulging in excessive negative emotions such as anger or grief, or knowing that certain habits (e.g., smoking) are harmful yet continuing them.

Pariṇāma – Climate Change

Pariṇāma in Āyurveda emphasises how seasonal timing influences human well-being. Extreme or unusual climatic events such as excessive rainfall, droughts, unseasonal cold or heat, floods, or other contrary seasonal influences are described in the texts and are increasingly reflected in modern climate change patterns. Climatic conditions impact human health both directly, through the physical effects of weather extremes, and indirectly, by influencing air pollution levels, agricultural and aquatic systems that provide food and water, and the vectors and pathogens responsible for infectious diseases.[119]

Chronic stress can result from the gradual impacts of climate change. For instance, infectious diseases, chronic illnesses such as asthma and allergies, nutritional deficiencies, and injuries can all contribute to heightened stress levels. Following a climate event or displacement, individuals may experience a diminished sense of self, difficulty relating to others, reduced social interaction, and solastalgia – the loss of a sense of place, solace, and security tied to one's physical environment. Communities may face broader consequences, including domestic abuse, child abuse, and various forms of violence, such as assault or civil conflict. Economic insecurity and physical damage are additional potential stressors. Dr. Vandana Shiva, an internationally recognised Earth Feminist, refers to such affected populations as Climate Refugees and had predicted this phenomenon years before it reached a statistically significant level. The Industrial Revolution marked the beginning of

---

119 McMichael, A. J., Campbell-Lendrum, D. H., Corvalán, C. F., Ebi, K. L., Githeko, A. K., Scheraga, J. D., & Woodward, A. (Eds.). (2003). *Climate change and human health: Risks and responses*. World Health Organization. Geneva.

alienation from our roots in nature, community, and living in harmony. Today, Industrial Era 4 has accelerated climate change to alarming levels, putting both the mental and physical health of humanity at risk. Addressing this challenge requires a holistic worldview that reconnects us with nature and community, rather than fostering xenophobia.

Chapter 04

Beyond Traits, Types, and Temperament – Svabhāva

In this chapter, we will explore the following themes:

- Understanding human nature: West and Bharat
- Personality or Svabhāva – an Āyurvedic Profile
- Pañca Mahābhūta, signature strengths, and innate talents
- Tridoṣa – balance and imbalance and their influence on human nature

Psychology: Bridging West and East

While Western Psychology is just over 150 years old, Indian perspectives on human behavior and consciousness have been explored for more than 5,000 years. For much of its history, Western Psychology focussed heavily on pathology and deficits, whereas positive psychology and well-being are relatively recent areas of research. The works of Mihaly Csikszentmihalyi, who rediscovered the FLOW state, and Martin Seligman, who popularised Positive Psychology, Authentic Happiness, and Flourishing, have been pioneering paradigms in the West. However, less widely acknowledged yet deeply significant contributions by Carl Jung and Abraham Maslow remain underintegrated in mainstream Psychology.

It is only very recently that interdisciplinary studies in immunology, neurology, cardiology, and biology are beginning to converge to understand the human being as a holistic entity. As far back as 1968, in the preface to the second edition of Towards a Psychology of

Being, Abraham H. Maslow wrote, "I consider Humanistic, Third Force Psychology to be transitional, a preparation for a still 'higher' Fourth Psychology – transpersonal, transhuman, centred in the cosmos rather than in human needs and interests, going beyond humanness, identity, self-actualisation, and the like."[120] This "cosmos-centred" perspective, which Maslow envisioned as the Fourth Psychology, has long been articulated in Āyurveda, offering insights into human nature, consciousness, and holistic well-being.

Understanding Human Nature

The Vedas assert that the Microcosm mirrors the Macrocosm.[121] In other words, as we understand ourselves, we understand the Universe – and vice versa. The journey of self-discovery can begin from either direction.

Most ancient cultures across the world recognized that humans are composed of Elements, although the number and classification of these elements vary across traditions. If all humans were made of the same five Elements, one might expect uniformity; yet, the incredible diversity of human nature is evident everywhere. Even identical twins exhibit notable differences in behaviour and tendencies.

Āyurveda explains this uniqueness by examining the dynamic interplay of the five Elements (Pañca Mahābhūta) and the three qualities (Guṇas). An Āyurvedic Profile can be constructed using a Pañca Mahābhūta–Triguṇa matrix, enabling a deeper understanding of oneself. This profile is not static; it must remain dynamic, reflecting ongoing changes due to environmental influences, lifestyle, and personal growth. A well-understood Āyurvedic Profile empowers conscious living and informed self-regulation.

---

120 Maslow, A. H. (1968). *Towards a psychology of being*. D. Van Nostrand Company, New York, USA.

121 Vasishtha, S. (2009). *Nadi Tatva Darshanam* (p. 71). Ramlal Kapoor Trust, Sonipat, Haryana, India.

Correlation with Western Theories

Temperament theory has its roots in early constitutional psychology, which dates back to ancient Greece. It is holistic, viewing individuals as integrated, functioning systems, and explaining the "why" behind behaviour. Hippocrates (460–377 B.C.) described four temperaments – Melancholic, Sanguine, Choleric, and Phlegmatic – attributing them to internal body fluids or 'humours', rather than experience or learning.[122] In the 16th century, Paracelsus, the Swiss physician and chemist, proposed four natures influenced by the four humours: Gnome/Earth, Salamander/Fire, Nymph/Water, and Sylph/Air, linking behaviour and health to elemental composition.

Around 1940, American physician William Sheldon developed a personality typology based on body build, each type corresponding to a temperament. Gordon Allport (1897–1967) and Raymond Cattell (1905–1998) advanced the trait approach, with Allport defining traits as consistent and enduring predispositions to respond to the environment,[123] while Cattell classified traits into categories such as common, unique, ability, temperament, dynamic, surface, source, constitutional, and environmental-mould traits.[124]

Meanwhile, in psychoanalysis, Carl Jung (1875–1961) developed Type theory, emphasising innate preferences. He described the psyche as composed of distinct but interrelated systems – the ego, personal unconscious, and collective unconscious."[125] When we explore the Āyurvedic perspective on human nature, we find that it encompasses these Western theories and extends further. On one level, Āyurvedic Profiling aligns with temperament, trait, and type theories. At a deeper level, Jung's concept of the Collective Unconscious resonates with

122 Schultz, D. P., & Schultz, S. E. (2013). *Theories of personality* (10th ed., p. 191). Cengage Learning.

123 Ibid. page 197

124 Ibid. page 215

125 Ibid, page 92

the Universal Principles of the cosmos: the same forces that shape the Universe also shape us. Our individual mind, Anu Mānas, emerges from the Universal mind, Vibhu Mānas, reflecting this profound interconnection.[126]

Āyurvedic Profile

Based on the ancient Indian science of well-being, Jñāna of Life – Āyurveda, the Universal Principles of Elements form the foundation of every atom. The idea of an Āyurvedic profile is simple in concept but profound in application. Every individual body and mind are unique, like a fingerprint. Āyurvedic profiles do not confine us to stereotypes; rather, they provide insights into metabolic tendencies that are deeply ingrained, requiring continuous awareness and conscious balancing. As discussed in earlier chapters, individuals are similar in substance, reflecting the Microcosm, yet different in expression due to unique combinations of Mahābhūta and their balanced or imbalanced states.

Mahābhūta

Popularly referred to as Elements, Mahābhūta, like in many civilizations, offer a profound framework to understand ourselves and others. Sanskrit terminology carries nuances that often get lost in translation, so in this text, we retain the term Mahābhūta rather than using the English "Elements." The five Mahābhūta – Ākāśa, Vāyu, Agni, Jala, and Pṛthvī – are mentioned in the Taittirīya Upaniṣad as evolving sequentially, with each possessing dominance of specific Guṇas and its own Guṇa Dharma and Svabhāva.

The Mahābhūta combine as Doṣas, which determine form and function within the body-mind constitution. This constitution, known as Prakṛti in Āyurveda, is referred to here as the Āyurvedic Profile. The Profile

---

126 Lad, V. D. (2002). *Fundamental principles of Ayurveda* (Vol. 1, p. 193). The Ayurvedic Press.

transcends temperament, traits, or type, as all three have inherent limitations. It is grounded in Universal Principles and provides a deeper understanding of who we are.

The Elements and Doṣas function like our DNA, naturally expressing qualities associated with each Element in both body and personality, collectively termed Prakṛti. Here, Prakṛti is considered the Profile – a combination of Doṣas. Let us first understand Mahābhūta, our signature strengths, and inherent talents.

Etymologically, Bhūta derives from the root 'Bhū', meaning 'To Be', expressing growth, development, and the dynamic aspect of existence. Bhū also refers to a being in the process of creation – taking birth, becoming, and being enriched. Another meaning of Bhūta is a ghost or spirit, and literal translations without contextual understanding have led to misinterpretations of our sciences. Mahābhūta is a determinative compound of Mahat ('great' or 'gross') and Bhūta. Masculinely, it can denote a 'great living being', while neuter refers to the gross elements of the earth. Ākāśa, Vāyu, Agni, Jala, and Pṛthvī together constitute both the Macrocosm (the Cosmos) and the Microcosm (everything within it, including humans).

Āyurveda adds another dimension: the Pañca Mahābhūta along with Brahmā (Ṣaḍ Dhātuḥ) compose the Macrocosm and Microcosm. Brahmā represents Creative Energy infused with Intelligence and Information, akin to David Bohm's concept in quantum physics: Energy = Information = Intelligence (Field Energy). This Creative Energy underlies Svabhāva (innate nature) and Svadharma (personal duty). Modern science similarly observes the Universe as ever-expanding, dynamic, and filled with information.

Ākāśa, derived from the root Kāsa ('to shine' or 'to be visible'), represents space – the dimension in which all things manifest and become visible. It is the medium in which luminous entities, like the Sun, shine, enabling the expression and perception of all forms.

Qualities (Guṇa Dharma) of Ākāśa

- Akhaṇḍ – Indivisible, Whole
- All-Encompassing, All-Pervasive
- Omnipotent – unlimited potential; Omnipresent – present everywhere simultaneously
- Omniscient – knowing all
- Vast, Mysterious, Expanding
- Black Hole – both unmanifest and manifest

Dominance: Ākāśa Mahābhūta is Sattva-dominated.

Actions of Ākāśa Mahābhūta:

- Vibration and Expansion
- Non-Resistance, Freedom
- Self-expression
- In-formation (descent of intelligence into matter)
- Tanmātra – Śabda (Sound)
- Sensory Faculty – Hearing

Qualities (Guṇa Dharma) of Vāyu

- Vital Life Force (Prāna)
- Movement – initiates and sustains flow
- Absorbs and carries
- Rajas-dominated

Actions of Vāyu Mahābhūta:

- Prāna – Life energy and movement
- Energy, Enthusiasm (Utsah), Engagement, Communication
- Expansion
- Absorption of moisture, heat, coolness, and smell
- Tanmātra – Sparśa (Touch)
- Sensory Faculty – Tactile perception

Qualities (Guṇa Dharma) of Agni

- Transformation
- Awareness
- Perception
- Intelligence
- Upward Movement only
- Sattva-Rajas dominated

Actions of Agni Mahābhūta

- Brilliance and Luminosity
- Metabolism and Digestion
- Penetration
- Intelligence and Perception
- Tanmātra – Rūpa (Form/Visual)
- Sensory Faculty – Vision

Qualities (Guṇa Dharma) of Jala

- Water of Life – Creation
- Assimilation
- Solvent
- Flow
- Emotion
- Sattva-Tamas dominated

Actions of Jala Mahābhūta

- Downward Movement
- Cleansing and Purification
- Cohesiveness and Adhesiveness
- Percolation
- Memory and Emotion
- Tanmātra – Rasa (Taste)
- Sensory Faculty – Taste

Qualities (Guṇa Dharma) of Pṛthvī

- Firm Ground – supports life
- Provider and Nourisher
- Gravity
- Tamas-dominated

Actions of Pṛthvī Mahābhūta

- Gravitation – grounding
- Holding Together
- Provision of Nourishment and Resources
- Tanmātra – Gandha (Smell)
- Sensory Faculty – Smell

Note: The Pañca Mahābhūta and our Svabhāva can be better understood by examining their Guṇa Dharma (inherent qualities) and actions. Tanmātra is a complex theme requiring deeper exploration. Similarly, sensory faculties (Indriyas) play a critical role in human life. These aspects warrant further research and can form the foundation for Bhāratīya Mānas Śāstra (Indian Psychology).

Svabhāva – Signature Strength and Talent through Mahābhūta

What is a Signature Strength or Talent? These are relatively new constructs in the field of Positive Psychology. Traditionally, psychology focused on pathology, but in the last few decades, there has been a paradigm shift toward recognising human potential and strengths, building on Abraham Maslow's concept of Self-Actualisation. Focus on strengths enhances them. Focus involves involvement and attachment, which expands the possibilities of a strength becoming a talent. In Positive Psychology, signature strengths are often linked to character strengths and are considered either inherent or trained as cognitive skills. Mahābhūta Signature Strengths present a slightly different construct. Here, the strength is inherent in the Mahābhūta, and it may become an individual's strength through constitution (Prakṛti), which is genetically determined. Furthermore, by conscious focus, one can activate the strength of a Mahābhūta that may not be dominant in one's Prakṛti, since every person is composed of all Pañca Mahābhūtas. This is original work by the author, and further research is needed to expand this construct.

Talent is a special natural ability or aptitude—any recurring pattern of thought, feeling, or behaviour that can be productively applied. Behaviour depends on the formation of appropriate interconnections among neurons in the brain – the arousal of Smṛti in Mānas. Synaptic connections create talent. Self-actualisers tend to utilise their talents more consistently than others.

Talents Associated with Each Mahābhūta

Ākāśa Mahābhūta:

- Visionary, Big Picture thinking
- Detached, Spiritual, Non-judgmental
- Clairvoyance
- Accommodating
- Innovation
- Imagination Across Boundaries
- Open to New Ideas / Unexplored Territory
- Holds Everyone Together, Gives Space

Vāyu Mahābhūta

- Movement and Change
- Innovation
- Dreams
- Energy and Vitality
- Verbal Communication
- Imagination, Creativity
- Life Force – Fun Loving
- Enthusiasm

Agni Mahābhūta

- Turning Ideas into Action
- Strategic Thinking
- Inspire and Motivate
- Expansion and Achievement
- Purification / Filtering
- Intelligence
- Sharpness
- Passion and Drive
- Intensity

Jala Mahābhūta

- Flow and Adaptability
- Deep Emotional Nature
- Finds the Path of Least Resistance
- Inclusiveness – Takes Everyone Together
- Nurturing
- Creativity
- Emotional Intelligence and Compassion
- Team Player

Pṛthvī Mahābhūta

- Nurturing
- Hidden Talents / Resourcefulness
- Team Worker
- Attention to Detail
- Grounded and Practical
- Process-Oriented
- Patience
- Big Data / Organisational Skills

Mahabhoota and Talent/Strengths

ETHER	AIR	FIRE	WATER	EARTH
Big Picture	New Ideas	Action	Team Player	Traditional
Visionary	Communication	Planning	Harmonizers	Stable
Inter-disciplinary	Dreamers	Strategy	Perseverance	Process oriented
Good Listeners	Intuitive	Implementation	Memory	Detail Oriented
Create Organizations	Innovation	Risk takers	Negotiator	Documentation
Leave Legacy	Enthusiasm	Courage	Conflict diffuser	MIS Reports
	Utsah	Change Makers	Emotional	Manage Data
	Initiator	Inspire		
	Networking	Self- Motivated		

Tridoṣa and Prakṛti

Mahābhūta combine to create the Doṣas, and the combination of Doṣas forms a Prakṛti. Doṣa is a specific term used by Āyurvedic Ācāryas. As described: "Doṣa is organization. As long as doṣas are normal in quality and quantity, they maintain a harmonious psychophysiology... The doṣas – Vāta, Pitta, and Kapha – bind the five elements into living flesh. The concept of support is a natural function of these principles of physiology we call Vāta, Pitta, and Kapha. They are the agents of DNA which form the blueprint for the physiology. They are energy complexes; these complexes are known by their attributes, or Guṇas."[127]

Composition of Doṣas:

- Vāta: Ākāśa and Vāyu Mahābhūta
- Pitta: Agni and Jala Mahābhūta
- Kapha: Jala and Pṛthvī Mahābhūta

127 Lad, V. D. (2002). *Fundamental Principles of Ayurveda* (Vol. 1, p. 29). The Ayurvedic Press, Albuquerque, New Mexico.

Functions of Doṣas:

- Vāta: Principle of kinetic energy in the body; mainly governs the nervous system and all body movement.
- Kapha: Principle of potential energy; controls stability and lubrication of the body.
- Pitta: Balances kinetic and potential energies; involves all digestive and transformative processes, including "cooking" of thoughts into mental theories.[128]

Balance and Imbalance:

- Balance of Doṣas creates a healthy personality and emotional well-being.
- Living in accordance with one's Doṣa helps maintain health. This natural constitution is called Prakṛti, analogous to DNA for easy understanding.
- When Doṣas are imbalanced, or when we live against our natural makeup, it creates Vikṛti, an unnatural state that can lead to disease.

Dr. Vasant Lad explains: "There is also a state called Vikṛti, which reveals the present state of Doṣas…Vikṛti reflects any aspects of diet, lifestyle, emotions, age, environment, etc., that are not in harmony with one's Prakṛti."[129] Although originally a medical concept, Doṣa principles have tremendous potential for daily life.

Emotional Intelligence benefits from this understanding, helping us:

- Recognise our own type and the effects of lifestyle on Doṣa balance.
- Appreciate individual differences in interpersonal relationships.

---

128 Svoboda, R. E. (1994). *Your Ayurvedic Constitution* (p. 17). Motilal Banarsidas Publishers, Delhi, First Indian Edition.

129 Lad, V. D. (2002). *Textbook of Ayurveda, Fundamental Principles* (Vol. 1, p. 36). The Ayurvedic Press, Albuquerque, New Mexico, First Edition.

- Develop social awareness, understanding, respecting, and valuing the uniqueness of others.

Tridoṣa in Āyurveda Profiling:

- Vāta, Pitta, and Kapha are the Tridoṣa.
- Just as we have all Mahābhūta, we also possess all three Doṣas within us.
- The dominance of certain Mahābhūta influences the predominance of one or more Doṣa, forming our Prakṛti.
- In Āyurvedic profiling, one may be categorised as:
- Vāta-dominant (V-primed)
- Pitta-dominant (P-primed)
- Kapha-dominant (K-primed)

Knowledge of Doṣa not only aids in self-awareness but also enhances self-management, providing a framework to maintain physical, mental, and emotional equilibrium.

V-Dominated Profile

Vāta is composed of the Mahābhūta Ākāśa and Vāyu. It is the most dynamic and powerful governing principle, responsible for movement, flow, and life force within us. As such, Vāta leads the other two Doṣas in governing physiological and mental functions.

Personality Traits of V-Dominated Individuals:

- Active, alert, restless, and creative
- Changeable and unpredictable, like the wind
- Quick-moving thoughts and actions
- Light sleepers
- Enjoy excitement and novelty, but get bored easily
- Often have irregular habits
- Light-hearted, mentally agile but may have weak memory
- Can appear lacking in willpower, less tolerant, insecure, untrustworthy, or anxious

Balanced Vāta:

- Joyful, engaging, and fun to be with
- Creative, quick thinkers, adaptable, and dynamic

Imbalanced Vāta:

- Nervous, fearful, anxious, and hyperactive
- Susceptible to insomnia, constipation, and fatigue
- Experience energy fluctuations and moodiness
- May appear unfocussed, jumping from one idea to another
- Quick to see the big picture but may lack patience for logical explanation
- Sensitive to external changes and emotional fluctuations
- Prone to feelings of emptiness and loneliness due to the Ether element
- Weak memory may prevent strong imprinting of negative emotions, but vague anxiety can persist

Creative Strengths of V-Dominated Individuals:

- Ākāśa gifts them clairvoyance and visionary thinking
- Excellent writers, architects, sculptors, or any field requiring creative imagination
- Quick at forming and releasing attachments
- Rapid emotional responsiveness – express and process emotions swiftly
- Ākāśa, as the first Mahābhūta, is considered the mother of all creativity, providing the "blank canvas" for ideas to flourish

Factors That Increase / Imbalance Vāta:

- Sensory overload
- Excessive television or screen time
- Too much talking
- Overexertion – mental or physical
- Dry or uncooked food

- Late nights
- Windy, dry, or cold weather
- Absence of a routine
- Fear, nervous strain, or stress
- Emotionally upsetting relationships

Factors That Reduce / Balance Vāta:

- Meditation and deep breathing
- Disciplined daily routine
- Warm and heavy diet suitable for Vāta
- Massage with warm oil, sauna, or hot shower
- Soothing music

P-Dominated Profile

Pitta is composed primarily of the Mahābhūta Agni, contained within the protective Jala of the body, such as digestive enzymes and bodily fluids. Pitta governs transformation, metabolism, hormone secretion, and biochemical activities. It controls digestion, vision, body heat and temperature, complexion, and blood formation.

Personality Traits of P-Dominated Individuals:

- Fiery, intense, sharp, intelligent, and competitive
- Strong drive and willpower
- Piercing, focussed eyes
- Articulate, learned, and proud
- Precise, punctual, and structured; impatient with delays
- Good memory

Balanced Pitta:

- Witty, joyful, enterprising, and passionate
- Love challenges and excel under pressure
- Natural leaders who can take command of situations
- Creates awareness and clarity in thought

Imbalanced Pitta:

- Judgmental, sarcastic, egoistic, boastful, impulsive, rigid, irritable, angry, or aggressive
- Perfectionist, self-righteous, unforgiving, and overly demanding of self and others
- Excess Pitta can produce tension, anger, and suppressed sadness
- Confuses the mind instead of fostering awareness
- Tend to display Type A personality traits

Factors That Increase / Imbalance Pitta:

- Excess alcohol
- Hot, spicy, or pungent food
- Low fluid intake
- Excess red meat
- Constant anger or stress-generating environment
- Excessive sun exposure
- Frequent arguments or confrontations
- Lack of outdoor time, especially in nature
- Lack of secure and loving relationships

Factors That Reduce / Balance Pitta:

- Meditation and slow, controlled breathing (preferably through the left nostril)
- Opening the heart to individual differences and practicing acceptance
- Spacing out activities rather than overloading the schedule
- Pitta-friendly diet: moderate spice, cooling foods
- Soft, calming music

K-Dominated Profile

Kapha is composed of the Mahābhūta Jala and Pṛthvī, making it the most stable and grounding principle. Kapha governs the strength and structure of the body, maintaining stability, cohesion, and fluid balance.

It is the principle of potential energy, responsible for protection, support, and lubrication. However, its stability can also lead to inertia and lethargy.

Personality Traits of K-Dominated Individuals:

- Calm, slow, grounded, and relaxed
- Compassionate, nurturing, loving, and forgiving
- Steady and deliberate in action
- Loyal, dependable, and emotionally resilient
- Slow to absorb information and resistant to change

Balanced Kapha:

- Dependable, emotionally stable, and enduring in energy
- Long-term memory and sincere, loyal nature
- Calm temperament, patience, and consistency in relationships
- Ability to maintain physical and emotional endurance
- Strong connection to family, community, tradition, and values

Imbalanced Kapha:

- Greed, attachment, rigidity, and resistance to change
- Sluggishness, low motivation, and heaviness of heart
- Fondness for inactivity, excessive sleep, and comfort
- Difficulty adapting to new situations or people outside their immediate circle
- Prone to clinging to the past, storing negative emotions, and depression

Observations in Āyurvedic Texts:

K-dominant individuals are often praised for their stability and low susceptibility to illnesses, while V-dominant individuals are seen as fickle-minded. This perception stems from their natural resilience rather than inherent superiority or weakness.

Factors That Increase / Imbalance Kapha:

- Excessive liquid, dairy products, or cold foods
- Overeating, especially sweets
- Sedentary lifestyle and insufficient exercise
- Excessive sleep
- Hoarding and greed

Factors That Reduce / Balance Kapha:

- Active sports and vigorous exercise
- Sweating and movement-based activities
- Kapha-friendly diet: mild, spicy, and warm foods
- Practicing acceptance and adaptability to change
- Stimulating music: fast rhythms such as tabla or drums

K-dominant individuals may prefer staying at home and feel content within familiar environments. They are deeply attached to family, friends, community, religion, and country, but may be resistant to accepting anything or anyone outside this sphere. Compared to P-dominated (Pitta) types, they may lack drive, and compared to V-dominated (Vāta) types, they may have less initiative. Strong attachment often results in clinging – either to loved ones or to the past – leading to stored hurt and negative emotions. K-types are prone to depression and dullness.

In Āyurvedic texts, K-dominant individuals are generally praised, while V-dominant types are judged negatively. This bias arises because K-types tend to be less prone to illness, not necessarily because they are superior.

Tridoṣa and Prakṛti

Mahābhūta combine to create Doṣas, and the combination of Doṣas forms our Prakṛti, or natural constitution. "Doṣa is organisation. As long as doṣas are normal in quality and quantity, they maintain a harmonious psychophysiology... The doṣas – Vāta, Pitta, and Kapha – bind the five elements into living flesh. They are energy complexes known by their attributes, or Guṇas."

- Vāta: Ākāśa + Vāyu; principle of kinetic energy, governs movement and nervous system.
- Pitta: Agni + Jala; principle of transformation, governs digestion, metabolism, and intelligence.
- Kapha: Jala + Pṛthvī; principle of potential energy, governs stability, structure, and lubrication.

Balance of Doṣas leads to healthy personality and emotional well-being. Living in alignment with our Prakṛti maintains health; imbalance creates Vikṛti, resulting in disease. Knowledge of Doṣas aids self-awareness and self-management, as well as appreciation of differences in interpersonal relationships, thereby enhancing Emotional Intelligence (EI).

Triguṇa and Svabhāva

While Tridoṣa forms the structural template, Triguṇa are the energies that animate it. Āyurveda describes svabhāva (nature) based on each Guṇa. Unlike Tridoṣa, which remains constant, Triguṇa are dynamic and transformable.

Sāttvic Svabhāva

Characteristics: Strength of character (Śīla), devotion (Bhakti), cleanliness, sense control, equanimity, selflessness, ability to let go, interest in spiritual knowledge. Rarely angry; quick to forgive; enjoy serving others; aesthetic appreciation.

S-Dominant Subtypes: Knowledge-seekers, self-actualisers, creative in arts (poetry, music, dance). Noble, generous, compassionate, selfless, self-controlled, virtuous, endowed with good memory, able to discriminate and retain knowledge. Spiritual pursuits outweigh materialistic desires.

Lifestyle: Early rising, clean and aesthetic living space, simple and fresh diet, preference for white or pastel colours, fondness for fragrances.

Roles: Counsellors, educators, leaders of spiritual or charitable organisations.

Potential Pitfall: Sattva pride may make them intolerant of impure thoughts or conduct.

Rājasic Svabhāva

Characteristics: Ego-centric, love power, expansion, and victory. Courageous, aggressive, ambitious, restless, and materialistic. Prone to anger, jealousy, lack of empathy, and impulsiveness. Driven by worldly success and recognition.

Subtypes: Six; common in business leaders. Energetic, extroverted, action-oriented, with entrepreneurial spirit. Can be ethical and sustainable if guided by Sattva.

Weaknesses: Impatience, stress-prone, emotionally volatile, enjoy materialistic pleasures, prone to burnout.

Tāmasic Svabhāva

Characteristics: Rigid, ignorant, lazy, procrastinating, indulging in sensuous pleasures, resistant to change, trapped in habits or beliefs. Atheist or rigid in religious beliefs. Gross Tamas produces darkness and ignorance, affecting perception and mental activity.

T-Dominant Subtypes: Three; overindulgent, self-centred, dependent on substances, focused on materialistic enjoyment, slow to grow or accept new ideas. Fear, inertia, and resistance are dominant.

Transformation of Guṇas

The combination of Guṇas can be transformed through willpower and Sādhana. Sattva can be cultivated to guide Rajas and Tamas, leading to higher awareness and balanced behaviour.

- Sattva: Intelligence, balance, clarity
- Rajas: Energy, movement, potential for imbalance

- Tamas: Substance, inertia, potential for stagnation

Guṇas are subtle qualities underlying matter, life, and mind, forming our energy matrix. They vary from light to heavy, maintaining equilibrium through constant flux, reflecting principles akin to energy conservation in physics.

Integration of these insights can enhance psychology, self-development, and counseling. Āyurveda offers psychotherapies, such as Sattvavajaya, to cultivate Sattva as the guiding force (see Appendix). We can also create a matrix showing the influence of Tridoṣa and Triguṇa on the mental (mānas) and physical state of Vāta, Pitta, and Kapha.

Vāta Mānas: Vāta is combination of Ākāśa and Vāyu Mahābhūta, and Sattva-Rajas dominated. Rajas makes Vāta very strong in influencing both other Doṣas of Pitta and Kapha. Sāttvic influence creates comprehension, the need for unity and healing, and creates a positive mental outlook. Rājasic influence creates indecisiveness, unreliability, and hyperactivity. Tāmasic influence creates fear, a servile attitude, dishonesty, depression, self-destructiveness, addictive behaviour, sexual perversions, animal instincts, or suicidal thoughts.[130]

Pitta Mānas: Pitta is Sattva and Rajas dominated due to Agni and Jala Mahā Bhūta. Sāttvic influence creates clarity, intelligence, leadership, warmth, and independence. Rājasic influence creates wilfulness, ambition, anger, manipulation, vanity, impulsiveness, and aggressiveness. Tāmasic influence creates vindictiveness, violence, hate, criminality, and psychopathic behaviour.[131]

Kapha Mānas: Kapha is Tamas-dominated due to the predominance of Pṛthvī Mahābhūta. When Sāttvic influence is strong, Kapha brings calmness, peace, love, compassion, faith, nurturing, and forgiveness,

130 Swami Sada Shiva Tirtha. (2005). *The Ayurvedic encyclopaedia* (5th reprint, pp. 21–22). Ayurveda Holistic Center Press, Bayville, NY, USA.

131 Ibid. pg. 22

resulting in individuals who are steady, supportive, and balanced. Under Rājasic influence, Kapha manifests as greed for money, material comforts, and luxuries; such individuals may become overly sentimental, controlling, attached, and indulgent. Tāmasic influence, on the other hand, leads to dullness, sloth, lethargy, depression, lack of care, and in extreme cases, tendencies toward dishonesty or stealing.[132]

Svabhāva, as understood through the combination of Mahābhūta into Prakṛti and Triguṇa into the mānas (psychological tendencies), represents a unique contribution of Bhāratīya Mānas Śāstra to the field of Psychology. The term Bhāva refers to the process of creation—how an entity comes into being, evolves, transforms, and grows.[133] Sva in Sanskrit means Self, and together, Sva + Bhāva = Svabhāva, which can be understood as the "nature of the Self." In Āyurveda, Svabhāva is considered one of the causes of the Universe, as suggested in Sāṅkhya philosophy. In this context, Svabhāva becomes the starting point of self-discovery, moving beyond traditional constructs like Type, Trait, or Temperament. Each Mahābhūta carries its own svabhāva, which manifests within us as signature strengths. They form the foundation of our talents, abilities, and psychological tendencies. Many psychological challenges may arise because we are disconnected from our Svabhāva – either unaware of it or not fully utilising the natural strengths embedded within us. Recognising and aligning with Svabhāva enables individuals to thrive in daily life, express their authentic self, and cultivate well-being.

132 Ibid. p. 22

133 Mishra, R. K. (2012). *Before the beginning and after the end* (p. 363). Rupa Publications.

CHAPTER 05

Citta and Citta Vṛttis, Yama and Niyama

In this chapter we cover these themes:

- Āyurveda and Yoga as twin sciences
- The four faculties of the Inner Being – Antaḥkaraṇa
- Saṁskāra Theory
- Citta Prasāda and Citta Vikṣobha
- Citta Vṛttis: From emotional numbness and spiritual intelligence
- Yama and Niyama – the foundation for Yoga

Introduction

Yoga and Āyurveda are twin sciences. Until now, we have explored most insights from Āyurveda. In this chapter, we integrate insights from Yoga to develop Indic Psychology. Some constructs differ in terminology: for example, the Five Great Elements are Pañca Mahābhūta in Āyurveda, while Yoga refers to them as Pañca Tattva. Similarly, Āyurveda uses Mānas or Mana, whereas Yoga uses Citta. (Although Āyurveda occasionally mentions Citta, too.) Many confusions have arisen, and today, many practitioners struggle to see the connections between Āyurveda and Yoga to create an integrated psychological framework. Historically, these two sciences were likely one integral system, both arising from compassion for human suffering. Both serve as pathways to achieve the Four Puruṣārthas: Dharma, Artha, Kāma, and Mokṣa. Āyurveda ensures health – Svastha, rooted in the self. Yoga guides us toward Svarūpa, our true identity. Āyurveda is the science of balance and harmony of body and mind, while Yoga transcends the limited understanding of self beyond body and mind. Āyurveda precedes Yoga:

without a healthy body and Mānas, Yoga practices are difficult. Yoga facilitates the evolution of a healthy person, and Āyurveda provides the foundation by creating health.

Four Faculties of the Inner Being – Antaḥkaraṇa

In Patanjal Yoga, Pradeep Shree Swami Omanand Teerth provides a clear understanding of Mānas and Citta.[134] Mānas, Buddhi, Citta, and Ahaṅkāra are sometimes used as synonyms and sometimes as distinct concepts. They can be differentiated by their functions as Antaḥkaraṇa Catuṣṭaya – the four faculties of inner working:

- Mānas – responsible for Saṅkalpa-Vikalpa (thoughts and deliberation)
- Ahaṅkāra – expression of identity
- Buddhi – decision-making and closure
- Citta – repository of impressions, memories (smṛti), and life imprints

Ahaṅkāra exists in a seed form within Citta. Citta generates ripples of movements that extend outward; these are called Citta Vṛttis. Upon death, it is Citta that leaves the body and travels with the subtle body to the next incarnation. Even if one does not believe in reincarnation, understanding Citta and its movements is essential for achieving a healthy, happy, and optimal life.

In the chapter on Mānas, we explored its functions. When we integrate the understanding of Citta and Citta Vṛttis, the science becomes complete. As Vimala Thakar aptly states, "Knowing about the mind is one thing, and being acquainted with it while it is functioning, being aware of the movement of the mind, is another thing." And hence she adds, "Most of us are strangers to our own minds."[135] The movements of

134 Shri Swami Omanand Teerth. (2013). *Patanjal Yog Pradeep.* Gorakhpur: Gita Press.
135 Thakar, Vimala. *Mutation of Mind.* Holland: Vimala Thakar Foundation, 3rd printing, p. 99.

the mind are connected with Citta Vṛttis. Mānas, because of its atomic and fluctuating nature, cannot be directly controlled. However, Citta Vṛttis can be managed through Yoga practices. That is why we must transcend Mānas, rather than attempt to control or suppress it. Citta, on the other hand, can be tamed and purified through Yogic practices. The process of Citta Śuddhi (purification of Citta) is critical, as we will explore in detail in subsequent sections.

Citta – The Storehouse of Saṁskāra

How often do we notice our thoughts, actions and behaviours as patterns? We may even realise that they limit our spontaneous responses to life, keeping us trapped in repetition, yet feel unable change much. From being a psychological process, these patterns become physical imprints in our cells, forming cellular memories. That is how our biology and biography are interconnected. Past memories soaked in emotions are saṁskāras – seeds over which we have no control, yet which hold us captive and influence us involuntarily.[136] These seeds of memory are planted in the Citta. Hence, Sage Patañjali calls Citta 'Bhoomi' – the soil where saṁskāras sprout. Once sprouted, they create patterns of reactions. Etymologically, the word Saṁskāra comes from the roots: "sāma" – putting together, whole, joining, and *"kara"* – action, doing. Saṁskāras are the sum of all our actions, thoughts, behaviours, learnings, and memories – impressions that create patterns and tendencies, cycles of living maintained through repetition and practice, almost like conditioning.

One of the qualities of Jīvātma is Saṁskāra. Memory (smṛti) arises from saṁskāras, which come from past imprints. This process is known as bhavana of Cetanā Ātma. Experiences from past or current lifetimes accumulate and remain in our Antaḥkaraṇa in latent form. The subconscious or unconscious mind functions in the same way. With the right trigger, these latent memories are activated and respond, guiding

136 Tavaria, S. N. *Yoga Sutra of Sage Patanjali*. India, 1st impression, March 1992, p. 49.

our likes and dislikes. Though the memory bank is vast, most memories lie dormant. As seeds have their own timing to sprout, so do saṁskāras. At the right moment, when they are ready, they surface like a plant emerging from a seed.

Svabhāva is shaped by our saṁskāras. Every experience leaves an imprint as saṁskāra. In Western Psychology, Sigmund Freud uses the iceberg analogy to understand the human mind: only one-tenth is visible in our conscious behaviour; nine-tenths lies in the subconscious and unconscious, which is below the surface, invisible yet immensely powerful. The iceberg is a powerful metaphor for understanding saṁskāra's role in svabhāva. Consider the Titanic: what sank it? The invisible mass beneath the surface. Similarly, in our lives, the hidden forces of saṁskāra must be understood to navigate the journey of life successfully.

Western Psychology debates whether nature or nurture influences us more. Are we born with certain tendencies and patterns, or do our environment and upbringing shape us? According to Indic Psychology, nature – our Prakṛti and saṁskāras – exerts a profound influence. However, epigenetics and punaḥ saṁskāras through Vedic rituals and Yoga practices can modify these tendencies, though this requires constant awareness and practice.Saṁskāras operate through activators that either inhibit or encourage certain behaviors. Some activators are genetically determined, while others result from experience. Meditation (dhyāna) and self-study (svādhyāya) help block latent activators or establish new ones. Patañjali notes that this process is difficult and often painful. Thus, both nature and nurture play a role, and the mind has the capacity to transcend its limitations.[137]

These patterns of thinking, feeling, and behaving can form a vicious cycle, which requires conscious effort to transform into a virtuous cycle.

---

137 Kak, Subhash. *Mind and Self: Patanjali Yoga Sutra and Modern Science*. Mount Meru Publishing, 2016, p. 48.

These are the subconscious impressions left by acts of volition, mental and emotional patterns that shape our conditioning. Western Psychology has not fully illuminated this subconscious and unconscious aspect of the mind, which is a unique contribution of Indic Psychology, offering a holistic understanding of svabhāva.

Citta Prasāda and Citta Vikṣobha

Positive Psychology represents a shift from pathological approaches. In Indic Psychology, this is integrated as Mānas Swasthyavrutt and Citta Prasāda. Mānas Swasthyavrutt focusses on cultivating a healthy mind, while Citta Prasāda refers to the creation of Prasannatā, a deeper, higher construct than mere happiness. *Prasanna* denotes clarity, brightness, and tranquility, while *Prasāda* implies satisfaction. Citta Prasāda is thus the natural outcome of a healthy mānas.

As Mahārṣi Patañjali explains in *Yoga Darśana*:

मैत्री करुणा मुदितोपेक्षणां सुखदुःख पुण्यापुण्य विषयाणां भावनात्पश्चित प्रसादनम्।

This means that by cultivating feelings of friendliness, compassion, joy, and equanimity toward the happy, the distressed, the virtuous, and the wicked, one attains unbroken tranquillity of the mind. In contrast, pathological psychology is described as Mānas Roga or Citta Vikṣobha. meaning a disturbed Citta. Mānas, being Triguṇātmaka (composed of Sattva, Rajas, and Tamas), is influenced by internal and external factors. When Sattva predominates, it manifests as Citta Prasāda; when Rajas or Tamas dominates, disturbances arise, creating Vikṣobha – agitation, conflict, confusion, and violent motion. The term Vikṣobha derives from kṣubha, meaning turbulence. Vitiated Rajas and Tamas lead to Mithyā Yoga, or wrong associations, between our Indriyas and the inner or outer world. Emotions such as fear, grief, anger, greed, attachment (moha), pride and jealousy are manifestations of such Mithyā Yoga.

Āyurveda, as a science of Svasthya (health and balance), recognises the mind-body continuum and psychosomatic wellness. Balanced Sattva driving Rajas and Tamas creates psychosomatic wellness, whereas dominance of Rajas or Tamas produces psychosomatic disease. The Guṇas are dynamic, and one's Prakṛti (innate nature) reflects a tendency rather than a fixed state. Conscious efforts through Yoga and Āyurveda can evolve a person's Svabhāva.

- Sattva-dominant Prakṛti: Spiritual, compassionate, just, generous, knowledge-seeking, detached, self-regulated.
- Rajas-dominant Prakṛti: Achievement-oriented, expansionist, selfish, revengeful, sometimes violent.
- Tamas-dominant Prakṛti: Materialistic, rigid, ignorant, lacking prudence, discipline, and hygiene.

Sattva fosters Citta Prasāda, while Rajas and Tamas generate Citta Vikṣobha. By enhancing Sattva, one can guide Rajas and Tamas to act appropriately according to circumstances. Daily fluctuations in Sattva, Rajas, and Tamas influence Citta and mānas, shaping mental states over time and forming patterns that determine our behaviour.

Five States of Citta – From Emotional Numbness to Spiritual Intelligence

Based on the dominant Guṇa combination at a given time, Yoga describes five states of Citta: Kṣipta, Mūḍha, Vikṣipta, Ekāgra, and Niruddha.

Kṣipta State: In the Kṣipta state, Rajas predominates, resulting in a "monkey mind". Adi Shankarācārya aptly describes the mind as markaṭa – a monkey – agitated and restless. Characteristics include:

- Unsteady mindset; inability to focus deeply
- Lack of steadfastness or capacity for introspection
- Superficial existence, herd mentality, limited thinking beyond material concerns
- Potential for aggression, violence, and self-centredness
- Rapid operations of the mind, often acting without considering consequences, leading to frequent mistakes

- Oscillation between emotions such as love, hate, sadness, anxiety, tension, and excitement
- Tendency to adopt a micro perspective rather than a holistic view

Mūḍha State: Mūḍha represents the "donkey mind," dominated by Tamas. In modern psychological terms, this resembles emotional numbness. Characteristics include:

- Derived from Mugdha – meaning hypnotized or dulled state
- Inability to think, reflect, or discriminate; lack of Viveka (discernment)
- Dominance of fear, anger, and greed
- Entrapment in rigid belief systems, inflexibility, laziness, illusion, fatigue, jealousy, and inertia due to Tamas
- Inability to differentiate between good and bad, or respond adaptively to environmental situations while maintaining integrity and self-identity

Vikṣipta State: The Vikṣipta mind is a "butterfly mind," primarily Sattva-dominated, though Rajas and Tamas influence fluctuations. Characteristics include:

- More stable than Kṣipta, showing signs of emotional maturity
- Rajas and Tamas may still influence, but Sattva can assert dominance more easily
- When Sattva prevails, one can achieve steadiness, engage in Śravaṇa (listening) and Manana (reflection), and focus on higher knowledge
- Capacity for enlightenment in certain areas, insight generation, and development of Prajñā (wisdom)
- Occasional influence of Rajas or Tamas may disrupt Sattva, returning the mind to a Vikṣipta state
- Emotional qualities include happiness, forgiveness, faith, patience, high energy, and compassion

Ekāgra State: The Ekāgra state is Sattva-dominated, with minimal influence of Rajas and Tamas. This state can be equated with Emotional Intelligence. A concentrated (Ekāgra) mind represents internal strength and can be cultivated intentionally. The Ekāgra mind is also analogous to the modern concept of Flow State. As Csikszentmihalyi describes,

"The ego falls away. Time flies. Every action, movement, and thought follows inevitably from the previous one, like playing jazz. Your whole being is involved, and you're using your skills to the utmost."

However, unlike the temporary and often effortless Flow state, Ekāgra requires self-awareness and conscious effort to maintain this Sattva-dominant condition. Key characteristics include:

- Ability to maintain focus for extended periods, exercise discernment (Viveka), restrict the outward journey of senses (indriya), and live consciously
- Resilience against external distractions
- Easier practice of Abhyāsa (consistent practice) and Vairāgya (detachment)
- Sustained Sattva allows one to be steady, engage in Śravaṇa, Manana, and Nididhyāsa, and focus on higher knowledge
- Capacity for insight, enlightenment in specific aspects, and development of Prajñā (wisdom), which comprises Dhī (intellect), Dhṛti (firmness), and Smṛti (memory)
- Balance, discretion, resilience, macro perspective, and the ability to harness emotional energy to achieve desired results

Niruddha State: Niruddha represents a step beyond Ekāgra, moving from Emotional Intelligence to a higher dimension of Spiritual Intelligence. Characteristics include:

- A thoughtless mind, so calm that no thought vibrations arise
- The thoughtless mind represents the highest state, a condition of Yoga Samādhi – the apex of Yoga practice and ultimate refinement of mental culture

- Beyond Guṇas – Svarūpa Sthiti (state of pure being)
- Heightened intuition, bliss, and transcendental awareness

These five states of Citta are summarised as follows in Patanjal Yoga Pradeep.[138] Here, Mj refers to the major or dominant Guṇa, and Mn refers to the minor or secondary Guṇa. The state of Guṇa in the Citta determines the corresponding manifestation in emotional and biological states. The selection of activities and behaviours is influenced by the prevailing state of Citta.

- When consciousness (Cetanā) contracts, Tamas predominates, leading to inertia, rigidity, and reduced awareness.
- When consciousness expands, Sattva predominates, supporting clarity, balance, and the potential for self-transcendence beyond all Guṇas.

Thus, the journey from a disturbed mind (Citta Vikṣobha) to a tranquil and harmonious mind (Citta Prasāda) is facilitated by the regulation and awareness of these states.

State Name	Dominance of Guna	Manifestation in the Emotional State	Biological State	Activities
Emotional Numbness (mudha)	**Tamas-Mj** Rajas & Sattva-Mn	Fear, Rigidity, Anger, laziness, illusion, sleep, greed, fatigue, jealousy, inertia.	Heavy & Dark	Violence, self-centeredness, ego-centric
Agitation & Anxiety (Kshipta)	**Rajas-Mj** Tamas & Sattva-Mn	Love, hate, sadness, anxiety, oscillation between tension & excitement, Micro perspective	Oscillate between heavy & light	Extends from myself to family & society
Emotional Maturity (Vikshipta)	**Sattva-Mj** **Rajas** & Tamas-Mn	Happiness, forgiveness, faith, patience, high energy, compassion.	Dominated By luminosity & lightness	Extends to larger circles of nation & the world
Emotional Intelligence (Ekagrata)	**Sattva-Mj** Rajas & Tamas-nominal	Balance, Discretion, Resilience, Macro perspective, able to use emotional energy for creating desired result	Luminous & lightness sometimes dulled by darkness	Extends to humanity & universe
Spiritual Intelligence (Niruddha)	Beyond Guna	High Intuition, Bliss	Luminous	Universal to Cosmic

138 Shri Swami Omanand Teerth. (2013). *Patanjal Yog Pradeep*. Gorakhpur, India: Gita Press.

Duryodhana Syndrome

As one progresses from Tamas dominance to Sattva dominance and ultimately transcends the Triguṇas, one becomes increasingly aware of the challenges posed by Tamas. Tamas exhibits the greatest resistance to change, adhering to the status quo even when life experiences are suboptimal. This challenge can be termed Duryodhana Syndrome.

Tamas creates xenophobia – a contraction of the soul. The saint-poet Dadu Dayal beautifully illustrates this in a couplet emphasizing that the expansion of Brahmā (Consciousness) within Puṇya and the contraction of Consciousness (Brahmā Saṅkoca) is a sin. Tamas is driven by the fear of survival, activating the medulla oblongata in the brain, which triggers fight, flight, or freeze responses, all characteristic of Tamas-dominated reactions, in contrast to heart-centred responses, which are more situation-appropriate.

The challenge of Tamas is analogous to the Duryodhana Syndrome. The Mahābhārata character Duryodhana exemplifies the knowing-doing gap. His own admission captures this:

"Jānāmi Dharmaṁ na ca me Pravṛttiḥ, Jānāmi Adharmaṁ, na cha me nivṛtti"

(I know what Dharma is, but I am unable to follow it in my actions; I am aware of what is Adharma, yet I still engage in it.)

In modern terms, management scholars Jeffrey Pfeffer and Robert I. Sutton describe this as the Knowing-Doing Gap – a phenomenon where individuals and organisations recognise optimal practices for growth but fail to implement them. While Western scholarship has theorised and quantitatively studied this gap, it requires integration with Indic wisdom on Citta and Triguṇa to truly transcend the Duryodhana Syndrome. Incorporating Dharmic frameworks into Western models can facilitate the evolution of human nature. Ultimately, each of us must reflect: How will we transcend the Duryodhana within ourselves?

Transformation of Guṇas

Sri Aurobindo's insights into the Triguṇas provide a framework for the journey from emotional numbness to spiritual intelligence. Even before transcending the Guṇas, they can be transformed into their purer forms through consistent practices and tapas. The three Guṇas can be purified, refined, and elevated into their divine equivalents:

- Sattva becomes Jyoti – the authentic spiritual light.
- Rajas becomes Tapas – the intense, tranquil divine force.
- Tamas becomes Sama – the divine quiet, rest, and peace.[139]

Many misconceptions surround the nature of Triguṇas. Tamas is often regarded as negative. However, subtle Tamas is essential for rest, rejuvenation, sound sleep, and enhanced receptivity. Gross Tamas, on the other hand, induces confusion, arrogance, and rigidity, exemplified by Duryodhana. There is, however, a ray of hope. Sri Aurobindo says, "The dominant Guṇas are not the essential soul-type of the embodied being but only the index of the formation he has made for this life or during his present existence and at a given moment of his evolution in Time."[140]

In psychotherapy, integrating the understanding of Citta and its various states can help humanity live healthier and more fulfilling lives. How can we practically transform the Guṇas? Yoga Sūtras provide guidelines for attitudes, thoughts, and behaviors through Yama and Niyama as part of Aṣṭang Yoga. While Āsana, Prānayama, and meditation have gained popularity, their benefits are limited if not practiced alongside Yama and Niyama.

Yama and Niyama – Foundation for Yoga

Yama and Niyama form the core foundation of a Yogic lifestyle and are essential attitudes to be cultivated through consistent practice. There

139 Sri Aurobindo, Greater Psychology, Sri Aurobindo International Centre for Education, January 2001, page 118

140 Ibid. (2002). *Light on the Yoga Sutras of Patanjali* (p. 115). Harper Collins Publishers India.

are five Yamas and five Niyamas, each serving as a psychological commitment, and all ten are interconnected. An important aspect of Yama and similarly of Niyama is that they operate on three levels: manasā (thought), vācā (speech), and karmaṇā (action). True practice involves integration across all three levels: when a principle is practiced at one level, it simultaneously influences the others.

Yama: Ahiṁsā, Satya, Asteya, Brahmācārya, Aparigraha (Yama 2.30)[141]

Yama has been translated in various ways. One of the interpretations is as a "perspective of life aligned with Absolute Truth." When Yama is described merely as restraint or control, it can feel like an imposition, and naturally, people resist force. However, when Yama is understood as a perspective of life, it becomes far easier for individuals to accept and integrate it as a way of living. As Vimala Thakar aptly states, "These are absolute values of human life. It is not a code of conduct. Unless there are some absolute values which cannot be bargained and the consciousness is rooted in those values, it seems to me that sane and healthy societies cannot come into existence."[142]

Ahiṁsā: Widely translated as non-violence, non-injury, or harmlessness. The prefix 'A' denotes absence, and 'Hiṁsā' means to harm. It is intriguing that Patañjali begins with ahiṁsā. When we value ahiṁsā, we intentionally refrain from harming anyone and aim to cultivate harmony in relationships. The Yamas, as absolute truths, must be actively cultivated within us. Why cultivated? Because it is not innately programmed in the current functioning of our brain. We have the potential to reformat and rewrite our mental programming, so Ahiṁsā must be consciously cultivated to replace ingrained tendencies of Hiṁsā. Hiṁsā often arises to protect our ego, identity, and sense of existence. However, if we

141 Iyengar, B. K. S. (2002). *Light on the Yoga Sutras of Patanjali* (pp. 135–136). Harper Collins Publishers India.

142 Thakar Vimala, Glimpses of Raja Yoga, Vimal Prakashan Trust, India, 1991

consistently practice Ahiṁsā at all levels, we experience inner and outer harmony, and fear naturally diminishes.

Ahiṁsā at the Action Level: Physical violence, abuse, killing, harming others, or cruelty ceases. This principle extends beyond humans to all of Nature. Capital punishment, cultural genocide, and ecocide are all forms of Hiṁsā. Practicing ahiṁsā means revering life in its entirety.

Ahiṁsā at the Speech Level: While physical violence is visible, violence through speech is subtler and equally impactful. Sarcasm, ridicule, belittling, condemnation, shouting, or harsh words all constitute Hiṁsā at the speech level. Many people are physically non-violent, but true awareness begins with speech. One must ask: *Am I harming anyone through my words, expressions, or even silence?* Intention determines whether an act is violent. Silence used to punish or invalidate someone is also violent – children, for example, often feel hurt by adults who remain silent rather than communicate effectively.

Ahiṁsā at the Thought Level: Thoughts are the subtlest dimension, making them most difficult to identify and regulate. Justifying violence by others – for national, religious, or "noble" causes – constitutes mental Hiṁsā

We need deep introspection to root out violence. According to Vyas, the most recognized commentator of Patañjali Sūtras, Ahiṁsā in Vedic concept is not just absence of Hiṁsā; it is harmony, Maitri and sadBhāva to Nature and all living beings.[143] This definition makes Ahiṁsā a broad, harmonious construct and an absolute value for life.

Satya: Satya is commonly translated as Truth. Are we truthful in our actions, speech, and thoughts? Truth is always filtered through perception, which means my truth and your truth often conflict. What does Patañjali intend when he calls truth a Yama? It is about being

---

143 Shrimat Swami Hariharanand Aaranya. (2000). *Patanjal Yoga Darshan* (2nd ed., reprint). Motilal Banarasidas. (p. 244)

truthful – truthful to one's intentions and motives. Commentaries explain truth as communicating without addition, dilution, or distortion. The Seer-Scientist recognised that personal truths are always partial. Hence, practicing Satya involves expressing how one truly feels or thinks, accepting one's limitations, and respecting others' truths. This path not only enhances inner harmony and relationship integrity, but also purifies perception filters, allowing Absolute Truth to reveal itself.

Connection between Satya and Ahiṁsā: Intent matters. When communicating, is the purpose to heal or to hurt? Clarity of intention links truthfulness directly to non-violence. Social conditioning and brain programming often work against Satya. No child is born untruthful, yet as children grow, consequences such as punishment, invalidation, denial, or rejection shape their communication. To protect themselves and maintain external harmony, children learn to speak half-truths or fabricate stories, inadvertently compromising their inner harmony, even though they inherently desire to be truthful. Speaking the truth requires outgrowing fear and cultivating courage. Satya is the commitment to follow the guidance of one's inner compass. When we strive to live truthfully at all three levels – thought, speech, and action—our dedication to inner values is continuously tested. For instance, the short-term focus of businesses from quarter to quarter may tempt one toward untruthful practices. Yet the inner compass constantly asks two questions: "Does this feel right?" and "What are the deeper implications of this action?" Self-questioning fosters self-governance and intrinsic morality.

Asteya: Asteya literally means "non-stealing," derived from steya, which means to steal. Like the previous Yamas, Asteya carries a profound, multi-layered understanding. On a superficial level, most of us might think that simply refraining from theft fulfills this principle. However, in the Vedic sense, Asteya extends much deeper: it means not taking anything that is not rightfully yours. Asteya also embodies the recognition of the Universe as interconnected, emphasizing the importance of sharing what we have with all other beings. Within this absolute value, living selfishly or consuming more than necessary is considered a violation. The Bhagavad Gītā states, "Yo Bhunkte Stena Eva Saḥ" – one who consumes without giving to the Deva (Universal Energy or Higher Beings) is a thief. Thus, Asteya safeguards us from the pitfalls of consumerism.

Asteya on the Action Level: Of course, refraining from taking what is not rightfully ours from others is fundamental. Equally, not exploiting Nature or consuming more than what is truly needed is an essential practice of Asteya.

Asteya on the Speech Level: Not claiming others' ideas or words as your own constitutes Asteya at the level of speech.

Asteya on Thought Level: Asteya, even at the level of thought, requires that one refrains from desiring or contemplating taking what belongs to others. This mental discipline is closely interlinked with ahiṁsā (non-violence) and Satya (truthfulness). Plagiarism is a common modern example of stealing, particularly in academic contexts. Similarly, taking anything that is not rightfully ours, even if offered freely, constitutes theft. People often engage in such acts unconsciously, for example, in relation to welfare benefits or insurance claims. Demanding more than a fair price or a just wage is another prevalent form of stealing.[144]

Brahmācārya: "'Brahmā' is a Sanskrit word, and the root meaning is that which contains inexhaustible potential of creativity."[145] This term has often been misunderstood and understated as merely observing celibacy. In reality, Brahmā signifies Supreme Intelligence, and creativity is its inherent characteristic. "Caryā" comes from the root word cara, meaning to walk, move, or live. Therefore, Brahmācārya is the practice of living in alignment with Supreme Intelligence, being guided by its creative potential, and consciously living with awareness of Divinity.

---

144 Atmajyoti. (n.d.). *Foundations of Yoga*. Retrieved September 16, 2025, from https://www.atmajyoti.org/med_foundations_of_yoga.asp

145 Thakar, V. (1991). *Glimpses of Raja Yoga*. Vimal Prakashan Trust, India.

Whatever I do, whether in business, daily living, socialising, or entertaining, I remain constantly aware of the Supreme Creative Energy. When one is conscious of such a vast and all-encompassing field, thoughts of selfishness or short-term gain naturally diminish. Consciousness expands to become compassionate, ethical, empathetic, philanthropic, and ecological, guided by the wellbeing of all. Profits and money may follow, but never through harming others, dishonesty, or theft. As Satish Kumar says, "Money is not wealth; real wealth is land, forest, rivers, animals and people. Wealth is created by the imagination, creativity and skill. Bankers and business leaders in search of ever-increasing profit are not the wealth creators; at best they are wealth counters and at worst wealth destroyers. So, let's honour the true wealth creators: skilled workers, architects and artists, craftsmen and women, teachers and doctors, builders and farmers; the economy is safe in their hands. Let us respect the generous Earth and wild Nature, the eternal source of wellbeing and prosperity. If we take care of people and Nature, then the economy will take care of itself."[146]

Aparigraha: Aparigraha is often translated as "non-possessiveness." However, it fundamentally concerns the inner attitude of possessiveness, which leads to acquisition and attachment, and requires correction. When one practices ahiṁsā (non-violence and harmony with Nature), Truth, Asteya (non-stealing), and Brahmācārya (self-restraint), outer Aparigraha naturally follows. One does not see oneself merely as a consumer of the external world, but as interconnected with Nature and all beings. Therefore, whatever wealth one possesses is not solely for personal enjoyment or social prestige but as a trustee, to be shared with others. In today's era of commercial consumerism, this value is essential to prevent further deterioration of ethical and ecological balance.

146 Kumar, S. (2012, January–February). Money and morality. *Resurgence & Ecologist*, (270). Retrieved from https://www.resurgence.org/magazine/issue270-a-new-moral-compass.html

Aparigraha prevents one from being consumed by the insatiable fire of desire. To equate ourselves with what we "have" is to forget our true nature and purpose. Aparigraha facilitates the shift from 'having' individuals to 'being' individuals.

Universality and Practical Application of Yama:

Jāti Deśa Kāla Samaya Anāvacchinnaḥ Sārvabhaumaḥ Mahāvratam (2.31)

Sage Patañjali refers to these Yamas as Mahāvratam, indicating that they are universal principles for people of all walks of life, at all times. They are absolute values. Vimala Thakar explains, "The word 'vratam' is derived from the root Vre, Vrethe, meaning choiceless acceptance based on understanding. Vratam is one's commitment, and Mahāvratam is commitment without interruption."

Often, we make New Year resolutions that are forgotten within days. Yama and Niyama, however, provide practical principles for sustainable, holistic, and organic growth. They are not merely intellectual concepts to be theorized, but lived experiences applied in daily life and relationships. They are truly result-oriented; one need not believe in them as dogma. Instead, they are experiential truths, not abstract philosophical concepts.

Niyama: ***Śauca, Santoṣa, Tapas, Svādhyāya, Īśvarapraṇidhānāni Niyamaḥ*** **(2.32)** Śauca: Śauca refers to Śucitā, or purity. While we commonly associate purity with the physical, Śauca encompasses all three levels: action, speech, and thought. On a superficial level, the practice of outer Śauca – cleanliness in homes and offices – is emphasised. Yet, in modern lifestyles, outer purity is often compromised, especially among younger generations. Purity cleanses, refreshes, and rejuvenates. Cleanliness extends beyond the home and clothing to include diet. Consuming toxic foods contaminated with fertilisers and artificial colours abuses the body. Equally important is purity of thought. Modern individuals are contaminated by messages of greed, consumerism, and television programs that distort relationships. Śauca penetrates as deeply as the cellular level. Recent research in immunology and kinesiology affirms many Yogic truths: chemically toxic food and negative thoughts damage the body at the cellular level, weakening health and causing disease.

Organisations are now recognizing the importance of Śauca in decluttering office spaces, using frameworks like 5S and other Japanese management tools. But what about the "5S" of our mind and thoughts? Patañjali's teachings serve as a practical manual for applying 5S principles at all levels – body, mind, and spirit.

Santoṣa: When one is pure, transparent, and organically aligned in inner nature, a person naturally experiences the inner bliss of contentment. Santoṣa means a "non-competitive, non-comparative approach to oneself, one's actions, and acquisitions in life" (Vimala Thakar). Much of our conditioning – evaluating ourselves and building self-esteem – arises from comparison and competition. The moment this mindset is removed, the true potential of one's being is revealed. Santoṣa leads to Centering, and Centering reinforces Santoṣa; it is a virtuous cycle. Santoṣa is the contentment virtue of the heart. While the brain is conditioned to follow a "more is better" script, the heart understands that inner happiness is independent of more or less. Santoṣa is the formatting of Citta Vṛttis (mental fluctuations).

Tapas: At one level, Tapas signifies austerity. Much repression and suppression arise from misunderstanding this term. Tapas is the creation of a transformative fire that burns away millions of years of conditioning, purifying us from emotional and intellectual toxins and debris accumulated in daily life. Tapas reconditions neurochemical habitual patterns, which Patañjali calls Saṁskāras. Thus, Tapas educates the body and mind through Āsana, Prānayama, Pratyāhāra, and Svādhyāya. As Vimala Thakar notes, "Tapas requires the alertness and the creativity of your own perception."

Svādhyāya: The term comes from 'Sva' (Self) and 'Adhyāya' (study). It encompasses both continuous self-learning and the study of oneself. A person who is self-vigilant, observant, and continuously formatting their own being will develop an inner compass for integrated decisions involving heart, head, and spirit. Self-study and the study of self together constitute Svādhyāya.

Īśvara Praṇidhāna: The word Īśvara is often translated as "God," which leads to misunderstandings. Īśvara literally comes from the root Īśa, where Īṣate means "to permeate." As expressed in "Īṣate Rājate Iti Īśvaraḥ," Īśvara is that which permeates everything. In modern terms, it can be viewed as the Creative Energy encompassing the Universe. Praṇidhāna is not surrender but a conscious following of a path. When one is told to surrender, the ego often raises questions. But by choosing to follow a path, one internally resolves all questions.

Following the path of supreme creative energy naturally leads to feelings of expansion and boundlessness. Thus, Īśvara Praṇidhāna is possible even without belief in God, making it a logical, scientific, and accessible practice.

Tapas, Svādhyāya, and Īśvara Praṇidhāna together constitute Kriyā Yoga.

Yama and Niyama provide the foundation for āsana, prānayama, dhāraṇā, dhyāna, and ultimately samādhi. For beginners, this foundation is essential both at the cognitive level and in the practical application through manasā (thoughts), vācā (speech), and karmaṇā (actions).

Chapter 06

Science of Aesthetics and Psychology

In this chapter, we will explore the following themes:

- Emotions and Emotional Intelligence – the Western construct
- The science of aesthetics (Nāṭya Śāstra) and emotions
- Sahṛdayatā and Hṛdaya Granthi
- Psychoneuroimmunology and Sthāyī Bhāva from Nāṭya Śāstra
- Saṃskāra Theory, Sthāyī Bhāva, and the transformation of emotions
- Abraham Maslow and the need for aesthetics
- David R. Hawkins – Map of Consciousness and emotional transformation

Introduction:

Emotions are universal experiences shared by all living beings. The expression of emotion may be culture specific. English Dictionary defines emotions as "a complex experience of consciousness, bodily sensation, and behaviour that reflects the personal significance of a thing, an event, or a state of affairs."[147] From Aristotle to contemporary literature on emotions and emotional intelligence, numerous definitions and classifications of emotions have emerged. The Latin root of the word emotion, emotere, literally means "energy in motion."

Why do some people experience certain emotions more frequently? Why do some emotions feel more intense, while others seem almost

147 Slomon, C. R. (n.d.). Encyclopaedia Britannica. Retrieved September 16, 2025, from https://www.britannica.com

absent? We often neglect the inward journey needed to understand the emotional landscape of our own psyche. Most people go through life without fully understanding their emotions. Whether we are aware of them or not, whether we express or suppress them, emotions are integral to our identity. Yet, emotions are often associated with the heart and perceived as weakness rather than intelligence. The common head-versus-heart conflict is usually resolved by favouring the brain's logic over the wisdom of the heart. Emotion is essentially a form of energy. We know that energy cannot be created or destroyed – it can only be transformed. When we fail to acknowledge and fully integrate our emotions into conscious awareness, they simmer below the threshold of consciousness. Emotions impact not only our mental state but also our gut health and immunity. Therefore, the science of emotions should be an important component of education. Bhāratīya psychology contains this understanding in the form of the science of aesthetics, or Nāṭya Śāstra. Though the Śāstra was primarily written as a guide for performing arts and artists, it contains profound insights into the human psyche and the science of emotions. In modern times, the science of psychoneuroimmunology is rediscovering this wisdom, viewing the body-mind-soul as an interconnected continuum.

While Western perspectives often connect emotions primarily to the brain, and most emotional intelligence training focuses on cognitive skill-building, the Bhāratīya perspective relates emotions to the body-mānas-ātma continuum. In this chapter, we explore this holistic connection.

Emotions and Emotional intelligence – The western Construct

There is extensive literature in psychology, positive psychology, and emotional intelligence (EI) available today. Emotional Intelligence (EQ or EI) is a term originally coined by Peter Salovey and John Mayer and later popularized by Daniel Goleman in his 1996 book of the same name. EQ is commonly defined as the ability to recognize one's own emotions, as well as those of others, and to make healthy choices in action and behavior. The term EI is more appropriate, as EQ suggests a numeric measure similar to IQ, which is a misnomer. Emotions and emotional intelligence are qualitative experiences, not easily quantified. The author has been trained under two international organisations for Emotional Intelligence – Six Seconds and EQ Map. Both approaches provide a uniquely qualitative understanding of Emotional Intelligence. However, their training remains primarily cognitive and does not fully integrate the 'whole' person – heart, body, and mānas. It is important to acknowledge the literature, courses, programs, and papers that have emerged over the last two decades since the construct of Emotional Intelligence became popular. Despite the wealth of research, psychology academia has not fully clarified the nature of emotions for the general public. Terms such as emotional numbness, emotional hijacking, and emotional alexithymia have become more widely understood. Emotional numbness is akin to an anesthesia to painful emotions, preventing one from enjoying positive emotions as well. It can be compared to having local anesthesia for a dental treatment; even if the dentist advises having ice cream afterward, the taste cannot be fully relished. Many individuals live life with such numbness without awareness. At the other extreme is emotional hijacking, where the intellect is overridden by rage or depression. Both extremes are unhealthy. Perhaps more harmful is the unidentified syndrome of difficulty in identifying and naming one's feelings – alexithymia. Many people around us suffer from this without realizing it. They may take pride in being logical and rational while neglecting emotions.

However, emotions are essential for living a meaningful and purposeful life. Gallup surveys indicate global lack of engagement at work, which is largely a function of emotions rather than rationality. Emotional intelligence, therefore, is the ability to be self-aware, manage emotions, express them appropriately, and live optimally. Robert K. Cooper and Ayman Sawaf's book Executive EQ provides insightful guidance on this subject.

Science of Aesthetics or Nāṭya Śāstra and Emotions

There are many Indian scholars who have synthesized the science of aesthetics as described in the Nāṭya Śāstra with contemporary theories of emotions. Anand Patwardhan is a leading pioneer in this area. Girishwar Misra and Shilpa Pandit have also highlighted this connection. The indigenous Indian approach to the psychology of emotions, originating from Bharata's ancient classical work, the Nāṭyaśāstra, is articulated and its conceptual framework is situated within contemporary psychological scholarship and discourse on emotion (Paranjape, 2009)[148]. One observes a bias in Western scholarship, which often treats its theories as universal while considering other indigenous theories as culture-specific. Here, the contributions of Anand Paranjpe become particularly significant. He asserts, "I wish to explain why the rasa-śāstra approach may be legitimately called psychology and indicate where it may stand in the spectrum of contemporary Western approaches." The primary purpose of Bharata's detailed studies was to provide guidelines for actors and directors of drama. We need not focus on the exhaustive details of Bharata's account of emotions but rather on the psychological insights embedded in his tradition.[149]

In this chapter, the focus is on Sthāyī Bhāva narrated in Rasa Theory within Nāṭya Śāstra. However, some historical context of the theory provides a good pathway to understand the concept holistically.

The authorship of the Nāṭyaśāstra is traditionally attributed to Bharata Muni. It is regarded as the earliest comprehensive treatise on drama (Raghavan, 1991).[150] This magnum opus of Bharata is held in high

148 Paranjape, A. C. (2009). In defence of an Indian approach to the psychology of emotion. Psychological Studies, 54(1), 3–22. https://doi.org/10.1007/s12646-009-0001-0

149 Ibid.

150 Gurjar, K., & Yadav, S. (2024). Shaping user experience in virtual reality: A study with special reference to Nāṭyaśāstra. Bodhi: An Interdisciplinary Journal, 10(2), 112–124. https://doi.org/10.3126/bodhi.v10i2.69684

esteem within the Hindu tradition, with its origins believed to be of "great antiquity, next only to that of the Vedas" (Adhikary, 2014)[151]. The entire text guides the reader toward the objective of universalization (Sādhāraṇīkaraṇa), aiming to evoke aesthetic pleasure (Rasa) through Bhāva (thought-emotions) with the help of Abhinaya (tools for knowledge and information transfer) via Asvādyatva Nāṭya (audio-visual experiences that are worth consuming), thereby creating Sahahṛdayata in the impacted environment. The Nāṭyaśāstra was created for the masses to cultivate higher mānas and to divinise the buddhi. Bharata refers to the human soul as Bhāva-Jagat (the world of emotions). The concept of "Rasa" is arguably the most important and significant contribution of the Indian intellect to the field of aesthetics. The study of aesthetics concerns the realization of beauty in art, the relish or enjoyment derived from it, and the awareness of joy that accompanies the experience of beauty. Rasa has no direct equivalent in any other language. The closest explanation might be "aesthetic relish."

Sage Bharata states that Nāṭya is the imitation of life (lokānukṛti), in which various human emotions must be dramatically glorified (bhāvānukīrtanam), allowing the spectator to experience the pleasure and pain portrayed (lokasya sukha-duḥkha) as Nāṭya Rasa. This Rasa experience both entertains and enlightens the spectator, who becomes a 'Rasika' – one capable of enjoying a Rasa.

The word Rasa is derived from the root rasaḥ, meaning sap, juice, taste, flavor, or relish. The extract of a fruit is called 'rasa,' representing its essence, the ultimate flavour. The term "Bhāva" is derived from the root 'Bhū'—bhavati, meaning "to become" or "to come into existence." Bharata attributes a causal quality to Bhāva, stating "bhāvayanti iti Bhāva," meaning a thing or mental state that brings awareness of itself

151 Adhikary, N. M. (2014). Theory and practice of communication – Bharata Muni. Bhopal: Makhanlal Chaturvedi National University of Journalism & Communication.

or makes one conscious of it, pervading the individual.[152] We have looked at Svabhāva earlier. One's own Bhāva at a deeper level in the psyche become our Svabhāva.

Bhāva (psychological states): In the context of the Nāṭyaśāstra, it is described as a dynamic force that permeates the heart and mind of both the performer and the spectator. Bhāva represents the emotions we experience, arising from situations and interactions, which in turn shape our behavior. To illustrate Bhāva practically, imagine a conversation in which someone expresses joy, sorrow, or anger. These emotions (Bhāvas) are conveyed not only through words but also through body language, facial expressions, and vocal tone. When a person is joyful, their smile, the brightness in their eyes, and the warmth in their voice can infuse their surroundings with happiness. Similarly, when a person is upset, their posture, gestures, and facial expressions communicate their emotional state without the need for words. Thus, Bhāva serves as the vehicle through which emotions are conveyed, perceived, and shared, creating a deeper human connection in both artistic and everyday contexts.

Sthāyī Bhāvaa: The nature of Sthāyī Bhāva is enduring, stable, and latent, remaining with an individual from birth to death. These emotions transcend time, culture, religion, region, race, and gender, though their intensity may vary slightly. While they are ever-present, they remain in a latent state, residing deep within the mind. There are eight Sthāyī Bhāvas as per the Nāṭyaśāstra authored by Bharatamuni. A ninth, Sama, corresponding to Śānta Rasa, was added later by Abhinavagupta.

रतिहासश्च शोकश्च क्रोधोत्साहौ भयं तथा ।
जुगुप्सा विस्मयश्चेति स्थायिभावाः प्रकीर्तिताः ॥ ६.१७ ॥

152 Thiagarajan, R. (n.d.). *The Rasa theory of Bharata – Indian aesthetics and fine arts*. Retrieved from https://ebooks.inflibnet.ac.in/icp04/chapter/the-rasa-theory-of-bharata/

The 6th chapter of Nāṭya Śāstra by Bharatamuni explains the eight Sthāyī Bhāvas. The ninth, Sama, associated with Śānta Rasa, was later added by Abhinavagupta. Anand Patwardhan provides a deeper understanding, correlating these concepts with modern psychological constructs of emotions. Bharata, in his Nāṭyaśāstra, identified eight major and thirty-three minor emotions. The major emotions are: erotic feeling (rati), mirth (hāsa), sorrow (śoka), anger (krodha), energy (utsāha), fear (bhaya), disgust (jugupsā), and astonishment (vismaya). He considered these major or basic emotions (Sthāyī Bhāva) for two main reasons: they are more enduring than the relatively short-lived minor emotions, and they are common to humans as well as animals. Bharata's list of major emotions overlaps with, but does not exactly coincide with, the basic emotions identified by contemporary psychologists such as Ekman and Plutchik.[153]

The families of emotions and corresponding feelings described by P. Ekman closely resemble the major and minor emotions outlined in Nāṭya Śāstra. Ekman defines emotions as: "Emotions are a process, a particular kind of automatic appraisal influenced by our evolutionary and personal past, in which we sense that something important to our welfare is occurring, and a set of psychological changes and emotional behaviors begins to deal with the situation." (Paul Ekman)[154] The phrase "automatic appraisal influenced by our evolutionary and personal past" closely aligns with the Indian concept of Saṃskāra Theory.

153 Paranjpe, A. C. (2009). In defence of an Indian approach to the psychology of emotion. *Psychological Studies, 54*(1), 3–22. https://doi.org/10.1007/s12646-009-0001-0

154 Ekman, P. (n.d.). *Paul Ekman*. Retrieved September 16, 2025, from https://www.paulekman.com

Families of Emotions
P. Ekman

ENJOYMENT	Happiness, relief, contentment, delight, amusement, pride, pleasure, euphoria, ecstasy, pathological: mania
LOVE	Acceptance, friendliness, trust, kindness, affinity, devotion, adoration, infatuation, agape
DISGUST	Contempt, disdain, scorn, abhorrence, aversion, distaste, revulsion
SHAME	Guilt, embarrassment, remorse, humiliation, regret, mortification, and contrition
ANGER	Fury, outrage, resentment, wrath, indignation, irritability, hostility, pathological: hatred, violence
SADNESS	Grief, sorrow, gloom, self-pity, loneliness, dejection, despair pathological: severe depression
FEAR	Nervousness, concern, wariness, dread, terror psychopathology: phobia, panic
SURPRISE	Shock, astonishment, amazement, wonder

Now compare with Sthāyī Bhāva:

1. **Rati (Love)** –Reflects beauty, attraction, and romantic or compassionate love.
2. **Hāsya (Laughter)** – Emotion of joy, humour, and mirth.
3. **Śoka (Grief)** –It manifests as sorrow, pain, and lamentation.
4. **Krodha (Anger)** –This is the feeling of rage, frustration, and wrath.
5. **Utsāha (Enthusiasm)** –This reflects bravery, courage, and positive energy.

6. **Bhaya (Fear)** –This involves horror, anxiety, and dread.
7. **Bībhatsa (Disgust)** –It reflects repulsion, loathing, and distaste.
8. **Adbhuta (Wonder)** –This emotion is one of amazement, curiosity, and awe.
9. **Sama (Peace/Equanimity)**: A sense of inner calm, serenity, and detachment, a state of transcendence.

The Sthāyī Bhāva represent the latent emotional makeup or the underlying emotional landscape of an individual. They are dormant traces of undigested emotions. In Nāṭya Śāstra, it is the performance, or in literature, the author, that evokes and appeals to these dormant emotions, bringing them to conscious awareness. In personal and professional life, different people and various situations can trigger these latent emotions. Essentially, Sthāyī Bhāva serves as a template that makes us more prone to react with certain emotions over others. Often, we rationalize our habitual emotional responses as natural, inborn, or inherited from parents or ancestors, without understanding why certain emotions come more naturally to us. Compassion, for instance, is a response to another's suffering, and some individuals possess this as their intrinsic svabhāva, sometimes guiding them to choose vocations where compassion is expressed. Conversely, some individuals have sorrow as their template, resulting in chronic unhappiness, while those with bhaya as a template experience fear in new situations or live under persistent anxiety without clear cause.

Psychology helps us comprehend our svabhāva as an emotional template. Often, we remain unaware of the patterns of thinking, feeling, and behaving that arise from this template. Unconsciously, we select life situations aligned with our Sthāyī Bhāva, allowing us to 'experience' them as a rasa. This is the author's interpretation of the relationship between bhāva, rasa, and behavioural patterns. In Emotional Intelligence training, one effective exercise is identifying personal emotional triggers. However, this often remains a cognitive exercise: awareness alone rarely leads to lasting change. Even with recognition and a plan to alter the pattern, individuals frequently revert to habitual responses.

To achieve deeper transformation, wisdom and practices from Āyurveda and Yoga must be integrated with Emotional Intelligence frameworks. As discussed earlier, Rasa represents the joyful experience arising from our Sthāyī Bhāva. To deepen our understanding, we can explore which Rasa emerges from specific Bhāva patterns.

The Nava Rasas

Sthayi Bhava	Rasa	Definition
Rati (Passion)	**Sringara** (Love)	**Love, beauty, and creativity** in all forms Not just desire or lust, about beauty and aesthetic
Haasa (Joy)	**Hasya** (Laughter)	**Laughter, playfulness, glee**
Shoka (Sorrow)	**Karuna** (Sadness, Compassion)	**Sadness or pity** due to **distress or anguish**
Krodha (Anger)	**Raudra** (Fury)	Often denoted through roaring and terrible **rage**
Utsah (Eagerness, Excitement)	**Veer** (Heroism)	**Heroism or the attitude of a hero**
Bhaya (Fear)	**Bhayanaka** (Fearful)	Fearful, terrible, or dreadful A temporary state.
Jugupsa (Disgust)	**Bibhatsa** (Disgust)	Experience of **disgust, aversion, or to detest** Commonly a **reaction as if something tastes bad**
Vismaya (Surprise)	**Adbhuta** (Wonder)	**Wonder, amazement and surprise** Sense of **being present in the moment**
Shanta - Sama	**Shanta** (Peace)	**Peaceful, tranquil, contented**

Paul Ekman began his pioneering research on emotions through the study of facial expressions, later expanding his work to include families of emotions and feelings. In contrast, the Nāṭya Śāstra offers not only a detailed description of facial expressions but also a comprehensive account of how the entire body responds to specific emotions. Although this chapter does not cover those aspects in detail, both perspectives highlight the universal science of emotions.

Nāṭya Śāstra and the Transformation of Emotions

In Western models of Emotional Intelligence, self-awareness of one's emotions is considered the first step, followed by self-management. However, according to Bhāratīya Mānas Śāstra, the ultimate goal is not merely management but the complete transformation of emotions. The emotional template we are born with is a continuation of our Saṃskāras, as will be explored later. Nāṭya Śāstra, however, provides a profound framework for reshaping and transcending these patterns. Dr. Shilpa Pandit has beautifully penned them in her paper.[155]

According to Abhinavagupta, the soul is immortal and has accumulated countless experiences in its journey, stored within as vāsanas, or latent "residues." In the process of artistic expression, these hidden vāsanas are brought into awareness. This is called sādṛśīkaraṇa. The next and perhaps most significant step is sādhāraṇīkaraṇa. In this state, the emotion is no longer tied to the "I" – it transcends personal identity, time, and context. As a result, even so-called "negative" emotions such as Raudra (anger), Bībhatsa (disgust), or Bhaya (fear) are experienced as universal movements rather than personal disturbances. This explains why watching intense emotions in performance can still generate joy and satisfaction.

155 Pandit, Shilpa Ashok. (2011). *The Concept of Rasa in Indian Psychology: A Preliminary Qualitative Study.* Journal of Psychological Research, New Delhi, 6(1), 139–148.

At this point, the boundaries between the performer and the spectator dissolve. The rasika (spectator) becomes the sahṛdaya (one with a resonant heart). This profound connection is described as hṛdaya-saṁvāda (a heart-to-heart dialogue). Abhinavagupta further calls the sahṛdaya's state of mind camatkāra – an awe-filled, mirror-like state (vimala), cleansed of personal biases and ready to experience rasa. Ultimately, the heart feels deeply rested in a state of saṁvid (awareness and satisfaction). This ancient wisdom holds immense relevance today, offering modern psychologists' therapeutic pathways to healing through the transformation of emotions.

For emotional training at any age, role plays based on Sthāyī Bhāva and Rasa serve as powerful exercises. As early as 1999, such practices were experimented with at an MBA institute among Human Resources students, eventually evolving into a transformative training method over the decades. Cheriyan insightfully observed that "Bharata has analysed with clinical precision the entire range of human emotions, from the basic to the transient, and his notion of the Sthāyī Bhāvas parallels the modern psychological theory of basic human instincts." This observation underscores Bharata's extraordinary foresight in mapping the emotional spectrum – a contribution that not only aligns with but also predates many of today's psychological theories.

Saṃskāra Theory and Rasa Theory Integration

According to Abhinavagupta, the Kashmiri philosopher and aesthetician, a permanent emotion (Sthāyī Bhāva) is already present in the mind of the spectator as a Saṃskāra (latent impression). These permanent emotions are inborn, innate, and deeply rooted in the human psyche; they cannot be acquired through training or education. The Sthāyī Bhāva serves as the core emotion around which all other transitory feelings revolve, much like a king surrounded by subordinate servants (Masson & Patwardhan,

p. 39)[156]. Similarly, Satya D. Chaudhary[157] defines *Sthāyī Bhāva* as basic instincts that exist in a dormant state in every human mind.

We have already discussed *Saṃskāra Theory* in earlier chapters and how the imprints of emotional memories form our subconscious and unconscious psyche. One way to understand *Saṃskāra* is through the *Sthāyī Bhāva* concept from the *Nāṭya Śāstra*. In daily life, we encounter numerous *bhāvas* at different times, and the traces of these experiences remain with us as impressions. These impressions constitute *Saṃskāras*. The *bhāvas* persist in us in the form of *vāsanās*. The *Sthāyī Bhāvas* can thus be seen as dispositions or *citta-vṛttis*. When these *bhāvas* are recognized through enlightened bliss in the self, they are transformed into rasa.[158]

Consider a simple example: a group of friends is planning to watch a movie. Will there be immediate agreement on which one to watch? Or a family sits together before the television – will there be unanimity in choosing the program? One person may prefer action, another romance, another comedy, while someone else chooses a sad soap opera. Why such variation in what people "enjoy"? The answer lies in integrating Rasa Theory with Saṃskāra Theory. We are all born with certain emotional predispositions. This is why even horror shows that evoke fear or those that evoke disgust can still be "enjoyed." What emotions we relish at the rasa level depends on the Sthāyī Bhāva with which we are born – our Saṃskāra. This connection between *Rasa* and *Saṃskāra* is well established in Indian aesthetics but needs deeper integration into modern psychology literature on emotions and emotional intelligence. While it may be difficult to trace the

156 Masson, J. L., & Patwardhan, M. V. (1970). Aesthetic rapture (Vols. 1–2). Poona: Deccan College.

157 Chaudhary, S. D. (2010). The glimpses of Indian poetics. New Delhi: Sahitya Akademi.

158 Misra, G. (n.d.). The science of affect: Some Indian insights. Indian Psychology Institute. Retrieved September 16, 2025, from https://www.ipi.org.in

exact *saṃskāra* (deep-rooted impression), we can still understand its manifestation through the *Sthāyī Bhāva* (dominant emotional state). The *Sthāyī Bhāva* acts as a bridge between the unseen, subconscious *saṃskāra* and the visible emotional and behavioural patterns of an individual. Though Saṃskāras are complex and buried within layers of consciousness, their influence is reflected in recurring emotional tendencies. For example, if someone's Sthāyī Bhāva is predominantly fear (bhaya) or anger (krodha), it signals that certain saṃskāras tied to these emotions have shaped their psychological makeup. By identifying such dominant states, we can indirectly understand the type of saṃskāra influencing a person – even if the precise saṃskāra itself remains inaccessible.

Therefore, while the original *saṃskāra* may not always be traceable, studying *Sthāyī Bhāva* provides a valuable method for discerning how *Saṃskāras* manifest in daily life. This understanding enriches both psychology and emotional development, offering a practical pathway to addressing and elevating an individual's emotional landscape.

Sthāyī Bhāva and Psychoneuroimmunology

Known as the Queen of PNI, Candace B. Pert[159] once observed: "If you look in the index of recent textbooks on psychology, you are not likely to find 'consciousness,' 'mind,' or even 'emotions.'" Her pioneering work in Psychoneuroimmunology (PNI) explores the intricate relationship between emotions and physiology, shedding light on the so-called "black box" of the mind – an area traditional psychology often overlooks.

Dr. Pert, formerly Chief of the Brain Biochemistry Section at the National Institute of Mental Health (NIMH) and later Professor at the Center

---

159 Pert, C. B. (2002). The wisdom of the receptors: Neuropeptides, the emotions, and bodymind. Advances in Mind-Body Medicine, 18(1), 30–35. https://pubmed.ncbi.nlm.nih.gov/12523304

for Molecular Behavioral Neuroscience at Georgetown University, is credited with the discovery of the opiate receptor along with many other peptide receptors in the brain and body. She famously described neuropeptides as "biochemical units of emotion."

Her research emphasises the pivotal role of the autonomic nervous system in emotional processing. Pert noted that every peptide she mapped and many more are found within the autonomic system, suggesting an emotional coding embedded in its functioning. This framework resonates with the Indian aesthetic concept of Sthāyī Bhāva, understood as enduring emotional states imprinted on the psyche and expressed in the body. Could Pert's discovery of neuropeptides be viewed as a modern rediscovery of this ancient insight? The present author proposes this as an original perspective and a possible first step toward future cross-disciplinary research.

According to Pert, our bodies are in fact our subconscious minds: "In the end I find I can't separate brain from body. Consciousness isn't just in the head. Nor is it a question of the power of the mind over the body... because they're flip sides of the same thing. Mind doesn't dominate body, it becomes body."[160] But why – and when – did this split between body and mind occur, leading even to the exclusion of consciousness?

The roots lie in the work of René Descartes, the 17th-century French philosopher known for the dictum *"I think, therefore I am."* This so-called "Cartesian Split" created a false dualism. Descartes, in agreement with the Church of his era, left matters of the soul, mind, and emotions to theology, while reserving the physical body for scientific study. Descartes declared, "Anything to do with the soul, mind or emotions, I leave to the clergy. I will only claim the realm of the body."[161] Candace Pert, however, was a pioneer in reconnecting

---

160 Healing Cancer Naturally. (n.d.). *Book section.* Retrieved from http://www.healingcancer.info/book/export/html/34

161 Ibid.

body, mind, and consciousness, and in introducing psychosomatic wellness into Western science. Yet, surprisingly, her revolutionary work has often been sidelined, and the Cartesian split continues to dominate even today. Ironically, this very dualism can sometimes be seen even in the holistic field of modern Āyurveda practice, which traditionally emphasized integrality.

Pert emphasised that emotions are real – tangible, existing in both time and space, spread throughout the body and mind. If we accept that peptides and their receptors are the actual biochemicals of emotion, then the nervous system's widespread receptor sites reveal that the body itself can be understood as the unconscious or subconscious mind. She explains further: "As investigations continue, it is becoming increasingly apparent that the role of peptides is not limited to eliciting simple and singular actions from individual cells and organs systems. Rather, peptides serve to weave the body's organs and systems into a single web that reacts to both internal and external environmental changes with complex, subtly orchestrated responses. Peptides are the sheet music containing the notes, phrases and rhythms that allow the orchestra – your body – to play as an integrated entity. And the music that results is the tone or feeling that you experience subjectively as your emotions."

This highlights the centrality of emotions and Sthāyī Bhāva in our lives. Without Rasa – the essence of emotions – life becomes *nirāsa*, devoid of joy and vitality.

Emotions, Mānas and healing

Psychoneuroimmunology (PNI) has demonstrated that receptor sites for neuropeptides are distributed throughout the body. The brainstem and the intestines are particularly rich in such receptors, which explains why both breathing and digestion are so directly influenced by emotional states. Intestines are not under our conscious control, but breathing is a powerful tool that we have in detecting and controlling emotions.[162] To make this book on Bhāratīya Mānas Śāstra a holistic experience, the Appendix includes 3SRB refining exercises and 3SRB breathing practices. Breath is directly connected with the heart (Hṛdaya), from where the Manovaha Srotas originate. Through these channels, emotions circulate throughout the body, clearly demonstrating the heart–mind connection.

Dr. Candace Pert understood this link deeply through her research:

"We are all aware of the bias built into the Western idea that the mind is totally in the head, a function of the brain. But your body is not there just to carry around your head. I believe the research findings.... indicate that we need to start thinking about how the mind manifests itself in various parts of the body and, beyond that, how we can bring that process into consciousness...the neuropeptides and their receptors are the substrates of the emotions, and they are in constant communication with the immune system, the mechanism through which health and disease are created." "Think of (stress-related disease) in terms of an information overload, a situation in which the mind-body network is so taxed by unprocessed sensory input in the form of suppressed trauma or undigested emotions that it has become bogged down and cannot flow freely, sometimes even working against itself, at cross purposes."

However, long before modern science articulated these ideas, Bharata Muni and Ācārya Abhinavagupta had already explored this 'black box.' They not only theorized about the workings of Mānas but also offered practical tools to address it – working not just at the mental level, but at the cellular level. This resonates strongly with today's psychological concepts such as cellular consciousness, the mind–body connection, and neuropeptide functioning. Thus, this integrated approach merges the eternal wisdom of India with modern neuroscience, demonstrating how

---

162 Kapadia, Mala. (2018). Heart Skills. Mitra Foundation, Mumbai, India.

emotions stored in our cellular consciousness can be activated, refined, and transformed into higher vibrations. The result is an elevated state of peace, joy, and harmony – both individually and collectively.

Map of Consciousness and Emotions

The Map of Consciousness[163] outlines the relationship between levels of awareness and emotional states in human experience. Developed by Dr. David R. Hawkins, this framework links emotional states with vibrational energy frequencies, presenting them as expressions of consciousness. According to Bhāratīya Mānas Śāstra, emotions are seen as expressions of Ātma, whereas Dr. Hawkins refers to this dimension as Consciousness. His model demonstrates how our spectrum of emotions reflects the way we perceive and live life at a given level of awareness. In this sense, the Sthāyī Bhāvas of Indian psychology find parallels within Hawkins' emotional spectrum.

To deepen this understanding, we can integrate insights from the Triguṇa theory, which associates different emotions with Sattva, Rajas, and Tamas, as well as from the Citta Vṛtti framework, which maps states of mind from Kṣipta to Niruddha. When compared with the Map of Consciousness, clear overlaps emerge: the lowest emotional states correspond to Tāmasic qualities, the mid-level states resonate with Rājasic tendencies, and the highest emotions align with Sāttvic states. This correlation is a significant original insight that invites further research.

Each individual is born into a particular level of consciousness – an energetic frequency within the greater field of awareness. Through the Map of Consciousness, we can grasp the full spectrum of human consciousness, ranging from its lowest to its most exalted states.

---

163 Hawkins, D. R. (1995). Power vs. Force: The Hidden Determinants of Human Behavior. Veritas Publishing, Sedona, USA.

Using a method of applied kinesiology (muscle testing), Dr. Hawkins conducted over 250,000 calibrations across 20 years of research, defining a logarithmic scale from 1 to 1,000 that links emotions, attitudes, and values to levels of consciousness. He first presented this model in his seminal work, Power vs. Force. The Map charts the entire continuum – from the lower levels of Shame, Guilt, Apathy, Fear, Anger, and Pride, to higher states such as Courage, Acceptance, and Reason, and ultimately to the expanded fields of Love, Joy, Peace, and Enlightenment. These higher frequencies are described as "carrier waves" of immense life energy, radiating transformative potential.

An essential introduction to these ideas can be found in The Map of Consciousness Explained, organisation which offers visual charts, practical applications, and guidance for personal growth, healing, and spiritual evolution. This work serves as a beacon for anyone seeking to expand effectiveness, wellbeing, and awareness in all areas of life.

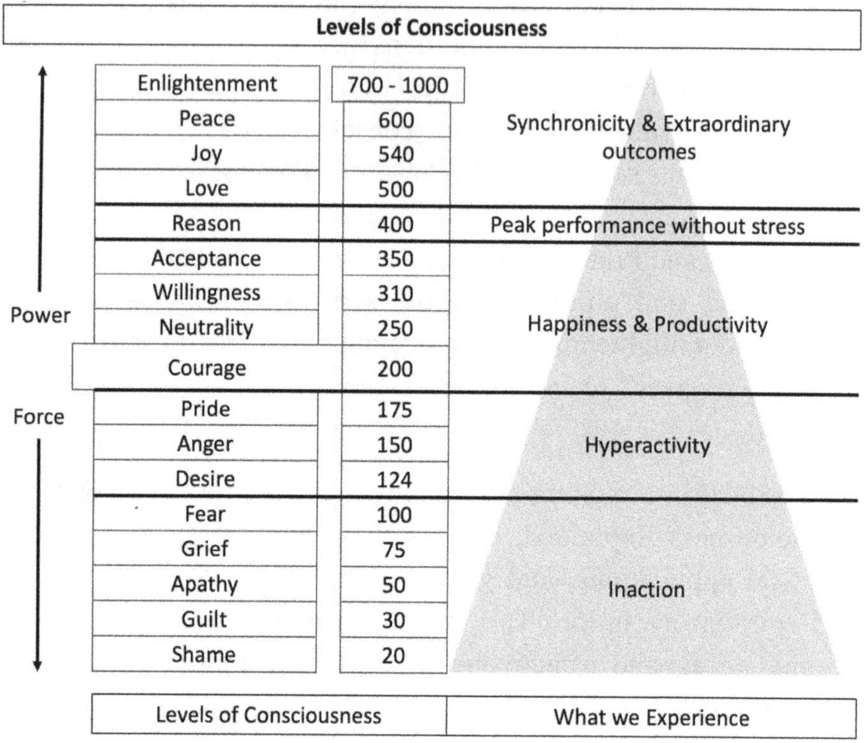
Levels of Consciousness
Power
Force
Enlightenment
700 - 1000
Peace
600
Joy
540
Love
500
Reason
400
Acceptance
350
Willingness
310
Neutrality
250
Courage
200
Pride
175
Anger
150
Desire
124
Fear
100
Grief
75
Apathy
50
Guilt
30
Shame
20
Synchronicity & Extraordinary outcomes
Peak performance without stress
Happiness & Productivity
Hyperactivity
Inaction
Levels of Consciousness
What we Experience

www.megankamei.com

Power vs. Force allows us to reflect deeply on the emotional patterns in which we remain stuck. Low-energy emotional algorithms can be directly connected with diminished immunity, vitality, and overall health. While transformation of emotions may be achieved through many approaches discussed in this and earlier chapters, spirituality, or the expansion of consciousness beyond the xenophobic concept of self, emerges as the ultimate path.

The wisdom of the Nāṭya Śāstra offers a way to cultivate Sahṛdayatā (sensitivity of the heart) and dissolve the Hṛdaya-Granthi (knots of the heart), enabling us to live an optimal life. This is further elaborated in the chapter on the Heart. To truly enjoy the Rasa of life, one requires a healthy heart, filled with compassion and free from biases that harden into knots.

All eight Sthāyī Bhāvas carry within them the potential for the perception of truth about the real nature of the world and the possibility of transcendence. Each of them, therefore, can ultimately lead to the state of Śānta-Sama, the equilibrium of Sattva. We have already considered Sri Aurobindo's insights on the transformation of Guṇas, and those insights can be meaningfully applied here as well.

Transformation of the Bhavas

Srinagar	**Rati Bhava**	Creation of beauty and aesthetic in the world
Haasya	**Haasa Bhava**	Joyful, Laughter in Life
Karuna	**Shoka Bhava**	Personal Sadness can become compassion for others
Raudra	**Krodha Bhava**	Anger can lead to positive change and movements
Veera	**Utsah Bhava**	Creates resolution, excitement, eagerness, courage, and positive action
Bhayanaka	**Bhaya Bhava**	Temporary alertness, attention, increase in information intake
Bibhatsa	**Jugupsa Bhava**	Changing the situation causing distaste, leaving unhealthy spaces.
Adbhuta	**Vismaya Bhava**	WOW

Abhinavagupta was the first practitioner–theoretician to connect the concept of emotion with emotional transformation. Ācārya Abhinavagupta demonstrated how raw emotional experience and expression can be elevated into a spiritual experience and expression.[164] In this way, he bridged aesthetics, psychology, and spirituality. Interestingly, contemporary dialogues in the West also reflect a similar trajectory, as modern psychology and neuroscience explore how emotions shape consciousness – suggesting that East and West may be converging in their understanding of the science of emotions.

Maslow's Motivational Model[165]

Abraham Maslow contributed deep and profound insights into the human psyche. Unfortunately, his original, nuanced work is often overshadowed by the popularised, simplified, and sometimes distorted version of his theories.

Humanistic psychologists, such as Carl Rogers and Abraham Maslow, emphasised the free will of human beings and their natural striving to grow and unfold their inner potential. They argued that behaviourism – with its emphasis on behaviour as determined solely by environmental conditions – undermines human freedom and dignity, reducing human nature to a mechanistic process. Maslow's Towards a Psychology of Being remains an excellent but underappreciated work, where he makes striking observations about human nature and expands psychology's scope to what he called the "Psychology of Health."[166] The insights are so profound that they need much more research even today.

---

164 Pandit, Shilpa Ashok. *The Concept of Rasa in Indian Psychology: A Preliminary Qualitative Study*. *Journal of Psychological Research*, New Delhi, Vol. 6, Iss. 1 (2011), pp. 139–148.

165 Ward, David & Lasen, Marta. (2009). *An Overview of Needs Theories behind Consumerism*. *Journal of Applied Economic Sciences*.

166 Maslow, Abraham H. (2013). *Toward a Psychology of Being*. First Start Publishing, eBook edition, October 2012.

The basic assumptions of this point of view are:

1. Each of us possesses an essential, biologically based inner nature that is, to some degree, natural, intrinsic, given, and relatively unchanging.
   (This resonates with the concept of Pañca Mahābhūta and Prakṛti in Āyurveda.)

2. This inner nature is partly unique to the individual and partly universal to the human species.
3. It is possible to study this inner nature scientifically and discover its character (not invent, but discover it).
4. This inner nature, as we know it, is not intrinsically evil, but rather neutral or positively good. What we call "evil" behaviour often appears as a secondary reaction to frustration of this intrinsic nature.
   (Comparable to the Āyurvedic understanding of Vikṛti.)

5. Since this inner nature is good or neutral rather than bad, it is best to bring it out and to encourage it rather than to suppress it. If it is permitted to guide our life, we grow healthy, fruitful, and happy[167]. *(Signature strengths and Talent of Pañca Mahā Bhūta)*

Way back in 1968, while writing a preface to the second edition of 'Towards A Psychology of Being', Abraham H. Maslow mentions, "I consider Humanistic, Third Force Psychology to be transitional, a preparation for a still "higher" Fourth Psychology, transpersonal, trans human, centred in the cosmos rather than in human needs & interest, going beyond humanness, identity, self-actualization, and the like."[168] This preface is missing from the eBook of the same title.

---

167 Ibid. Page 16

168 Maslow, Abraham H. Towards a Psychology of Being. New York, USA: D. Van Nostrand Company, 1968.

In his work on Motivation and Personality,[169] he states very clearly, "Holism is obviously true- after all, the cosmos is one and interrelated; any society is one and interrelated; any person is one and interrelated, etc.- and yet the holistic outlook has a hard time being implemented and being used as it should be, as a way of looking at the world."

Modern psychology has since witnessed paradigm shifts in the form of health psychology, wellness, well-being, and positive psychology. In fact, Maslow (1962) was among the first in psychology to describe "well-being" through the characteristics of a self-actualised person. His framework foreshadowed later models like Seligman's PERMA model and the Wellbeing Theory (WBT). Bhāratīya Mānas Śāstra insights – such as Mānas (Mind), Hṛdaya (Heart), Citta Vṛttis, Triguṇa, and Sthāyī Bhāva – offer pathways to make these constructs more holistic through integration. Finally, when revisiting Maslow's Hierarchy of Needs, it is important to note that the popular five-stage model is incomplete. Maslow's revised eight-stage model includes Cognitive, Aesthetic, and Self-transcendence needs – integral aspects of human experience. These correspond to the Need for Knowledge, Need for Beauty, and the Need to transcend the limited sense of self into Sva-Rūpa (true self in Yoga), ultimately remaining in the state of Svasthya (wholesomeness and health) as understood in Āyurveda – the true goal of human existence.

---

169 Maslow, Abraham H. Motivation and Personality. 2nd ed. New York, USA: Harper & Row, 1970, Preface ix.

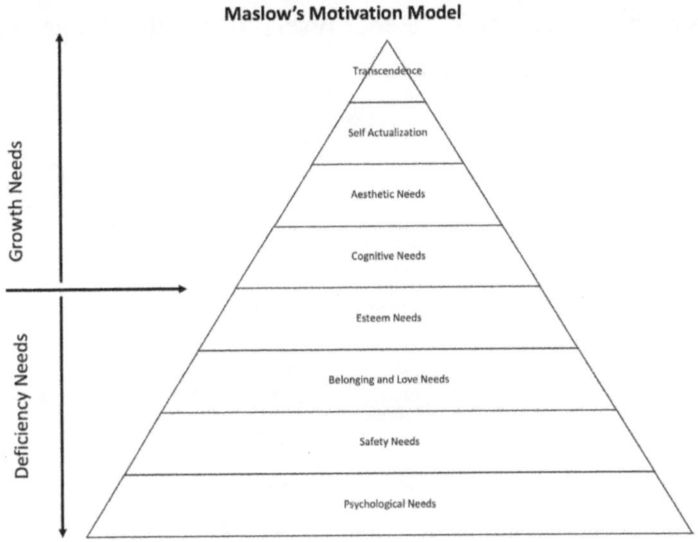

In Maslow's extended hierarchy of needs, the addition of cognitive and aesthetic needs in the 8-stage model bridges the gap between the more basic "deficiency needs" and the higher "being needs." Cognitive needs reflect the innate drive for knowledge, understanding, and insight, while aesthetic needs signify a yearning for beauty, balance, and harmony in one's surroundings and experiences. These needs act as stepping stones toward self-actualisation, with aesthetic experiences playing a crucial role in evoking deeper emotional and reflective states. In the Indian context, this process parallels the cultivation of Sahahṛdayata – a state of empathic resonance, inner balance, and harmonious engagement with life.

Map of Consciousness, Triguṇa, and Growth

Maslow's hierarchy, the Map of Consciousness, and the Triguṇa framework overlap meaningfully.

- Deficiency needs keep us trapped in Tamas and Rajas, below the frequency of 200 in the Map of Consciousness.
- When Sattva drives our growth needs, we rise into higher states of being, expanding our consciousness and flourishing.

This integration of Maslow's hierarchy with Indian psychological insights opens pathways for deeper research into the science of human growth, health, and transcendence.

Chapter 07

Future Frontiers of Bhāratīya Mānas Śāstra

Psychology as a Meta-Science for Human and Planetary Flourishing

Bhāratīya Mānas Śāstra is not merely an ancient body of wisdom but an evolving discipline, now seeking integration into mainstream education, research, counselling, therapy and organisational culture. The following directions highlight possible frontiers for future research and application:

1. Psychology as a Meta-Science

A discipline that offers a deeper and higher understanding of the human experience. Bhāratīya Mānas Śāstra aligns with the vision of Abraham Maslow's Towards the Psychology of Being, which sowed the seeds of Transpersonal Psychology. In Bhārat, this very foundation was already laid in the Vedic literature. The Atharva Veda – also called Brahmā Veda, Ātma Veda, or Mano Veda – holds profound insights applicable to Transpersonal Psychology, Social Psychology, Public Leadership, and Educational Psychology.

2. Psychology of Soil, Society, and Soul

- Soil: Our life and health are rooted in Mother Earth.
- Society: Human flourishing depends on community and collective living.
- Soul: The spirit incarnates into body–mind to participate in conscious evolution.

Understanding this trilogy brings wisdom to life choices. Bhāratīya Mānas Śāstra offers a path toward human and planetary flourishing through this integration.

3. Bhāratīya Anatomy and Psychology

- Pañca Tanmātra, Pañca Mahābhūta, Triguṇa, Pañca Kośa/Ātma, Tridoṣa Matrix.
- Cakra psychology and their role in mental health.
- Gorakṣanāth's Siddha Siddhānta Paddhati as a source for advanced psychology.

4. Hṛdaya and Well-Being

Exploring the role of the heart (hṛdaya) as the seat of sattva, rajas, tamas, and manovaha srotas, and its influence on mental health and overall well-being.

5. Educational Psychology

Jñānotpatti – the emergence of insight and knowledge – is profoundly tied to the heart's role in learning and memory. How does knowledge arise? Ancient wisdom offers significant insights into this process.

6. Motivation

The aspiration for self-growth and development as rooted in Indic psychology.

7. Engagement

- Career and profession through the lens of Mahābhūta and Tridoṣa.
- Engagement at work linked with utsāha as sthāyī bhāva.
- The heart (hṛdaya) as the origin of manovaha srotas and ojas.

8. Psychosomatic Well-Being

- Role of the heart in psychosomatic health.
- Insights from Candace Pert on emotions and the body.
- The significance of hṛdaya granthi in wellness.

9. Intergenerational Trauma

Exploring how trauma, sthāyī bhāva, and saṃskāra theory intersect in shaping psychological health across generations.

10. Consciousness and Growth

- Mapping overlaps between the Triguṇa, Maslow's Hierarchy of Needs, and the Map of Consciousness.
- Deficiency needs keep one bound in tamas and rajas, below the threshold of 200 on the consciousness scale.
- When sattva becomes the driver for growth needs, frequency expands, elevating consciousness.

(This is an original insight of the author, requiring further research.)

Wider Applications

Child Psychology, Social Psychology, Health Psychology, Ecological Psychology, Evolutionary Psychology, Psychotherapy and Counselling, Coaching and Mentoring, Sports Psychology – all these domains can draw richly from the wisdom of Bhāratīya Mānas Śāstra.

This book marks one of the baby steps on this long but fulfilling journey. The path ahead is vast and inspiring. I warmly invite all readers to participate in this shared quest for integrating Bhāratīya Mānas Śāstra into the flourishing of humanity and the planet.

Śubham Astu.

Appendix 1

Excerpts from the teachings of **Shri S. N. Tavaria "Total Health Through Rhythmic Breathing."**

I express my gratitude to *Shri Digant Desai* for granting me permission to quote and share these practices. These exercises are profoundly effective for holistic health. They enhance emotional intelligence by dissolving negative emotions, erasing deep engravings of *Saṃskāras*, and liberating us from fear. From my personal experience, I affirm that regular commitment to these exercises enables one to overcome the life script and connect more meaningfully with one's *Role Script.*

About 3SRB:

3 Step Rhythmic Breathing (3SRB) is an ancient yogic technique that calms the mind while promoting total physical, emotional, and mental well-being in the body–brain system. Rooted in the *Yoga Sūtra* of Sage *Patañjali*, this practice was preserved in secrecy for thousands of years through the *Guru–Śiṣya Paramparā.*

How to Practise 3 Step Rhythmic Breathing

1. Technique

- Both the chest and abdomen should rise and fall together in equal measure.
- The chest naturally requires more expansion because of the ribs, while the abdomen must not be forced outward unnaturally.
- *Tip:* To check balance, lie down in front of a mirror with two books – one placed on the chest and the other on the abdomen. Both books should move up and down simultaneously.

2. Volume

- Breathing should fill the space from the neck down to the navel, engaging the upper, middle, and lower abdomen to their natural capacity.
- The amount of air inhaled and exhaled must feel normal – not excessive or forceful – since 3SRB is not a strenuous exercise but a correction of natural breathing.
- *Note:* In the beginning, breaths may be deeper to establish rhythm. Once technique and volume are mastered, the breath naturally returns to its normal, effortless state.

3. Rhythm

- One complete breath takes approximately 5 seconds or 6 pulse beats.
- Count 1-2-3 while inhaling and 5-6 while exhaling (*4 is skipped*). Unlike other breathing practices or *prāṇāyāma*, inhalation here is longer than exhalation, mimicking natural breathing.
- This rhythm equals about 12 cycles (breaths) per minute.
- There should be no pause between inhalation and exhalation.

Practice Guidelines

- Begin by practising with taped music to internalise the rhythm.
- Try it in conventional postures: lying down, sitting, standing, and walking.
- Gradually increase practice by 5 minutes every fortnight, aiming to reach 1 hour of conscious 3SRB within six months.
- Once this level is achieved, one may practise 3SRB while going to sleep with soft taped music. This supports the transfer of the practice from conscious regulation to unconscious integration, thereby sustaining 3SRB naturally for 8–10 waking hours daily.

PRACTICALS

Refining Exercise No. 1

This exercise focuses on the heart and lungs.

Method: Take deep, rapid breaths at a pace of 36 breaths per minute, coordinated with musical rhythm (available on YouTube – 3SRB or via the 3SRB app). Place both palms on the chest. Ensure that the chest expands during inhalation and contracts during exhalation, while keeping the rest of the body still. Breathing must remain restricted solely to the chest/lung area.

Time Limit: Begin with a maximum of one minute. Once comfortable, increase the duration gradually by ¼ to ½ a minute per month until reaching three minutes. Do not exceed three minutes. Benefits –

1. Physical:

    - This practice addresses issues related to the lungs. With age, unused portions of the lungs, especially the upper regions, tend to stagnate. This exercise reopens them, improving respiration and circulation, thereby alleviating asthma and respiratory conditions such as congestion or "wet lungs."
    - Since this is also the region of the heart, the practice benefits cardiac health, supporting conditions such as weak heart, blocked arteries, and valve irregularities. It aids in regulating blood flow.
    - Oxygenated blood from the heart reaches every cell of the body. Each cell, as Tavaria Ji explained, carries an organic memory, often shaped by conflict. By practicing at the 3SRB rhythm, this rhythm is carried through the blood to each cell. Gradually, the cells adopt this rhythm, replacing conflict with harmony, thereby promoting overall systemic health.

2. Emotional:

    - This is the region of love, but it is also the birthplace of the Ego (I-consciousness). Love, in its truest sense, requires the transcendence of Ego.
    - Ego emerges from birth, beginning with the assignment of a name – my name, my family, my house, and so on. The desire to preserve and satisfy this Ego leads to self-centredness, manipulation, and the pursuit of power. This restricts the ability to truly love, as genuine love demands the will to love.
    - This exercise nurtures willpower and gradually balances the practitioner through life's ups and downs, fostering emotional resilience.

3. Endocrine Connection:

    - The thymus gland, located in this region, is linked in the astral plane with the Anāhata Cakra. The thymus supports overall physical growth. It is large in childhood, but shrinks at adolescence as bodily growth slows. Around the age of three, it also begins influencing personality development.
    - Most significantly, the Anāhata supplies energy to the thymus, fostering growth in a new, inner dimension – the path of inner evolution. Tavaria Ji referred to this as our point in time, the first step toward spiritual awakening.
    - Because this exercise initiates the practitioner on this path, it is considered the first refining exercise.

Refining Exercise No. 2

Method: Place both palms on the stomach, just above the navel. In this exercise, the upper portion of the stomach above the navel should remain light. Take deep, swift breaths in rhythm with music, at the speed of 36 breaths per minute (as in Exercise No. 1). Ensure that the stomach expands while inhaling and contracts while exhaling, with the breath restricted solely to the abdominal region.

Time Limit: Begin with a maximum of one minute. Once comfortable, increase the duration by ¼ to ½ a minute per month, gradually reaching three minutes. *Do not exceed three minutes.*

Benefits:

1. Physical:

    - This exercise stimulates the digestive fire, ensuring good health and toning of the abdominal glands.
    - It enhances intestinal peristalsis, easing food passage and preventing constipation.
    - Organs such as the kidneys, liver, pancreas, and spleen receive a gentle massage.
    - The pancreas, through its Islets of Langerhans, secretes insulin for sugar metabolism and valuable digestive juices. Balanced pancreatic function also helps regulate adrenaline production.
    - The adrenal glands, located atop each kidney, produce adrenaline, vital for self-preservation. This exercise tones and balances these glands.

2. Emotional:

    - Improper adrenal function may cause passivity, moodiness, or depression.
    - An imbalance between the pancreas and adrenals can lead to irritability, impulsiveness, and anger. Proper functioning of both glands restores vitality to the lethargic and calmness to the overly anxious.
    - The pancreas acts like a sponge for negative emotions, storing and repeating them, creating a *granthi* (knot) of fear in this area.

- This exercise dissolves the *granthi* of fear, transforming it into positive biological energy. With this, one experiences awe and joy in simple living.
- Balanced adrenal activity, combined with higher energy connections through the Maṇipūra Cakra, allows one to face "fight or flight" situations consciously and calmly.

With practice, the practitioner gains deeper receptivity – whether listening to birdsong, witnessing a sunrise, or walking mindfully. This newfound openness brings joy, laughter, and lightness, akin to becoming a "Laughing Buddha." The Maṇipūra Cakra, literally the *City of Jewels*, symbolises the transformation of lower instincts into higher living – where life itself shines like a true "City of Jewels."

Refining Exercise No. 3

This exercise primarily engages the backbone, pelvic girdle, and knees.

Method: Stretch the legs and hold the toes with the fingers of both hands. If this is not possible, hold the ankle joints instead. The legs should remain straight without bending at the knees, and the head should be held upright. Take deep, swift breaths in a rhythmic manner at a speed of 36 breaths per minute, as in the previous exercises. In this practice, we take a complete breath – not restricted to any single area – using the chest, stomach, and abdomen together.

Time Limit: Maximum one minute in the beginning. Once you are comfortable with a minute increase by about 1/4 to 1/2 a minute per month till you reach 3 minutes. (Please note that the duration should not be extended beyond 3 minutes.)

Benefits

1. Physical: This exercise strengthens and relaxes the backbone, pelvic girdle, and knees. A strong, flexible spinal cord enables us to sit upright and walk tall, helping us face the challenges of life. In contrast, slouching under tension reflects the burden of

heaviness in life. Tensions tend to accumulate about two inches on either side of the spinal cord, largely due to the emotions of jealousy and anger. These manifest as acidic deposits in joints, hips, and other regions, leading to pain. Chronic accumulation can cause rheumatism and arthritis.

Over time, such tensions weaken the spine and contribute to back conditions like spondylitis, slipped discs, and lumbar degeneration. Practicing this exercise at the 3SRB rhythm (36 cycles per minute) helps dissolve accumulated acids throughout the body. The backbone becomes free of tensions and resumes its natural role as the body's shock absorber. Additionally, the practice alleviates abdominal disorders, stimulates and tones the lower body plexuses (chakras), and particularly strengthens the perineum.

2. Emotional: Jealousy and anger are two dominant emotions that strain the body and mind. With consistent practice, this exercise helps transform these emotions, freeing one from their negative influence. Shri Tavaria ji described it as a "vacuum cleaner for the backbone (Sushumnā nāḍī)," as it pumps breath up and down the spine, cleansing the Sushumnā nāḍī and enabling the rise of higher regenerative energy.

Refining Exercise No. 4

This exercise deals mainly with the blood circulation, lung capacity, and a specific area of the brain

Method: *Staccato breathing:* Take five short, quick inhalations totalling one full breath, followed by one forceful exhalation through the mouth emptying the lungs completely.

Time Limit: Start with three repetitions, gradually increase by one or two repetitions every fortnight or longer (depending on how comfortable the performance feels) until the exercise can be continued for three minutes. Do not extend beyond this time.

Benefits

1. Physical: This exercise improves circulation by clearing blockages, helping prevent skin problems, varicose veins, etc. The better the circulation, the better the overall health. On a physical level, nervous impulses are transmitted as electrical signals through the nerves. Due to muscular tension (arising from various causes, sometimes very deep-rooted), these impulses can be blocked, leading to an accumulation of static electricity in the muscles. This may cause involuntary muscular contractions or spasms, and in severe cases, paralysis. Thus, smoother blood circulation reduces muscular tension.

Breathing in short installments and then fully improves lung elasticity and capacity. Like the first exercise, this practice also benefits those with heart or asthma conditions and trains the lungs for higher prāṇāyāma practices at later stages of yoga.

The body has its own electromagnetic field, which reflects physical health – the stronger the field, the healthier the body. This exercise increases sensitivity to one's circulation; the more aware we are of blood flow, the stronger our magnetic field, vitality, and resilience. Many adepts have cultivated such deep sensitivity to circulation that they developed powerful and charismatic personalities. Finally, this practice stimulates vibrations in brain cells, which enhances memory, vitality, and overall brain well-being.

2. Emotional: In yoga literature, the astral counterparts of the nerves are called nāḍīs. "Nāḍī" literally means a channel for the flow of emotional energy or prāṇa. Vital forces of prāṇa flow through them (amperage), and they must be trained to withstand higher pressures (voltage). This exercise increases awareness and enables one to extract higher-quality prāṇa from incoming

impulses. Without such preparation, the nāḍīs may not withstand these high pressures, leading to breakdown and imbalance in the body–brain system.

Refining Exercise No. 5

This exercise helps oxygenate the blood, introduces a small amount of carbon dioxide (CO_2) into the bloodstream, and activates the parasympathetic nervous system.

Method: Square breathing – (1) Inhale for three seconds (2) Retain the breath for three seconds (3) Exhale for three seconds (4) Hold with lungs empty for three seconds. Gradually increase the duration up to five seconds.

Time Limit: Start with three repetitions, gradually increase by one or two repetitions every fortnight (or longer, depending on comfort) until the exercise can be continued for three minutes.

Benefits

1. Physical: Yoga says that holding the breath for three seconds oxygenates the blood, making one feel more alive, sensitive, and vibrant. Holding the breath for an additional two seconds adds a small amount of CO_2, not the CO_2 released as cellular waste into venous blood, but CO_2 absorbed directly from the air into the arteries. In small amounts, this CO_2 acts as a natural antibiotic that keeps the body free from minor ailments such as colds and fevers. Holding the breath in and out slows both respiration and pulse rate.

It activates the parasympathetic nervous system, creating a calming effect on the entire body. At birth, the parasympathetic system functions at only a small percentage of its full capacity – enough to neutralise excess endocrine secretions and prevent anger and irritation. With age, its functioning diminishes, leading to accumulated irritation and anger due to imbalanced secretions (especially adrenaline). This exercise helps re-ignite the parasympathetic system, restoring balance to the body–brain mechanism.

2. Emotional: On a psychological level, we live in a constant cycle of action and reaction, which produces ongoing irritation. Irritation drains subtle psychic energy, and when excessive, leaves us feeling spent. It also creates a groove that makes us increasingly prone to irritability. In this agitated state, we constantly react and often regret our actions afterward.

Refining Exercise No. 6

This exercise primarily stimulates the throat (larynx), the thyroid gland, the four tiny parathyroid glands, the sinuses, and the pituitary gland.

Method: Throat bandha (bundh) – Take a deep breath through the nose, close the mouth, block both nostrils with the fingers and thumb, press the chin tightly into the hollow of the throat, and swallow five times as if drinking water. Then release the bandha and unblock the nostrils.

Time Limit: Start with three repetitions, gradually increase by one or two repetitions every fortnight (or longer, depending on comfort) until the exercise can be continued for three minutes.

Benefits

1. Physical: It activates all five senses (sight, taste, hearing, smell, and touch), enhancing their sensitivity. It clears the sinuses and alleviates throat and thyroid-related problems. The thyroid gland regulates breathing efficiency and heat balance in the body–brain system. The minute parathyroid glands, embedded within the thyroid, influence growth and sexual balance. Another crucial thyroid function is producing hormones that ensure calcium is deposited in the bones and removed from the blood.

The thyroid also secretes hormones that influence metabolism, especially the growth of bones, teeth, and the brain. Thus, this exercise promotes optimal glandular functioning and protects against disorders of the bones and blood. Poor thyroid activity can produce individuals who are pathologically nervous, jumpy, and hypersensitive – even to minor stimuli. Proper thyroid function enhances positive sensitivity, while balanced parathyroid function fosters calmness and gentle composure.

Just above the palate, at the base of the brain, lies the pituitary gland – a small organ about the size of a cherry stone. It has two lobes: anterior and posterior. The anterior pituitary controls involuntary muscles of the intestines, bladder, and uterus, and regulates milk production in mothers. The posterior pituitary influences the skeletal system, auditory perception of abstract thought, and capacity for self-control. Yoga describes the brain as powered by the posterior pituitary. The pituitary is often called a master gland because, in addition to releasing thyroid-stimulating hormone, it regulates the activity of several other glands. It also governs overall growth and initiates the dramatic hormonal changes of puberty. If it malfunctions, conditions such as pituitary dwarfism, gigantism (acromegaly), or precocious ageing may result. Proper functioning ensures balanced physical development.

2. Emotional: On a subtler level, this exercise addresses the granthi of pain formed at the Viśuddhi cakra. As this knot becomes chronic, it embeds deeply and causes us to feel pain at the slightest provocation. We gradually lose the ability to absorb life's pain because of this blockage. The exercise dissolves the pain-knot, helping us regain resilience and later enabling us to transform pain into higher creative energies for inner growth. The throat centre is also the seat of communication, since the larynx (voice box) is located here. Thus, this practice strengthens both expressive and communicative energies.

Appendix 2

Sattvavajaya Cikitsā and Cognitive Behavioural Therapy

Symbiotic Integration

Dr Mala Kapadia, Professor, Resident Mentor & Director, Centre for Well-being & Wellness, Rashtram School of Public Leadership.

Paper presented at the Conference on *Hinduism & Modern Psychology*, INDICA, August 2021.

Abstract

Contemporary psychology has traditionally focussed on the physical and pathological, yet current trends in research indicate a gradual shift towards its philosophical roots. As points of intersection emerge between the realms of Western psychotherapy and the practice of Āyurvedic Cikitsā, this paper seeks to explore the analogous nature of Sattvavajaya Cikitsā in Āyurveda and Cognitive Behavioural Therapy (CBT) in Western psychology. CBT views psychological distress as arising from individual perceptions of events, while Sattvavajaya Cikitsā attributes it to both cognitive and psychospiritual drivers of behaviour. Both therapies place the client at the centre, and emphasise the independent management and control of the *mānas* (mind) through structured techniques and practices. The distinction lies in the psychospiritual dimension of Sattvavajaya Cikitsā, which emphasises cultivating Sattva Guṇ and moving towards overall healthy living.

The present paper outlines these points of intersection and distinction between the two modalities and highlights the scope for integration in developing a more holistic model of mental health and healthcare. It further explores the wisdom of Āyurveda as a holistic science, now being rediscovered by modern disciplines such as psychoneuroimmunology (PNI) and energy physics, and examines its integrative possibilities with psychological frameworks like CBT, along with limitations and strengths of both approaches.

Keywords: Psychology, Āyurveda, Sattvavajaya Cikitsā, CBT, Psychospiritual, Psychotherapy

Introduction

Hinduism traces its origins to Sanātana Dharma. *Sanātana* literally means eternal, and *Dharma* is loosely translated as a way of life. The etymological root is captured in *dhārayati iti dharma* – that which sustains and holds is Dharma. Thus, Dharma is the way of life that sustains us and makes living sustainable. Āyurveda, an Upaveda of the Atharva

Veda, the last of the four Vedas containing India's oldest cultural and civilisational wisdom – is deeply rooted in this worldview. इह खल्वायुर्वेदो नाम यदुपाङ्गमथर्ववेदस्य ॥ (*Su. Su.* 1/6) In fact, the very first chapter of the *Suśruta Saṃhitā Sūtrasthāna* is *Vedotpatti*, which establishes beyond doubt that the knowledge of *āyu* (life) is contained in the Veda and originates there.[i] The major themes of the Atharva Veda concerned discovering the Self and living in effective interconnectedness with the Cosmos. According to Āyurveda, its two primary aims are to protect the health of the healthy and to heal those who have deviated from health.

Psychology in Sanātana Dharma is embedded across philosophical and medical literature. Constructs such as positive psychology, subjective well-being, and resilience, often considered recent developments in Western psychology, are already articulated in the Vedas, Upaniṣads, six Darśanas, and many Śāstras, including Āyurveda. Psychotherapy in Sanātana Dharma is not merely a treatment for mental illness once it has developed; it also aims to safeguard mental health as a positive construct – preventive and proactive in nature.

In contrast, psychology in the West has undergone several paradigm shifts, influenced not only by the migration of scholars from Germany and Europe to America but also by evolving approaches to the very definition of psychology. Within this larger context, the present paper focusses on a comparative study between Cognitive Behavioural Therapy (CBT) in modern psychology and Sattvavajaya psychotherapy in Āyurveda. Here, it is important to clarify that "modern" does not necessarily mean better, more evolved, or more effective – it simply denotes what is more recent in time.

Modern Psychology (Western Psychology) & Psychotherapy

Psychology in the Western world is comparatively recent when measured against the Vedas. Like in India, psychology in its early phases belonged to the domain of philosophy. In 387 BCE, Plato proposed that mental processes occurred in the brain, while in 335 BCE, Aristotle argued that they resided in the heart. However, this philosophical continuity often appears fragmented when we read standard textbooks on history of Psychology.

The field took a decisive turn when Wilhelm Wundt established the Institute for Experimental Psychology at the University of Leipzig in 1879. This event is generally regarded as the birth of modern psychology, and Wundt is often honoured as the "father of psychology."

Psychology, derived from Psyche, meaning soul, spirit, or consciousness – still lacks a consensus on the meaning of consciousness in the West. Consciousness is typically understood in a narrow, literal sense as awareness or attention, localised in the brain and treated as a cognitive process. The American Psychological Association defines psychology as "the study of the mind and behaviour", embracing everything from brain function to child development, aging, and social phenomena. It is the study of the mind, how it works, and how it affects behavior, and "embraces all aspects of the human experience, from the functions of the brain to the actions of nations, from child development to care for the aged." Though the definition seems positive, Psychology as a field of study has focused more on pathology of the mind than health. When the word mind is used, the word means brain or processes of the brain, and not mind or mānas as understood by Indic Psychology.

The wave of behaviourism dominated Western psychology for decades, shaping both scholarship and curriculum. Later, health psychology, emerged as a subfield within psychology, shifting focus from the biomedical to biopsychosocial model. This newer framework emphasizes health promotion, prevention and treatment of illness, exploration of the causes and correlates of dysfunction, and improvement of health care systems. However, spirituality has been excluded from these evolving models, while ecology and collective consciousness remain largely absent. Western psychology continues to take a brain-centred approach, with the role of the "mind" yet to be fully recognized or integrated. Terms such as "well-being" appeared only much later in the history of health and positive psychology. Even as late as 2017, mental health was not considered integral to the health psychology by the APA. An editorial marking the 38th anniversary of Division 38 (Society for Health Psychology) observed: "With due respect to holistic conceptions of human health, the field of health psychology is fundamentally concerned with physical health, not with mental health."[ii]

In India, unfortunately, the introduction of psychology became associated primarily with Western frameworks rather than with its own Indic roots and wisdom. Western or "scientific" psychology was formally introduced in 1905 at Calcutta University[iii]. In 1915, a full-fledged Department of Psychology was established, and Girindrashekhar Bose, a physician, earned the first doctorate in a doctorate in psychology in 1921. He went on to found the Indian Psychoanalytic Society in 1922. After independence in 1947, India established premier mental health institutions to provide preventive, curative, and rehabilitative care. National Institute of Mental Health and Neurosciences (NIMHANS) in Bangalore and Central Institute of Psychiatry in Ranchi. These institutions also became centres for higher education in psychiatry, psychiatric social work, and clinical psychology, where psychotherapy became an essential component of training.[iv]

CBT as Psychotherapy

Psychotherapy is a therapeutic approach designed to support individuals experiencing a wide range of mental illnesses and emotional difficulties. Its primary aim is to reduce or eliminate troubling symptoms, enhance functioning, and promote overall well-being. Cognitive Behavioural Therapy (CBT), one of the most widely practiced forms of psychotherapy, focusses on identifying and altering harmful or ineffective patterns of thought and behaviour, replacing them with more accurate thoughts and functional behaviours. By helping individuals focus on present problems and practical problem-solving. CBT often incorporates exercises that encourage applying newly learned skills in real-life situations.

CBT has proven ineffective for treating numerous conditions, including depression, anxiety, trauma-related disorders, and eating disorders. For example, in cases of depression, CBT can assist individuals in recognising and maladaptive thought patterns and behaviours that reinforce depressive states.[v]

The roots of CBT lie in Rational Emotive Therapy, pioneered by Albert Ellis in the mid-1950s.

Ellis argued that our emotions and behaviours are strongly influenced by irrational thinking. He proposed several typical irrational thoughts that people tend to hold, which often lead to dysfunctional ways of being in the world (e.g., the need to be loved by everyone, or the belief that we must rely on others for our happiness). His approach gained wide popularity in the latter half of the 20th century and continues to be practiced today.

Ellis introduced the A-B-C model, where A refers to the activating event, B represents our belief system, and C is the consequence of our reaction to A, mediated by B. The model follows a linear process and is based on the idea that core beliefs, though not always immediately accessible at the cognitive level, shape our reactions. To extend this framework, Ellis added D (disputation of irrational beliefs by the therapist) and E (the more effective outcome that emerges as a result).

In the 1960s, Aaron Beck developed Cognitive Therapy, diverging from Ellis in some methods. Beck avoided using the term "irrational" and instead emphasised that core beliefs and schemas – deep, embedded patterns of interpreting the world – produce dysfunctional behaviours and negative feelings. Within Cognitive Behavioural Therapy (CBT), three major levels of cognition are often identified:

1. Full consciousness – a state of heightened awareness and optimised judgment.
2. Automatic thoughts – rapid, often unexamined cognitions that arise in daily life. Though typically outside conscious awareness,

they can be accessed when attention is drawn to them. The growing popularity of Mindfulness practices has helped individuals become more aware of these automatic thoughts, marking a shift from purely rationality-based models toward approaches that emphasise attention and self-discipline.

3. Schemas (core beliefs) – fundamental rules, templates, or imprints in a person's psyche that shape the processing of information and form the underlying scripts by which life is interpreted.

If psychotherapy is defined as an "interpersonal method of mitigating suffering," it is worth noting that India has long nurtured psychotherapeutic systems. Unlike Western approaches, these traditions have not been shaped by clinical frameworks but instead offered broader, more holistic models of the mind and wellbeing. The future of psychotherapy – both Eastern and Western – likely lies in discovering a conceptual framework with universal validity, within which more targeted, ad hoc therapies (for symptom relief, personality growth, or interpersonal adjustment) can be developed.

Psychotherapy in India

Āyurveda, as an Upaveda of the Atharva Veda, and the Patañjali Yoga Sūtras contain an ocean of wisdom on Psychology and Psychotherapy. However, in this paper, we focus only on Sattvavajaya as psychotherapy within Āyurveda. The primary sources of Āyurvedic knowledge are the Bṛhat Trayī – the three foundational texts: Caraka Saṃhitā, Suśruta Saṃhitā, and Aṣṭāṅga Saṃgraha. The first objective of Āyurveda is to preserve the health of the healthy, while the secondary objective is to heal the diseased.

स्वस्थस्य स्वास्थ्य रक्षणमातुरस्य विकारप्रशमनं च ॥ (Ch. Su. 30/26)

Āyu means life and Veda means knowledge – hence, Āyurveda is the knowledge of how to live life. The central concern of this śāstra is not merely curing illness but guiding individuals to live a balanced and healthy life. Health in Āyurveda is defined positively as a state of equilibrium at the physical, psychological, and spiritual levels.

Suśruta defines health as follows:

"sama doṣa sama agniśca sama dhātu mala kriyāḥ prasanna ātmendriya manaḥ svastha iti abhidhīyate" – ***Suśrutaa Saṃhitā***

One is considered in perfect health when:

- The three doṣas (vāta, pitta, kapha) are balanced
- Digestive fire (agni), which governs digestion, assimilation, and metabolism, functions properly
- All tissues (dhātus) and bodily components are stable
- Excretory processes are well-regulated
- And most importantly, the mind, senses, and spirit are content and clear.

Āyurveda identifies four modes of living:

हिताहितं सुखं दुःखं आयुस्तस्य हिताहितं । मानं च तच्च यत्रोक्तं आयुर्वेदः स उच्यते ॥ (Ch. Su. 1/41)

What is a good and happy life? What constitutes a harmful or unhappy life? Hita means good, beneficial, and aligned with well-being. The root of Hita connects it with love and sustainable well-being.

A Hitāyu (life guided by Hita) is one where the individual lives with love and consideration for all beings, animate and inanimate, leading to harmony and sustainability.

A life is considered "good" when one:

- Is a well-wisher of all creatures
- Does not covet others' possessions
- Speaks truth, acts peacefully, and with deliberation
- Balances the three ends of life – virtue, wealth, and enjoyment – without conflict

- Respects elders, pursues knowledge, and lives with humility
- Practices self-restraint in passion, anger, envy, pride, and conceit
- Is charitable, contemplative, and devoted to knowledge, tranquillity, and spiritual insight

The opposite of this worldview is Ahitāyu – a life against well-being. Thus, Hitāyu (life in harmony with society and environment) precedes Sukhāyu (a life of personal happiness). For Āyurvedic ṛṣis, social and ecological well-being came before individual pleasure. This ancient view resonates with modern positive psychology, which emphasizes social well-being. For instance, Keyes (1998) proposed a five-component model including social integration, social contribution, social coherence, social actualization, and social acceptance – all of which align with Āyurveda's worldview.

Nature and Function of Mānas

The constitution and functioning of the mind (Mānas) are described in detail in Āyurvedic texts. Mānas is considered subtle and the 11th sense organ, linking the external world to the internal world through the ten senses. Its natural tendency is to move outward, attracted by artha (objects of pleasure). Each sense organ drags the mind toward its object (e.g., nose toward smell, tongue toward taste). Through memory and association, these attractors activate indulgence.

However, the senses in conjunction with mānas lack the discriminating power of Viveka Buddhi (higher intellect). Thus, when guided only by desires, the mind can fall into Ahita (unwholesome patterns), leading to duḥkha (suffering)

Classical references describe Mānas as follows:

- "उभयात्मक मनः" (Su. Śā. 1) – Mānas is dual in nature
- "मनो दशेन्द्रियाण्यर्थाः प्रकृतिश्चाष्टधातुकी । चतुर्विंशतिको ह्येष राशिः पुरुषसंज्ञकः । करणानि मनो बुद्धिर्बुद्धिकर्मेन्द्रियाणि च ।" (Ch. Śā. 1)
- "उभयात्मकमत्र मनः संकल्पकमिन्द्रियञ्च साधर्म्यात् ।"

- "गुणपरिणाम विशेषान्नानात्व बाह्यभेदाश्च" (Sāṃ. Kā. 27)
- "अन्तःकरणं त्रिविध दशधा बाह्य त्रयस्य विषयाख्यम्" (Sāṃ. Kā. 33)

Bhūt Vidyā and Āyurvedic Psychotherapy

Bhūt Vidyā, the branch of Āyurveda dealing with mental health and psychiatry, has largely been lost over time. However, concepts such as Sattvavajaya preserve valuable psychotherapeutic wisdom for scholars and practitioners seeking to expand their approaches.

Sattvavajaya as Psychotherapy

The Carakā Saṃhitā is the earliest known text where Sattvavajaya is mentioned. In Āyurveda, Sattva is one of the Triguṇa energies that constitute the cosmos, the mind (mānas), and human psyche. 'Sattva' represents the psyche, while 'Avajaya' refers to conquest. Together, Sattvavajaya implies the control or conquest of the mind.

सत्त्वावजयः पुनरहितेभ्योऽर्थेभ्यो मनोनिग्रहः ।[vi]

Carakā defines Sattvavajaya with three key terms – Ahita, Artha, and Manonigraha:

- Ahita: That which is harmful or unwholesome
- Artha: Objects of attraction for each sense (Indriya)
- Manonigraha: Mastery or restraint of the mind

However, one critical aspect often overlooked in literature is Punaḥ, meaning "again" or "to return". This term emphasises the restoration of the mind to its original state of Sattva, from which a person may have deviated. Sattvavajaya is therefore not about acquiring new skills, attitudes, or behaviours; it is about reconnecting with the mind's inherent state of balance and clarity. The mānas, naturally inclined outward, also possesses the Bala (willpower or inner strength) to turn inward and restrain itself. Sattvavajaya provides therapeutic support to cultivate this Bala and guide the mind back to its natural equilibrium.

Unfortunately, Carakā Saṃhitā provides only this single verse on Sattvavajaya, and no further description is available in classical texts. However, Todarananda, a 17th-century scholar, expanded on this concept. In addition to Manonigraha, he included Dhīdhairyādi Vijñānam – a deeper understanding of intellect (Dhī), fortitude (Dhairya), and related capacities (vijñāna) – as integral to Sattvavajaya.

अहितेभ्यः सदार्थेभ्यो मनोनिग्रहणं तथा । धीधैर्यादि विज्ञानं सत्त्वावजयमुच्यते । (आ.सौ. 2/170) [vii]

Research on Todarananda's work can greatly contribute to Bhāratīya Psychology, as his texts are not widely accessible.

Vāgbhaṭa, a follower of Carakā who presented Āyurvedic knowledge concisely, also references Sattvavajaya in the context of mental health (mano doṣa): धीधैर्यात्मादि विज्ञानं मनो दोषौषधं परम् . (अ.हृ.सू. 1/26)

In explaining mānas, it is emphasised that transcending the mind allows buddhi (intelligence) to function effectively. Hence, Dhī becomes very important in Manonigraha. Carakā, in another context has also included Smṛti or memory and Samādhi, or mental equanimity as important aspects of mental health.

मानसो ज्ञानविज्ञानधैर्यस्मृतिसमाधिभिः । (च.सू. 1/58)

In Āyurveda, both mental and physical health are deviations from Buddhi or Prajñā. Illness is considered a Prajñāparadha – a result of living against the natural wisdom of Prajñā. Therefore, the therapeutic goal of Sattvavajaya is to restore Dhī or Prajñā, bringing the mind back to its natural clarity, balance, and resilience.

CBT and Sattvavajaya - A Comparison

	Sattvavajayaa Cikitsā	Cognitive Behavioural Therapy
Basic Principles	Considered to be a means of countering/ alleviating distress through controlling the mind and it's urges. Sattva – guiding towards Hita, away from Ahita (Sarma et al., 2016) The victory of sattva, over the demands of rajas and tamas, (Dhī, Dhṛti, Smṛti) (Sarma et al., 2016) through Jñāna (self-knowledge) Vijñāna(psycho-education), Dhairya(patience & will power) Smṛti (memory) and Samādhi (self-transcendence)	Ultimately aims to teach patients to be their own therapist, by helping them to understand their current ways of thinking and behaving, and by equipping them with the tools to change their maladaptive cognitive and behavioural patterns. Essentially being aware of one's responses, and actively changing them.
	Aims to provide (i) Assurance to the patient of the return of lost objects or persons – Empathically, emotional support is given to the patients who are in grief or sudden loss. It declares that when a person is stressed by the loss of some desired subject, he should be treated by supplementing the same, if not at least through a minimal empathy or consolation	Aims to break down the problem step by step, in a structured manner, whilst focused on the present and alleviating current needs and manifestations of the problem. Problem oriented approach, focused on SMART (specific, measurable, achievable, realistic and time-limited) goal setting

	(ii) Works at inducement of emotions opposite to those associated with patient's distress - Substitution or replacement of emotions with opposite ones is another novel method induced by SC. It is advised that if the patient has developed psychosis due to emotional disorders, he/she should be treated by inducing the opposite nature of the respective attained emotions.	Focuses on understanding and unlearning Negative automatic thoughts, Dysfunctional assumptions, and negative Core beliefs (Donohue et al. 2008).
Cause of Distress	Disturbance is caused via imbalance of the Guṇas, excessive rājasic or tāmasic living. Aims to increase sattva Guṇa, hence the name. Disturbances are also caused through the actions of the senses (taste, tactile, visual, auditory & olfactory) as well as the objects of the mind and thinking in various malfunctioning patterns/ states. It is advised that if the patient has developed psychosis due to emotional disorders such as excessive *Kāma* (desire), *Bhaya (*fear), *Krodha* (anger or aversion), Harṣa (happiness), *Īrṣyā* (jealousy), and *Lobha* (greed), he/ she should be treated by inducing the opposite nature of the respective attained emotions.	CBT hypothesises that people's emotions and behaviours are influenced by their **perceptions of events**. It is not a situation in and of itself that determines what people feel but rather the way in which they construe a situation' (Beck, 1964). Therefore, illnesses are caused more due to negative or dysfunctional perceptions as compared to the event itself. Attempts to tackle faulty cognition at 3 levels Negative automatic thoughts - are thoughts that are involuntarily activated in certain situations. In depression, NATs typically centre on themes of negativity, low self-esteem and uselessness. For example, when facing a task, a NAT may be 'I'm going to fail'

		Dysfunctional assumptions - rigid, conditional 'rules for living' that people adopt. These may be unrealistic and therefore maladaptive. For example, one may live by the rule that 'It's better not to try than to risk failing'. Core beliefs - or schemas, are deeply held beliefs about self, others and the world. Core beliefs are generally learned early in life and are influenced by childhood experiences and seen as absolute. (Byrne, 2013) (analogous to our inherent saṁskāras)
Domains covered	1. *Dhī Cikitsā* (Uplifting Intelligence) This domain focusses on uplifting and refining the intellectual mind and thought process. Its primary mode of action is the judgment and discrimination of negative thoughts, thereby guiding the patient towards healthier cognition. (Cintya – ability to do Cintana, i.e., thinking at a higher and more constructive level) 2. *Dhairya Cikitsā* (Boosting Confidence and Determination) The aim of this domain is to cultivate firmness and strength in the disturbed mind while preserving mental stability. Support is provided through deep empathy and guidance that nurtures a mature level of awareness and judgment. (i.e. Self-monitoring and control)	A – B – C Components of the problem are understood before treatment. Each component is targeted for holistic treatment, and since the components constantly interact with each other A – Affective- Emotions: Types of emotions experienced post event (e.g., anger, anxiety and depressive problematic emotions) B- Behavioural – Problematic behaviors, outward expressions of how the thoughts and feelings manifest themselves. Usually outwardly visible C- Cognitive - Thoughts: What is the patient thinking/ how did they perceive the event

	3. *Ātma vijñāna Cikitsā* or stimulating the consciousness or to set self-realization-This domain brings mental tranquillity through understanding the hidden conflicts which are the source of the emotional illness. (Belguli and Savitha, 2019)	
Process	***Jñāna*** The word *Jñāna* stands for *Ātmajñāna* – knowledge of the self and the soul; spiritual knowledge and true understanding. For attaining *Ātmajñāna*, Ācārya Caraka has described various methods, with special emphasis on *Satya Buddhi* (true knowledge or true understanding). *Adhyātma Jñāna* further refers to the complete and holistic knowledge of both *Śarīra* (body) and *Mānas* (mind). (i.e. Self-knowledge)	**Assessment** This may include filling out questionnaires to help you describe your particular problem and to pinpoint distressing symptoms. You may also be asked to complete forms periodically, so that both you and your therapist can monitor progress and identify symptoms that require additional attention. *(i.e. Initial and ongoing evaluation of symptoms and progress tracking)*
	2. *Vijñāna* Vijñāna refers to scriptural and textual knowledge that leads one to true and valid understanding. It is not mere accumulation of information but a transformation where knowledge (Jñāna) is processed through reasoning, tested against scientific principles, and verified by repeated observation until it becomes practically usable and reliable (jñānam tadartha niścita).	**Personal education** In CBT, personal education involves providing the patient with written materials (brochures, handouts, or books) to enhance their understanding of their condition. The principle "knowledge is power" forms the foundation, when individuals gain clear and accurate knowledge about their psychological problem, they are better equipped to dismiss unfounded fears.

	Through this refinement, Vijñāna gradually reduces the Rajasik and Tāmasik qualities of the mind, while enhancing Sāttvik tendencies. (i.e. Psychoeducation – structured learning that empowers individuals with accurate knowledge about their condition and equips them to manage it effectively.)	This educational process not only reduces anxiety but also lessens other negative emotional responses, empowering the patient to actively participate in their healing journey. (i.e. Psychoeducation through written resources – enhancing self-understanding to reduce fear and anxiety.)
	3. *Dhairya* *Dhairya refers to mental steadiness and stability. It enables the mind to withdraw from unwholesome objects and regulate itself with discipline. Cultivating Dhairya is essential in restraining the mind and serves as an important tool in Sattvavajaya Cikitsā (i.e. Self-monitoring and self-control).*	**Goal setting** In therapy, goal setting involves creating a clear list of the objectives you wish to achieve (for instance, overcoming shyness in social situations). Together with the therapist, you develop practical strategies to reach these goals. Practice of Strategies – These newly developed strategies are rehearsed during sessions. For example, you may role-play challenging social interactions or engage in realistic self-talk, replacing negative or unhelpful inner dialogue with healthier patterns.
	4. *Smṛti* Smṛti refers to higher mental faculties like memory, cognition, perception of the past, and mastery of knowledge. In essence, it is the preservation of acquired understanding.	**Homework** In therapy, active participation is essential. Clients are encouraged to practice the strategies learned during sessions in their daily lives and report their experiences back to the therapist. For instance, they may be asked to keep a diary and consciously work on modifying negative or unhelpful memories and instincts.

	According to Yoga, mental functions can be quietened through Abhyāsa (regular practice) and Vairāgya (detachment). This cultivates refined memory and self-mastery. In modern psychology, this can be compared to EMDR (Eye Movement Desensitization and Reprocessing), where distressing or distorted memories (Vikṛt Smṛti) are processed and replaced with healthier, adaptive associations (Samyak Smṛti).	Once skills are acquired, they should be consolidated and applied across real-life contexts – both within and beyond the clinic. The goal is to ensure generalisation and long-term maintenance of these skills. (CBT, Mayo Clinic)
	5. *Samādhi* *Samādhi* a state where, after fully connecting with the *Ātma* (self), the *Mana* (mind) withdraws from external objects and unites only with the *Ātma*. In Yogic tradition, it is seen both as a spiritual and psychological practice. The purpose is to shape an ideal personality by transforming one's character and guiding the person toward the ultimate life goal – salvation, or Self-Transcendence. (i.e. Self -Transcendence) (Belaguli and Savitha, 2019)	

Techniques	***Cintya* – regulating the thought process** Some important techniques or steps in promoting Jñāna include: recognising and correcting negative automatic thoughts, teaching reattribution strategies, increasing objectivity in perspectives while keeping a spiritual understanding of life, identifying and testing maladaptive assumptions, and practicing decentering. It may also include behavioural techniques such as activity scheduling, homework assignments, graded task assignments, behavioural rehearsal, role playing, diversion strategies and structured problem-solving skills training. Re-education and Insight (Punarśikṣaṇa and Vicāraṇa) are strongly encouraged. (Tripathi, 2012)	**–Activity Scheduling and Behavioural Activation** If there is an activity you tend to put off or avoid due to fear or anxiety, scheduling it in advance can help. Once the burden of decision-making is removed, you may be more likely to follow through. Activity scheduling not only helps in building good habits but also provides consistent opportunities to apply therapeutic learnings in daily life. **Journaling and Thought Records** Writing is a time-honoured way of getting in touch with your own thoughts. A therapist may ask you to record negative thoughts that occurred between sessions along with alternative, more constructive thoughts you could adopt instead. Another helpful exercise is to track newly practiced thoughts and behaviours since the previous session. Recording them in writing provides perspective and helps you recognise your progress over time.

	Vicārya – **by replacing negative ideas and thinking patterns** *Vicārya* refers to the reflective process of examining and transforming unhealthy cognitive patterns. In this method, negative thoughts such as hopelessness, worthlessness, helplessness, and pessimism are actively replaced with healthier and more constructive ideas. **Dharma Artha Vākya:** This involves correcting depressive cognitions by aligning one's thoughts with the principles of Dharma (righteousness) and Artha (purpose/meaning). By reframing ideas through these guiding values, the patient is encouraged to move from negativity toward a sense of responsibility, meaning, and balance. **Pratidvanda Cikitsā (Replacement of Emotions)** Āyurveda emphasizes balancing emotions by invoking their opposites. For example, krodha (anger) is countered by kāma (love/affection), śoka (grief) by harṣa (joy), īrṣyā (envy) by saṃbhāvanā (appreciation). As stated, Kāma śoka bhaya krodha, harṣeṣya lobha, saṃbhāvan, paraspara-pratidvandvaireva śamam nayet (C. Chi. 9/86) Meaning: Excess desires, grief, fear, anger, delight, envy, or greed should be pacified by bringing forth their opposites to neutralise the disturbance.	**Cognitive Restructuring or Reframing** Perhaps you tend to overgeneralise, catastrophise (assume the worst will happen), or place excessive importance on minor details. Such thinking patterns can affect your behaviour and even become self-fulfilling prophecies. In this method, the therapist explores your thought process in certain situations so you can identify negative cognitive patterns. Once you become aware of them, you can learn how to reframe these thoughts into healthier, more constructive practices. Example: Instead of thinking, "I blew the report because I'm totally useless," you might reframe it as, "That report wasn't my best work, but I am a valuable employee and contribute in many ways."

	This structured replacement helps restore emotional equilibrium and cultivates a healthier mindset, in line with the principles of Sattvavajaya Cikitsā.	
	Ūhya – by channelling the presumptions *Ūhya* refers to the process of directing and refining one's assumptions or presumptions in a constructive way.	**Behavioural experiments** Behavioural experiments are structured activities designed to test the validity of maladaptive thoughts, particularly catastrophic thinking common in anxiety disorders. Before engaging in a task that usually provokes anxiety, the individual is asked to make a specific prediction about what they fear will happen. After completing the task, the prediction is compared with the actual outcome. Through repeated trials, the discrepancy between expected catastrophe and lived experience becomes clear, reducing anxiety and reinforcing adaptive beliefs. Typically, tasks begin with low-anxiety situations and progress gradually to more challenging ones, building confidence step by step.
	Dheya – Clarification of Objective Dheya refers to refining and clarifying one's objectives. It involves polishing the goal or purpose so that the patient develops a clearer sense of direction and motivation in life.	**Successive approximation** This technique breaks overwhelming tasks into a sequence of small, concrete and achievable steps. Each successive step builds on the previous one, allowing gradual mastery and increasing confidence, bit by bit.

		Realistic Goal Setting Set goals that are SMART: Specific, Measurable, Achievable, Relevant, and Time-bound. Break long-term aims into short-term and mid-term objectives; use "if–then" plans to anticipate obstacles.
	Saṅkalpa (Resolution) – through proper guidance and advice for making the right decisions. Suhṛtvākya (Guidance and Suggestion) Patients are given guidance to make decisions with the help of principles of Dharma and Artha as described in classical literature. In this way, they can support themselves in coping with the illness. Patients should also be made aware of the pros and cons of both the diseased and healthy states. (Tripathi, 2012) **Dharmārtha Vākya** (Education of the Individual and Family) The patient's family should also be guided positively to support his or her needs. All family members are to be informed about the nature and course of the disease, as well as necessary precautions for effective management. They should be further educated on how to interact with and support the patient appropriately, regardless of the situation. (Tripathi, 2012)	**Guided Discovery** In guided discovery, the therapist first familiarises themselves with the patient's perspective. Then, through carefully framed questions, the therapist challenges underlying beliefs and encourages broader ways of thinking. Patients may be asked to provide evidence both supporting and contradicting their assumptions. Through this process, they learn to view situations from alternative perspectives, including ones they may have not considered earlier. This broadened outlook can help them choose more constructive and adaptive paths. Socratic Questioning Gentle Reasoning

		Exposure Therapy Exposure therapy is used to help individuals confront fears and phobias in a structured way. The therapist gradually exposes the person to the situations that provoke fear or anxiety, while providing guidance and coping strategies in real time. This process is carried out in small, manageable steps. Over time, repeated exposure can reduce fear, increase tolerance, and help the individual feel less vulnerable and more confident in their coping abilities.
	Yogic relaxation is an integral part of psychotherapy. It involves the promotion of Vijñāna (self-awareness and knowledge of one's own bodily responses).	**Relaxation and Stress Reduction Techniques** In CBT, you may be taught progressive relaxation methods, such as: deep-breathing exercises muscle relaxation guided imagery You'll learn practical skills to help lower stress and increase your sense of control. These techniques can be particularly helpful in managing phobias, social anxiety, and other stress-related conditions.

		Biofeedback Mechanisms Biofeedback involves the use of an instrument (usually electronic) that provides immediate feedback to the patient regarding his physiological activities that are not normally available to conscious awareness, (e.g. ECG, EEG, pulse rate, blood pressure, EMG, and galvanic skin response [GSR]). This feedback helps the patient gradually learn to control these responses, and relaxation can be effectively achieved through this method. A simpler form, known as relaxometer, uses only one parameter: the GSR. Other applications of biofeedback include the treatment of enuresis, migraine headaches, tension headaches, idiopathic hypertension, incontinence, cardiac arrhythmias, uncontrolled generalised tonic-clonic seizures, and neuromuscular rehabilitation (Tripathi, 2012). These methods are most effective when used in combination with other therapeutic approaches.

	Deśātana – *leaving space and going away; physical distancing from stressor*	**Role-playing** Role-playing is a therapeutic technique that helps individuals practice and work through different behaviours in potentially difficult situations. Playing out possible scenarios can reduce fear and anxiety and may be used for: Improving problem-solving skills Building familiarity and confidence in certain situations Practicing social skills Developing assertiveness Enhancing communication skills (*Techniques of CBT, Healthline*)

Conclusion and Future Research

Hinduism, as originated from Sanātana Dharma, offers vast reservoirs of wisdom that remain highly relevant to addressing the current crises facing humanity. Modern psychology is still grappling with its own evolution, gradually expanding its boundaries to include positive psychology, neuroscience, quantum physics, and other interdisciplinary domains. In contrast, Bhāratīya Psychology – even when considered only through Āyurveda and the Patañjali Yoga Sūtras – presents a holistic, inclusive, and forward-looking framework. The profound insights of the Ṛṣis are now being rediscovered and validated by modern sciences.

The limitations lie in the scarcity of original research in some areas and in the fact that the sūtras are encoded. Decoding them requires not only scholarly expertise but also intuition and sadhana, so that they may be integrated with modern language and made relevant to contemporary applications. The younger generation – navigating quarter-life crises, the aftermath of the pandemic and lockdowns, and uncertainty about the future – is seeking deeper meaning and spiritual anchoring. For this, the knowledge of Self, as well as of mānas, Dhī, Dhṛti, and Smṛti are important to create this deeper meaning.

Sattvavajaya is only one of the psychotherapeutic approaches described in Āyurveda. Many others remain to be systematically researched and applied, particularly when combined with Yogic Psychotherapy. The mind or psyche continues to puzzle modern psychologists, yet Āyurveda and Yoga together can provide a comprehensive framework for holistic healing. Human beings are not merely rational or cognitive; we are also emotional, spiritual, and in need of Logos in our lives. Therefore, modern psychology curricula should aim to integrate the wisdom of Āyurveda and Yoga into their core, rather than relegating it to electives where true integration is lost.

Endnotes

i V. Vasudevan, Ayurvedatatvaprakashini, Aug 2000, AVP, Coimbatore, India, 1

ii Freedland Kenneth E., **Health Psychology**, (2017) Vol. 36, No. 1, 1–4, EDITORIAL, A New Era for Health Psychology, Washington University School of Medicine, USA

iii Prasadrao, P. S. D. V., & Sudhir, P. M. (2001). Clinical psychology in India. *Journal of Clinical Psychology in Medical Settings, 8*(1), 31-38.

iv Bhatt Gayaitri, Encountering Culture: Psychotherapy and Counselling Practice in India, Parivartan.org

v Laxman ji Yadav1& J.S. Tripathi3 & Richa Rani Yadav2, Expanding horizons of satvavajaya chikitsa through EMDR&CBT, IJRAR- International Journal of Research and Analytical Reviews, VOLUME 5 I ISSUE 4 I OCT.– DEC. 2018

vi Ch su 11/54

vii Dr. A. R. V. Murthy, Rationale of Ayurvedic Psychiatry, Chaukhamba Orientalia, 2009, Varanasi, India, page 14

References for the Comparisons

Healthline. (n.d.). *9 CBT techniques for better mental health.* https://www.healthline.com/health/cbt-techniques

Shukla, V., & Tripathi, R. D. (2002). *Charak Samhita* (Vol. 1, 2nd ed., p. 447, Sutra 30/26). Chaukhamba Sanskrit Pratishthan.

Belaguli, G., & Savitha, H. P. (2019). An empirical understanding on the concept of Sattvavajaya Chikitsa (Ayurveda psychotherapy) and a mini-review of its research update. *Indian Journal of Health Sciences and Biomedical Research (KLEU), 12*(1), 15–20. https://doi.org/10.4103/kleuhsj.kleuhsj_182_18

Mayo Clinic. (n.d.). *Cognitive behavioural therapy*. Mayo Foundation for Medical Education and Research. https://www.mayoclinic.org/tests-procedures/cognitive-behavioral-therapy/about/pac-20384610

Fenn, K., & Byrne, M. (2013). The key principles of cognitive behavioural therapy. *InnovAiT*, 6(9), 579–585. https://doi.org/10.1177/1755738012471029

O'Donohue, W. T., & Fisher, J. E. (Eds.). (2008). *Cognitive behavior therapy: Applying empirically supported techniques in your practice*. John Wiley & Sons.

Sarma, D. R., Ali, K., & Sarmah, J. (2016). An Ayurvedic perspective to cognitive behavioural therapy vis-a-vis Satwavajaya Chikitsa. *International Journal of Ayurveda and Pharma Research, 4*(5), 42–45.

Tripathi, J. S. (2012). Dimensions of Sattvavajaya Chikitsa (Ayurvedic psychotherapy) and their clinical applications. *Annals of Ayurvedic Medicine, 1*(1), 31–38.

American Psychological Association. (n.d.). *What is cognitive behavioral therapy?* https://www.apa.org/ptsd-guideline/patients-and-families/cognitive-behavioral

Dhoriyani, D. D. (2014). *Applied concept of Sattva, Sattvabala and its promotion through Sattvavajaya and Yuktivyapashraya* (Doctoral dissertation). Department of Basic Principles, IPGTRA, Gujarat Ayurveda University.

Bagali, S. S., Baragi, U. C., & Deshmukh, R. A. (2016). Concept of Satwavajaya Chikitsa (Psychotherapy). *Journal of Ayurveda and Integrated Medical Sciences, 1*(1). p. 56–63.

viii Chakraborty, S. K. (2013). *Education in India: A Tree Without Roots*. Shastra Dharma Prachar Sabha. p. 49

ix Singh, H. G. (1977). *Psychotherapy in India* (p. 9). National Psychological Corporation.

x Sharma, R. C. (1928). *Atharva Veda Samhita*. Sayan Bhasya, Kand VI, Mathura

xi सातवलेकर, श्रीपाद दामोदर. (2008). अथर्ववेद मेधाजनन, संगठन और वजिय (भाग ५, pp. 10, 43). Swadhyaya Mandal (Vedic Research Centre), Pardi, Gujarat

xii ibid

xiii Rao, Ramachandra S. K. *Tantra of Sri Chakra Bhavanopanishad*. Sri Satguru Publications, A Division of Indian Books Center, New Delhi, India, 2008, p. 23

xiv https://www.wisdomlib.org/definition/medha

xv Bhagwat Sinh. (1986). *Bhagavadgomandal*. (p. 7357). Pravin Prakashan.

xvi सातवलेकर, श्रीपाद दामोदर. (2008). अथर्ववेद मेधाजनन, संगठन और वजिय - *(भाग ५)*. Swadhyaya Mandal (Vedic Research Centre), Pardi, Gujarat, India, Page 10

xvii https://www.wisdomlib.org/definition/vasotpati

xviii Ibid, page 43

xix Harshavardhana, Y. (2022). *Vidyā*. Garuda Prakashan PVT. LTD. p. 111

xx Sri Aurobindo. (1995). *On Original Thinking*. In *The Harmony of Virtue* (SABCL Vol. 3, p. 112). Sri Aurobindo Ashram.

Appendix 3

Peace Psychology

As we have already seen, Western psychology has been gradually evolving through several paradigm shifts, and Peace Psychology is one of its most recent developments. However, this chapter – included here as an Appendix – takes us beyond the Western framework into the deeper dimensions of Peace from Bhāratīya perspectives. With gratitude to the editor, Giri Anant Kumar, we present this contribution in the book.

Kapadia, M. (2024). Toward a New Dharma of Peace, Health, and Global Well-Being. In: Giri, A.K. & Varghese, S. (Eds.), *Towards a New Dharma of Peace Building*. Springer, Singapore. https://doi.org/10.1007/978-981-99-6066-8_9

Towards a New Dharma of Peace, Health, and Global Well-being

Dr. Mala Kapadia, Director, Transdisciplinary Research Initiatives, Anaadi Foundation, India

Abstract

Peace is generally seen as the absence of conflict, just as health is often seen as the absence of disease. However, when we review Vedic literature, both peace and health emerge as independent constructs, rather than as mere opposites of conflict or illness. Peace is an emotion and a state of being, while health is a positive state of alignment of mind, body, and spirit. Moreover, peace and health are deeply interconnected – peace creates health, and health creates peace. In all Vedic prayers, completion is marked by chanting "Om Śānti, Śānti, Śānti." The repetition of Śānti (peace) three times carries profound significance: the first Śānti is for the individual level, the second for the nation (*Rāṣṭra*), and the third for the world. Each level has distinct causes of disharmony that must be addressed to establish lasting peace.

When we review modern Positive Psychology and Peace Psychology literature, we find similar conceptual frameworks. Yet, modern literature largely views peace in relation to conflict or violence. In contrast, Vedic literature speaks of peace as a positive, self-sustaining construct. It provides guidelines and rituals to achieve this state, which this paper elaborates.

This paper also examines Indian aesthetics, particularly the Nāṭya Śāstra, which discusses emotions in depth and identifies peace (*Śānta Rasa*) as the ninth emotion – an addition by Kashmiri scholar Abhinavagupta. Modern neuroscience, especially the work of Candace Pert (*Molecules of Emotion*), offers insights into how emotions operate in the body and mind. Research from HeartMath, USA, further explores the relationship between emotions and the heart. Mechanisms to cultivate peace within oneself, and extend it outward to the world, are possible through Yoga, Āyurveda, and the integration of neuroscience. The heart is increasingly recognised as the locus for expanding consciousness and anchoring peace. These modern insights resonate with Vedic literature and Abhinavagupta's work. To establish peace as Dharma, the journey must begin with the self. Deep inner work is essential before peace can manifest at societal or global levels. This paper explores rituals and practices through which peace can be directly experienced and firmly established.

The tapestry of ancient and modern insights, Eastern and Western perspectives will generate better understanding of SDG and SDG+. Real victories are often small, and internal. This paper will expand on we begin our Dharma from Svadharma and connect with Viśva Dharma.

Keywords-Rta, Dharma, Śānta Rasa, Inner Peace, Heart Meditation, Wellbeing, Intergenerational Trauma, Psychoneuroimmunology

Introduction

The world today is witnessing a renewed interest in fundamental questions of life and existence. The boundaries between science and spirituality are increasingly merging, enabling humanity to recognise the fault lines in its ways of thinking and living. To grasp the meaning of Peace, humanity has endured wars; to comprehend Dharma, it has faced the devastation of Adharma. This raises a crucial concern: Can Peace and Dharma be understood not merely in contrast to conflict and Adharma, but as foundational constructs of human existence? In the wake of pandemic, it has become all the more Peace Dharma together.

Peace Psychology first emerged in the West as an area of research concerned primarily with the prevention of nuclear war. Western psychologists have engaged with questions of war and peace since the very beginnings of modern psychology. In the first issue of *Peace and Conflict: Journal of Peace Psychology* (Deutsch, 1995), William James is identified as the earliest peace psychologist. However, the idea of Peace – as a philosophy or ontology of worldview – extends much farther back in human history and evolution. What is needed now is a pause, a deliberate 'Point of Return', through which humanity can envision a new future shaped by the Dharma of Peace. This requires us to understand Peace as a construct in itself – not simply as the absence of war or conflict, which remains the dominant focus of much Western peace research. In 1997, the American Psychology Association (APA) changed the name of its "Division of Peace Psychology" to the "Society for the Study of Peace, Conflict, and Violence: Division of Peace Psychology", thereby signalling a broader scope of inquiry (Christie et al., 2008). Furthermore, some scholars have argued that peace psychology must give greater attention to inner (intrapsychic) peace (Nelson, 2007; Nelson & Milburn, 1999).

Peace Peace Peace- The Vedic Mantra

In this chapter, we explore the construct of peace as an inner state of being – aligned with the Cosmos and articulated by the sages (Ṛṣis) of India, one of the world's oldest civilisations. Peace, known as Śānti in Sanskrit, has various shades of meaning. Monier-Williams' Sanskrit-English Dictionary records its meanings as: tranquillity, peace, quiet, calmness of mind, absence of passion, the averting of pain (śānti! śānti! śānti! – may the three kinds of pain be averted!), and even indifference to objects of pleasure or pain [Kaṭha Upaniṣad; Mahābhārata], among others (Cologne Digital Sanskrit Dictionaries).

The earliest mention of peace appears in Vedic literature in the forms of Śānti Mantras. Modern science seems to have come full circle, with quantum physicist David Bohm rediscovering the idea that both the Cosmos and individuals are composed of energy, and that energy contains information and intelligence (Pearsall, 1998, p. 52). Mantras are powerful means to activate this energy, intelligence, and information. Śānti Mantras invoke peace at the cellular level and extend it to the Cosmic plane. The concept of Dharma emerged later, in the post-Vedic period. In the Vedas, the word Rta was used to denote what we understand as Dharma today. Rta is the all-pervading cosmic order that provides balance in both the natural world and human society. It is because of Rta that the seasons change, the rivers flow, and the sun rises and sets. Rta governs not only the forces of nature but also moral values and the cause of human suffering (What Is Rita? - Definition from Yogapedia, 2019). The etymological understanding of Dharma comes from dhārayati – it sustains, it upholds; therefore, Dharma is that which holds together. In his essay *Can Vedic Dharma Bring Peace to the World?*, Stephen Knapp (Nandanānanda Dāsa) clearly outlines the correlation between peace and Dharma. He argues that the ultimate human purpose is to live harmoniously with nature, society, and the world, thereby accomplishing the true goal of life. This is Sanātana Dharma – the timeless, universal spiritual truth. This, he asserts, is the uplifting nature of Vedic Dharma (Knapp, 2022).

In Vedic literature, the Śānti Mantras have special significance. They reflect the profound interconnectedness of the Cosmos, Nature, and human beings. The following mantra from the Yajurveda is one of the most well-known, recited to invoke peace universally:

ॐ द्यौः शान्तिरन्तरिक्षं शान्तिःपृथिवी शान्तिरापः शान्तिरोषधयः शान्तिः।
वनस्पतयः शान्तिर्विश्वेदेवाः शान्तिर्ब्रह्म शान्तिः
सर्वंशान्तिः शान्तिरेवशान्तिः सामा शान्तिरेधि॥
ॐ शान्तिः शान्तिः शान्तिः॥ – **Yajurveda**

Here, the Ṛṣi invokes peace for the Cosmos, the earth, the waters, the plants, medicinal herbs, all divine beings, Brahmā, and for all existence itself. This mantra profoundly illustrates that peace must permeate the Cosmos and the Earth in order for us. as individuals, to truly experience inner peace.

Peace at Three Levels: Individual, Collective, and Universal

All Indian prayers, Vedic or otherwise, culminate by invoking peace three times with the recitation Śānti, Śānti, Śānti. The first invocation is for peace at the individual level, the second at the national or collective level, and the third at the global or universal level. The Śānti Mantra establishes clearly that these three levels are interconnected; hence, peace must be invoked and cultivated at all levels. The sages realised that lack of peace arises due to disharmony at these levels, and therefore named them Adhyātmika, Adhibhautika, and Adhidaivika.

Adhyātmika, or Individual Level Peace

In Vedic literature, the individual shares responsibility with the collective and the universal. The individual needs to be aligned with Dharma – the universal principles of sustainability. As we saw earlier, one of these principles is rhythm, which in individual life is cultivated through self-discipline. Lack of rhythm creates Adhyātmika suffering – dis-ease at the body and mind level, manifesting as illnesses and disharmony.

When we reflect on our own lives and those around us, we realise there is hardly anyone who has escaped this suffering. Overindulgence in sensual gratification, misuse of intellect, and misguided aspirations for materialistic achievements are some causes of Adhyātmika suffering. We often believe we have progressed through technological advances and space exploration, yet we have neglected the deeper understanding of our own mānas (mind). The Ṛṣis had long understood that the mind can generate either peace or conflict through actions. In the Ṛgveda, the Ṛṣi expresses hope that humanity will protect Truth and practice actions that establish peace (Ṛgveda. 7/35/12). In the Atharva Veda, the connection between actions and mānas is emphasised: the mānas, the sixth sense organ, governs the five senses, and must be established in peace. "May our speech be established in peace" (Atharva Veda 19/9).

Inner peace is the antidote to Adhyātmika suffering. Body, mind, senses, intelligence, and spirit need to be rooted in harmony. When one experiences the self as Cosmos, the principles of Rta and Dharma are naturally followed. Rhythm is restored, and one can self-transcend beyond a xenophobic existence. Later sections reconnect this idea with self-transcendence in the work of Abraham Maslow.

The Ṛṣis had a deep understanding of how cellular memories can create psychosomatic illnesses – or, as Candace Pert's work in Psychoneuroimmunology reveals, how they can foster "psychosomatic wellness." Peace as an emotion, or one of the Sthāyī Bhāvas described in the Nāṭya Śāstra, highlights that peace is our innate svabhāva (nature). Pert's research connects this to the 'molecules of emotion' at the biological level. Similarly, David R. Hawkins' work on kinesiology describes the body's energy at different emotional levels. Peace, as an emotion, elevates our energy to higher states. Hawkins also demonstrates how individuals vibrating at higher energy levels can positively influence those at lower levels. Modern research thus reaffirms what the Ṛṣis proclaimed in Vedic times: peace within the individual level is the foundation of health, harmony, and well-being. Peace, harmony, and well-being form a virtuous circle, each strengthening the other.

The first Śānti is therefore a call to establish inner peace at the individual level – through the right orientation of mānas, and through dharmic living and action.

Collective Level Peace

An individual lives within the family, society, community, and nation. The second Śānti operates at the collective level. Humanity has not only experienced world wars and cold wars, but also an overall disintegration of the family and social fabric. Nations continue to allocate vast budgets to weapons and invest in technologies of war. At one level, peacekeeping forces are deployed, and at the same time, the right to carry weapons is supported as a constitutional right. Lack of peace at the individual level has contributed to rising mental health issues and violence in schools. In Vedic language, these disturbances are called Adhibhautika suffering. Even peace-loving individuals become victims of this suffering, because we live within an ecosystem that normalises and supports violence. Social inequity is on rise, and the divide between developed and underdeveloped countries is widening. However, a deeper insight into what we call "developed" countries needs to be cultivated through soul-searching. While the basic needs of individuals in these countries may be met, many still remain far from what Maslow describes as self-transcendence. We therefore need to address Adhibhautika suffering and establish peace at collective levels as well.

For Adhibhautika suffering, the leaders of communities and nations have a crucial role to play. They hold the power to establish peace and create safety. The national role in maintaining internal harmony is particularly critical. Some countries have enjoyed centuries without war, while others have struggled with internal conflict for decades.

Another collective sphere includes society, community, and organisations or workplaces. This requires our collective norms, practices, systems, and institutions to cultivate peace. A simple analogy that explains the reality is found in the works of Psychologist Paul Gilbert. He states,

"Despite our wealth and comforts, half of us will have a mental health problem at some point, with depression, anxiety, alcoholism and eating disorders topping the list. We are also becoming less trusting and feeling more threatened" (Gilbert, 2009, p. 9). Where is peace in this hurry-hurry culture? As Henry David Thoreau observed, we are living too fast rather than deep. Peace requires us to slow down at the collective level and to experience stillness.

Our collective way of life itself compromises peace. In the words of Thomas Merton, "There is a pervasive form of contemporary violence to which the idealist most easily succumbs: activism and overwork. The rush and pressure of modern life are a form, perhaps the most common form, of its innate violence...The frenzy of our activism neutralizes our work for peace. It destroys our own inner capacity for peace" (Merton, 2009). Taking a pause and reflecting on how we are collectively living is therefore the foundation for Peace as the New Dharma.

The second Śānti calls us to collective peace.

Global and Cosmic Level Peace

The third invocation of Śānti is at the global as well as cosmic level. Just as the individual belongs to a community and a nation, the larger unit is the unification of nations. Peace between nations is essential, but it depends on the presence of peace within society and community. At the cosmic level, peace is equally vital, for disturbances in cosmic harmony inevitably affect the internal peace of nations. In Vedic literature, this third Śānti is directed toward Adhidaivika forces – the forces of nature that can bring destruction and suffering: floods, excessive rainfall, famine, wildfires, earthquakes, tornadoes, and hurricanes.

The Vedic Ṛṣis believed that when both inner peace and collective peace are violated, these cosmic forces are activated and create havoc. To harmonise the forces of nature for protection and well-being, Śānti mantras and yajñas were performed. While natural calamities may appear beyond human control, Vedic belief holds that such events occur when dharma is violated at individual or collective levels, leading to disharmony in the forces of nature. As we propose Peace as the New Dharma, this interconnectedness between the individual, the nation, and the cosmos must be re-established. When Rta and Dharma are followed in both individual and collective life, peace becomes established at global and cosmic levels.

The third Śānti thus belongs to the global and cosmic dimension.

Many global or social initiatives for peace fail to achieve lasting impact because they overlook the foundational role of individual peace. Attempting to create world peace without inner transformation is ineffective. Although difficult, cultivating peace within the individual is the only sustainable way. As the Dalai Lama observes: "Peace must first be developed within an individual. And I believe that love, compassion, and altruism are the fundamental basis for peace. This atmosphere can be expanded and extended from the individual to his family, from the family to the community, and eventually to the whole world." (Dalai Lama, in Thich Nhat Hanh, 1991, p. vii).

Peace as Psychology and Human Nature

Why is peace so difficult for us to understand as an independent construct rather than merely as the absence of conflict or war? Is peace something that must be learnt and cultivated, or is it inherently ingrained in our nature and psyche? How is the experience of peace – or its absence – related to psychology? Earlier, we explored the collective culture that generates a lack of peace in our lives through three types of crises or concerns: Adhyātmika (individual), Adhibhautika (collective), and Adhidaivika (global-cosmic). A Vedic insight into our interrelatedness with the cosmos highlights xenophobia as a symptom of a limited sense of self. To experience peace, self-transcendence is required, as Abraham Maslow stated. Yet, self-transcendence seems difficult, because we have been conditioned to believe otherwise. Biologically, too, myriad ingrained emotions keep us locked in repetitive emotional and behavioural responses. Revisiting the Nāṭya Śāstra through the commentary of Abhinavagupta, the Kashmiri philosopher, helps us understand the biology of emotions. Connecting this with modern psychoneuroimmunology research by Dr. Candace Pert provides a fresh perspective on Maslow's idea of self-transcendence.

Abhinavagupta – Śānta Rasa

In Indian tradition, psychology has been an integral part of philosophy, performing arts, health systems like Āyurveda, and the Itihāsa–Purāṇas. The Nāṭya Śāstra provides insights into how the readiness to enjoy certain emotions is both innate and cultivable, and how it can also transcend. Emotions, or bhāvas in Sanskrit, are not only psychological but also biological, existing as Sthāyī (permanent) Bhāvas. The Nāṭya Śāstra, more than 2,500 years old, is the world's earliest treatise on performing arts. Sage Bharat was the first to compile the scattered sūtras into a systematic theoretical text. The origin and historical context of this work are especially significant. Time in ancient India was divided into Yugas. At the end of the Kṛta Yuga and at the onset of the Tretā Yuga, people became consumed by base emotions such as excessive desire, greed, jealousy, and anger. Their happiness became entangled with sorrow. Concerned, Indra and the devas approached Brahmā, the deity of creation, requesting an audio-visual form of entertainment – something that would be accessible to people of all places. (Bharadwaj, 2016). Thus, the Nāṭya Śāstra opens with the objective of the compilation and need of the hour. Interestingly, this aim resonates strongly with the crises of our modern world – pandemics, biowarfare, and terrorism. For our present discussion, two constructs from the Nāṭya Śāstra are most relevant to psychology: Sthāyī Bhāva, or ingrained emotions, and Rasa, the experience of those emotions when heightened and activated by external stimuli.

The word "Sthāyī" in Sthāyī Bhāva indicates its permanent nature. These are innate, latent emotions present in human beings from birth. They are timeless and universal, existing across all periods of human history, every caste, race, religion, culture, and nation. Their existence in the unconscious state is passive from birth, but they become active when stimulated or awakened by external excitants (Chaudhary, 2002). The absence of a particular Sthāyī Bhāva results in an inability to experience certain emotions personally, and this lack manifests in relationships as well. For example, absence of compassion reflects the lack of the Sthāyī Bhāva of śoka (sadness). Conversely, excessive anger indicates the dominance of Krodha (anger) as a Sthāyī Bhāva. In the Nāṭya Śāstra, Sthāyī Bhāvas are understood as the readiness of an individual to experience and enjoy emotions in performing arts. This work, however, extends the construct beyond aesthetics to everyday life experiences.

Rasa, a Sanskrit term, has multiple connotations depending on context – juice, essence, aesthetic experience, emotional pleasure, medicine, or plasma. Sage Bharata identified eight Sthāyī Bhāvas and their corresponding Rasas. The Sthāyī Bhāva represents an inherent readiness to experience emotions at the level of Rasa. Extending them beyond aesthetics into psychology is only natural, since they are both psychological and biological in nature. Without rasa, life becomes nir-rasā – empty of essence and joy, barren, monotonous, and lifeless. Rasas bring variety to the theatre of life, and this enjoyment is sui generis, self-generative. Abhinavagupta emphasises this uniqueness of rasa as an unmistakable "datum of consciousness."

In the 11th century, the Kashmiri philosopher Abhinavagupta expanded Bharata's theory of rasa through his commentary. Bharata described eight principal human feelings – delight, laughter, sorrow, anger, energy, fear, disgust, heroism, and astonishment – which correspond to eight rasas: erotic, comic, pathetic, furious, heroic, terrible, odious, and marvellous. Abhinavagupta's most significant contribution was the addition of Śānta Rasa (peace/tranquillity). He argued that "the eight rasas are like eight gods, and Śānta is like their highest centre, Śiva.'

The addition of Śānta Rasa not only enriched the theory of aesthetics but also offered a profound framework for understanding the human psyche. Abhinavagupta regarded Śānta Rasa as the fundamental state that permeates all others and into which they eventually dissolve. Unlike the transitory nature of other rasas, Śānta represents a mind at rest, steeped in tranquillity. Since Abhinavagupta, critics have acknowledged nine rasas (Saha, n.d.).

Three Sanskrit ślokas from the Nāṭya Śāstra expand our understanding of psyche and consciousness in relation to peace:

मोक्षाध्यात्मसमुत्थस्तत्त्वज्ञानार्थहेतुसंयुक्तः।
नैश्रेयसोपदिष्टःशान्तरसोनामसंभवति॥६.१०७॥

This śloka explains that Śānta Rasa evolves when one pursues liberation, engages in philosophy, analyses reality, and reflects on sustainable well-being.

बुद्धीन्द्रियकर्मेन्द्रियसंरोधाध्यात्मसंस्थितोपेतः।
सर्वप्राणिसुखहितःशान्तरसोनामविज्ञेयः॥६.१०८॥

Śānta Rasa arises when intellect and senses are withdrawn from external distractions and remain steady in self-knowledge, with thoughts devoted to the well-being of all. The author notes that in conceiving and writing this chapter, such deep peace was personally experienced.

नयत्रदुःखंनसुखंनद्वेषोनापिमत्सरः।
समःसर्वेषुभूतेषुसशान्तःप्रथितोरसः॥६.१०९॥
(Paudel & Mohan, 2020, pp. 116–119)

Here, Śānta Rasa is described as the state where there is no personal sorrow or joy, no jealousy or envy, but perfect equanimity toward all beings.

To achieve this state, self-transcendence is essential – expanding consciousness beyond narrow, self-centred existence. Several ślokas indicate that the other rasas are not our original nature, but deviations from prakṛti. Only through withdrawal from indulgence in them can Śānta Rasa be realised.

Śānta Rasa is rooted in the Sthāyī Bhāva of Nirveda or Sama. It is a state of pause, detachment, and reflection, viewing life and relationships with equanimity rather than entanglement. Sama Bhāva emerges through connection with the heart, consciousness, and oneness with the cosmos. While aesthetics scholars debated its inclusion, from a psychological perspective Śānta Rasa is vital for happiness and well-being. The Bhagavad Gītā (Ch. 6.22) explicitly states that one who is not at peace cannot experience true happiness. Yet in modern definitions, happiness is often equated with high arousal, active lifestyle, instant gratification, and indulgence in sensual pleasure. In contrast, Śānta Rasa points to withdrawal from futile pursuits and temporary satisfactions, guiding us toward deeper meaning, philosophy, and long-term fulfilment.

Abraham Maslow, Self-Transcendence, and Peace

The human psyche is so entangled in the short-term pursuit of happiness that the sustainable, long-term experience of calm and peace continues to elude both individuals and societies. Abraham Maslow describes self-transcendence as the highest human need. Once achieved, transcendence involves the dissolution of the separate self in one's perception of place in the universe. In its stead emerges a sense of connectedness and integration with humanity, nature, and the cosmos (James, 2017). The *Sthāyī Bhāva* underlying Śānta Rasa – Nirveda or Sama – can be described in same words. This becomes the very premise for experiencing Śānta Rasa. In Maslow's *Hierarchy of Needs*, which attempts to explain the structure of the human psyche, needs are driven by deficit and/or growth. At the level of transcendence, one can even move beyond individual differences in a profound sense. Maslow described the highest attitude toward differences as an awareness of them, an acceptance of them, an enjoyment of them, and finally a gratitude for them – as beautiful instances of the ingenuity of the cosmos, meriting wonder and recognition of their value (Maslow, 1972, p. 267).

However, a review of psychology, management, and leadership curricula reveals that Maslow's model is often taught in a distorted and incomplete way. Basic, safety, social, self-esteem, and self-actualisation needs are presented in the familiar pyramid. Yet the needs for knowledge, aesthetics and beauty, and self-transcendence are either minimised or entirely omitted. Maslow, in fact, provided clear analysis of the characteristics of self-actualizers and the centrality of self-transcendence. Abhinavagupta's insights can help us understand why such distortions persist. Most people remain stuck in the lower-level, deficit needs, which are governed not by joy or aspiration but by fear and insecurity Fear, as an emotion, is deeply connected with anger – when one fears loss of control – or with sadness and grief when one fears losing loved ones or possessions. Abhinavagupta noted obstacles to the enjoyment of Rasa, one of which is the *Hṛdayagranthi* (knot of the heart). This blockage preoccupies the mind and prevents the experience of Rasa (Ṣāstrī, 1940, p. 188). In exploring peace or Śānta Rasa, this obstacle plays a significant role. Many of us are unable to experience calmness or tranquillity because of these knots in the heart and the restless preoccupation of the mind. Fear creates such inner knots, which keep us trapped at the level of deficit needs. The final section outlined practices that can help cultivate inner peace. By dissolving the *Sthāyī Bhāvas* of anger, fear, and disgust, these practices can remove inner blocks and open the path to peace.

Most studies on peace focus on external conflict and war, not on transcendence. A paradigm shift is needed to recognise peace as *Dharma* – our inner compass and state of Being. Unless individuals achieve this state, collective Peace Missions will remain of limited value. Peace-makers or peace-making mechanisms must operate from their higher Self and expanded consciousness, not merely at a transactional level.

Working for world peace is, therefore, not simply a profession but an avocation – a transcendent goal that surpasses the pursuit of our basic needs. Together, we can move toward this vision (Arment, 2018).

Psychoneuroimmunology, Psychosomatic Well-being and Peace

Insights from Bhāratīya psychology and Abhinavagupta must be explored beyond their contributions to aesthetics. The concept of *Sthāyī Bhāva* and the possibility of experiencing it at the level of *Rasa* not only generate energetic shifts within us but also relate to neurotransmitter activity. Charles Darwin, in *The Expression of the Emotions in Man and Animals*, connected emotions to survival and emphasised the universality of facial expressions. Paul Ekman later expanded this work by classifying families of emotions. Yet, peace as an emotion is absent in both Darwin's and Ekman's frameworks. Similarly, Robert Plutchik (2003), a psychology professor at Hofstra University, proposed a theory of eight primary emotions – sadness, disgust, anger, anticipation, joy, acceptance, fear, and surprise. Once again, peace is conspicuously missing as a primary category. Candace Pert, however, connected emotions to biochemistry, offering a deeper understanding of the body-brain-mind-consciousness continuum. While she did not elaborate on a taxonomy of emotions, she linked peace directly to health and well-being, observing: *"Part of being a healthy person is being well integrated and at peace."*

She further explained: *"Thus, we might refer to the whole system as a psychosomatic information network, linking 'psyche,'...Mind and body, psyche and soma"* (The Research of Candace Pert, PhD, 2023).

Here science and spirituality intersect. Psychoneuroimmunology (PNI) and the *Nāṭya Śāstra* together illuminate the significance of *Sthāyī Bhāva* at the levels of consciousness, heart, and body. Pert's research provides scientific evidence that awareness and consciousness have a biochemical basis – that the mind and body are indeed one, and that emotions and feelings form the bridge linking the two. She wrote:

"The chemicals that are running our body and our brain are the same chemicals that are involved in emotion. And that says to me that we'd better pay more attention to emotions with respect to health."

Candace Pert was among the scientists who did not shy away from acknowledging spirituality: *"Yes, we all have a biochemical psychosomatic network run by intelligence, an intelligence that has no bounds and that is not owned by any individual but shared among all of us in a bigger network, the macrocosm to our microcosm, the 'big psychosomatic network in the sky.' And in this greater network of all humanity, all life, we are each of us an individual nodal point, each an access point into a larger intelligence."* This larger intelligence is what Vedic literature identifies as Consciousness, or *Brahman*. According to Pert, *"It is this shared connection that gives us our most profound sense of spirituality, making us feel connected, whole. As above, so below."*

Crucially, this Consciousness is not experienced cognitively but through the Heart. What the Vedic seers articulated millennia ago is being scientifically rediscovered today. Doc Childre, founder of the HeartMath Institute, states: *"Becoming our true self involves the fading of self-centredness, judgment and separation, and through the practice of compassion, kindness and cooperation, while learning to increase the coherence between our heart, mind and emotions in our day-to-day energy expenditures. This brings about the elusive 'peace' humanity has searched for forever."*

The Mother on Peace and Calm

Individual transformation through self-transcendence appears to be the path ahead. As pauses to review its collective life – marked by climate change, environmental degradation, and wars between nations – spiritual awareness emerges as the guiding light to lead us from darkness into illumination. Though not much literature is available on Śānta Rasa, The Mother placed great emphasis on the theme of peace and calm in her talks. She related peace to a dynamic inner force intrinsically connected with health and well-being. In the *Complete Works of Sri Aurobindo (CWSA)* and the *Complete Works of The Mother (CWM)*, peace is presented as the foundation of human awakening and sādhana.

In many of her interactions with aspirants, The Mother repeatedly emphasised the need to invite peace: *"Make peace and calm your friends and call them: Come, peace, peace, peace, peace, come"* (CWM, 6:314). She further insisted that peace must permeate even the physical body: *"Catch hold of peace deep within and push it into the cells of the body. With the peace will come back the health."* This illustrates the continuity of the Sthāyī Bhāva of peace deep within, and the psychoneuro connection that allows this inner emotion to spread through every cell, fostering health and psychosomatic well-being. According to The Mother, the ability to ward off illness depends less on physical strength than on inner strength, which is always associated with calm and peace.

Unfortunately, strength and power have too often been misunderstood as outer action and raw dynamism. Wars are the result of such flawed mental models. We must reframe power – not as restless activity, but as a quiet, steady force. Humanity remains unaware of the true nature of peace because it has rarely experienced its depths. The Mother described peace not as passivity, but as a dynamic force of great potency. She affirmed, *"...all those who are really strong, powerful, are always very calm. It is only the weak who are agitated... This true quietude is always a sign of force. Calmness belongs to the strong"* (Dalal, 1991, p. 149).

Individual Practices for Peace as Dharma

Our body and mind are like the strings of a musical instrument. Even with slight provocation from the outside, they produce sound. However, not all sounds create music. To create music, the musician must first prepare the instrument by tightening the string in right proportion, neither too tight nor too loose. With mindfulness, the musician can then create harmony. Similarly, if we wish to experience music in life through our body and mind, certain practices are essential. These practices create the right environment for harmony. Another powerful image is that of a flute. The flute, like our body and mind, must be free of blockages for the breath to flow through it and create music. The right attitude of body and mind, and health promoting lifestyle are integral to experience peace. We need to invite peace, as The Mother has explained, and invoke inner calm. This harmony can even create lasting changes in human DNA. The following practices can help take the first steps:

Practice 1. Peace can be experienced by stilling the mind. Breathwork – focussing on the rhythm and fullness of breath, or Prāna (Chi) brings peace. Inculcating this habit can gradually transform deep-rooted mental models.

Practice 2. Peace can also be experienced through meditation on the Great Elements (Pañca Mahābhūta) – especially Ether (Ākāśa) and Water. These elements exude peace and expand our consciousness when meditated upon. They allow us to step back from the superficial movements of the mind.

Practice 3. Consuming organic and natural food, grown and prepared with love rather than violence, supports inner peace. In contrast, modern industrial agriculture is violent toward Mother Nature and generates toxicity in both body and mind.

Practice 4. Physical well-being leads to mental well-being and opens the possibility of peace. Pratyāhāra – withdrawal from the external world – can be practiced daily before sleep. This involves turning the senses inward, disciplining the restlessness of the body through steady posture, and quietly observing the restlessness of the mind without judgement or reaction. Even a few minutes of this practice before retiring can rejuvenate the self.

Practice 5. Alternate nostril breathing (Nāḍī Śuddhi Prāṇāyāma) calms the sympathetic nervous system while activating the parasympathetic system, restoring pH balance and creating peace. Alongside this,

Bhrāmarī Prāṇāyāma – named after the Indian bee – instantly calms the mind, relieving agitation and anxiety. However, it is essential to learn Prāṇāyāma scientifically from a qualified Master. During the Covid-19 pandemic, research demonstrated the calming effects of Bhrāmarī Prāṇāyāma on the mind.

New Research Frontiers

Inner peace can generate vibrations of outer peace, creating an environment free from fear. Many places in India where *Ṛṣis* established their Ashrams were called *Abhayāraṇya* – forests without fear. These sages had conquered their inner fears and attainted a state of deep inner peace. Tradition holds that even animals such as lions and tigers, upon entering Abhayāraṇya, would become calm and refrain from harming others. The key question is: how do we create such safe spaces within our families, schools, colleges, workplaces, cities, and nations?

By practicing methods that clear negative emotions – emotions that often generate violence, individuals cultivate inner peace, which in turn enables the creation of safe external spaces.

One modern case study is the Cities4Peace initiative of the Art of Living Foundation in Cyprus, undertaken in collaboration with the UN Peacekeeping Force. With the goal of strengthening social cohesion and understanding between Turkish Cypriot and Greek Cypriot communities, UNFICYP sponsored a unique peacebuilding methodology developed by **Cities4Peace** (an initiative of the Art of Living Foundation and the International Association for Human Values). This program sought to empower community changemakers from both groups to enhance their mental well-being and leadership capacity, thereby enabling innovative approaches to peace and social harmony on the island.

Between March and June 2022, the **Cities4Peace** team customised and delivered two peacebuilding workshops for 20 women leaders drawn from both sides of the conflict. Participants were selected not only for the diversity of their professional and social experience but also for their commitment to becoming part of the solution and trusted bridges between Cypriots. The training included IAHV's evidence-based SKY (Sudarśana Kriyā) breathing and meditation practices to build inner resilience and improve mental well-being. In addition, interactive discussions and group processes helped participants strengthen systems thinking and develop networks of trust.

Effective peacebuilding requires disciplined approaches, structured processes, and coherent frameworks. Yet at its heart, it depends on individuals who are inspired, committed, and bold enough to implement innovative methods to promoting peace and harmony. Unfortunately, the well-being and socio-emotional needs of peacemakers, the very community leaders and changemakers who design and implement programs, are often overlooked. Equally ignored is their need to build leadership capacity and develop innovative skills for sustaining peace. Community changemakers are vital resources for holistic peace solutions. Rooted at the grassroots level, they understand local challenges intimately and thus play a critical role in maintaining safe and peaceful communities. The Cities4Peace program addresses this gap by equipping such stakeholders with evidence-based tools and strategies to improve mental health, heal trauma, enhance resilience, and strengthen socio-emotional skills – empowering them to design effective and innovative responses to the challenges that arise in peacebuilding work.

The second important research frontier concerns agriculture and our relationship with Mother Earth. When the food we consume is cultivated through violent and exploitative practices, how can we expect peace in our bodies, minds, and societies? Visionary barrister Polly Higgins argued that ecocide should be recognised as the fifth crime against peace. She pointed out that climate change, industrial deforestation, tar-sands oil extraction, oceanic dead zones, and other forms of ecological devastation cause wars, conflicts, suffering, and species extinction. "We can no longer profit out of damage to the Earth," Higgins stated. "Our laws are no longer fit for purpose,"

According to her, "Ecocide would impose 'superior responsibility' on those people who take decisions that ultimately destroy the Earth, so that they are responsible for the consequences of their actions and business decisions" (Higgins, 2012). Āyurveda, one of the oldest literatures on well-being, describes four types of lives one may live: Hita Āyu (sustainable life), Sukha Āyu (pleasant life), Ahita Āyu (harmful or unsustainable life), and Duḥkha Āyu (painful life). To live a Hita Āyu – sustainable and wholesome life – one essential condition is reverence for all life, including Mother Nature.

New Beginning or Point of Return?

Words like *Summary* or *Conclusion* seem too limiting to end this chapter. Indian civilisation is one of the oldest, and vedic literature is not just philosophy it is Sanātana Dharma. *Sanātana* means beyond time, eternal. *Dharma* comes from the root *dhri* – to uphold. The laws of Nature, whether in the external physical world or the inner world of the individual, are ultimately connected, for we are the microcosm of the macrocosm. Modern quantum physics is rediscovering truths that the sages already knew – that all beings are made of the same energy and are deeply interconnected. The seers encoded this wisdom in mantras, prayers, and rituals. Yet human beings remain in a transitional stage of evolution, where animal instincts still dominate daily living. At the same time, human consciousness is evolving beyond this mould, discovering the potential for self-transcendence. This is both a new beginning and a return to origins.

Satish Kumar, in his editorial for *Resurgence*, reminds us: "There is a word in Sanskrit for the point of return: *Pratikramaṇa*. Its opposite is *atikramaṇa*, which means stepping outside of our natural limits. *Atikramaṇa* happens when we break universal laws. Returning to the centre of one's being or to the source of inner wisdom is *Pratikramaṇa*" (Kumar, 2007).

The path from *atikramaṇa* to *pratikramana* passes through the heart and consciousness. It is about the journey of transcendence: rising beyond our lower, self-centred nature and connecting with an expanded sense of Self. In yogic psychology, the *Anāhata Cakra* (Heart Chakra) is described as the midpoint between the lower and higher chakras.

Modern research resonates with this ancient wisdom. Candace Pert advocates Heart Chakra mediation for psychosomatic wellness. Just as psychosomatic illness arises from imbalance between body and psyche, psychosomatic wellness emerges from their integration. Similarly, psychologist Carl Jung describes the transcendent function as arising from the union of conscious and unconscious contents. It is called *transcendent* because it enables the transition from one attitude to another organically, without the loss of the unconscious. This function, Jung notes, has a *synthetic* quality, marked by the birth of a *new attitude* (Odorisio, 2014).

Peace as the new dharma can therefore be seen as both a beginning and a return – a *pratikramana,* a U-Turn toward ancient wisdom centred in the heart. By not merely reciting but truly invoking *Śānti* – peace – from within the heart and radiating its vibrations outward to the cosmos, we foster psychosomatic well-being, societal harmony, and universal peace.

Aum Śānti Śānti Śāntiḥ

References Cited

Arment, J. F. (2018, February). *World Peace is Not Transactional.* International Cities of Peace. https://www.internationalcitiesofpeace.org/2018/02/

Āum Śānti Śānti Śānti. (2000). *Swādhyāya Mandal Pardi, Valsad, Gujarat* [Reference for Sūtras from Ṛgveda, Yajurveda and Atharva Veda)

Bharadwaj, A. (2016, September 3). The Story of the Origin of Natyashastra – 1. *Prekshaa.* https://www.prekshaa.in/story-origin-natyashastra-1

Chaudhary, S. (2002). *Glimpses of Indian poetics.* Sahitya Akademi.

Christie, D. J. (2006). What is Peace Psychology the Psychology of? *Journal of Social Issues, 62*(1), 1–17. https://doi.org/10.1111/j.1540-4560.2006.00436.x

Christie, D. J., Tint, B. S., Wagner, R. V., & Winter, D. D. (2008). Peace psychology for a peaceful world. American Psychologist, 63(6), 540–552. https://doi.org/10.1037/0003-066x.63.6.540

Dalal, A. S. (1991). *Psychology, Mental Health, and Yoga* (p. 149). Sri Aurobindo Ashram Press, 1991.

Deutsch, M. (1995). William James: The first peace psychologist. *Peace and Conflict: Journal of Peace Psychology,* 1, 27–36.

Gilbert, P. (2009). *The Compassionate Mind: A new approach to life's challenges* (p. 9). Constable.

Hawkins, David R. (2012). *Power vs Force,* Hay House Publishing, USA.

Higgins, P. (2012). What Will Your Legacy Be? *Resurgence.* https://www.resurgence.org/magazine/article3554-what-will-your-legacy-be.html

James, S. P. (2017). *A Psychology of Peace: Development of a Transcendent Ontological Worldview* [Doctoral dissertation, University of Hawai'i at Mānoa]. ScholarSpace. https://scholarspace.manoa.hawaii.edu/items/7844120d-74dc-48b3-9f6c-0b1e21ad8bba

Knapp, S. (2022). Stephen Knapp and his books on Spiritual Enlightenment and Vedic Culture. https://www.stephen-knapp.com/

Kumar, S. (2007). Welcome. *Resurgence.* https://www.resurgence.org/magazine/article120-welcome.html

Maslow, A. H. (1972). *The further reaches of human nature.* Penguin.

Merton, T. (2009). *Conjectures of a guilty bystander.* Image Books/Doubleday.

Odorisio, D. M. (2014). The Alchemical Heart: A Jungian Approach to the Heart Center in the Upanisads and in Eastern Christian Prayer. *International Journal of Transpersonal Studies, 33*(1), 5.

https://doi.org/10.24972/ijts.2014.33.1.27

Paudel, P., & Mohan, M. V. (2020). *Natyashastra Part 1* (pp. 116–119). Samkrit Promotion Foundation.

Pearsall, P. (1998). *The heart's code.* Broadway Books.

Pert, C. B. (2003). *Molecules of emotion.* Scribner.

Saha, S. (n.d.). Module 14: Bhāmaha and Indian Poetics. In *Indian Literary Criticism and Theory*. MHRD-UGC e-PG Pathshala.

Ṣastri, P. P. (1940). *The Philosophy of Aesthetic Pleasure, etc.* Annamalai University.

Śrīmad Bhagavad Gītā. (1997). Gorakhpur: Gītā Press.

The Research of Candace Pert, PhD. (2023). Healing Cancer. https://www.healingcancer.info/book/export/html/34

Yogapedia. (2019). What is Rita? – Definition from Yogapedia. https://www.yogapedia.com/definition/11563/rita

Appendix 4

This paper was presented at the Indica Conference on Ancient Indian Pedagogy, Ujjain, 2023

Atharvaveda Pedagogy, Knowledge, and Medhā Creation: The Educational Heritage of India

Mala Kapadia, Director, Transdisciplinary Research Initiatives, Anaadi Foundation, Palani, Tamil Nādu, India

Keywords – Meta-Knowledge, Medhā, Self-Mastery, Heart-Based Learning, Nature-Centric Pedagogy, Svabhāva and Svadharma, Self-Transcendence

Abstract-

Humanity today is facing four interconnected crises: Ethical, Economic, Emotional, and Ecological. However, the Ethical crisis appears to be the root cause of the other three. A major factor contributing to these crises is value-devoid education – education lacking the guidance of Dharma – which has led much of humanity towards xenophobia and a truly materialistic life. Modern education, a product of the Industrial Revolution and Machine-Age Thinking, reduces human identity to 'hands that work' and 'a brain that thinks,' overlooking the vital roles of the Heart and Consciousness and our interconnectedness with soil and soul. To reimagine humanity's way forward and to educate future generations, India must take a U-turn and draw upon the wisdom of the Ṛṣis for the intent, content, and pedagogy of education.

This paper draws upon the Atharva Veda, which teaches that one can be a competent teacher only after achieving self-knowledge and being able to transmit it to learners. Pedagogically, this results in nature-centric learning that leads to self-mastery and self-transcendence, as the learner realises that the macrocosm and microcosm are One. Methods such as joyful learning, student-centric learning, inquiry-based learning, and forest/nature-based are often celebrated as modern innovations. However, the Sūktas of the Atharva Veda reveal that such approaches were already integral to Vedic education.

The Atharva Veda also articulates a clear intent and outcome of education. The creation of Medhā or Higher Intelligence, the integration of Head and Heart, and the centrality of Dharma form the very foundation of learning. This paper explores Medhā as Right Temper, in contrast to the Western notion of Scientific Temper, which has heavily influenced contemporary education.

Medhā thus emerges as a guiding force for achieving life's goals, enabling the integration of Svabhāva and Svadharma into pedagogy.

Introduction

The World Today – Challenges and the Way Forward

Humanity today faces a fourfold crisis – Ethical, Economic, Emotional, and Ecological. Among these, the Economic crisis is felt most immediately, as our lives revolve around numbers. The Ecological crisis took longer to register, and only recently has climate change begun to be taken seriously. The Emotional crisis is visible in the growing prevalence of mental health issues. Yet underlying all of these is the Ethical crisis, and it is here that the root of the problem, and its solution, lies. The only lasting answer is education. Not mere information, but education that cultivates insight and intuition. In Bharat, this is called Vidyā. As the tradition declares: *"Sā vidyā yā vimuktaye"* – true Vidyā is that which liberates us from ignorance. Vidyā is rooted in Dharma, the First Principles that shape both worldview and self-view. Only Dharma-Vidyā can resolve the Ethical crisis, ensuring that the other three do not overwhelm us.

Here, Bharat has a distinctive role. Every individual, and every nation, has a destiny to fulfill. As S. K. Chakraborty notes: *"India has always existed for humanity and not for herself, and it is for humanity and not for herself that she must be great."*[viii]

This spirit is woven into our prayers: Sarve sukhinaḥ santu, sarve santu nirāmayāḥ – may all be happy, may all be free of illness. The Ṛṣis recited Śānti mantras not only for individual well-being, but also for global and cosmic peace. They recognised the profound interconnectedness of all existence. The macrocosm and microcosm are not merely related, they are one – Yat piṇḍe tat Brahmāṇḍe.

Hence, Vedic chants resonate with harmony, inclusiveness, and higher aspiration. This paper explores select Sūktas of the Atharva Veda to illustrate how the ancient Indian education system embodied these principles and offers insights for addressing the crises of our own time.

Significance of the Atharva Veda

The Atharva Veda, also known as Ātma Veda, Brahmā Veda, Bheṣaja Veda, and Amṛta Veda[ix], deals with multiple dimensions of life, including education. One of its central concerns is self-knowledge – understanding the Self as the Cosmic or Higher Self. R.C. Sharma observes, *"The Ṛg Veda, the Yajur Veda, and the Sāma Veda bless us for the other world, but the Atharva Veda blesses us both for the other world as well as for this one."*[x] This unique orientation makes the Atharva Veda deeply relevant to practical living.

Its Sūktas cover themes such as Ātma and Mānas, body and health, Ātma-bala (strength of the Self) and Indriya-jaya (mastery over the senses), warding off evil, and cultivating su-saṃskṛta individuals capable of building a Rāṣṭra (nation) worthy of the Devatās. They emphasise both internal harmony and external peace – and when necessary, strategies for confronting or conquering enemies. At its heart, however, the Atharva Veda is committed to the welfare of humanity. A healthy life, according to the AV, requires the balance of body and mānas (mind). Many Sūktas outline this foundation of health while addressing relationships, society, environment, and education – presenting them as deeply interconnected.

The authors of these Sūktas were the Atharvan and Āṅgirasa Ṛṣis. In ancient times, Ṛṣis devoted to Agni were called Atharvans. The etymology itself is instructive: Tharva signifies distraction, fragmentation, or lack of mindfulness, whereas Atharva denotes one who is mindful, steadfast, focussed, and rooted.[xi] In AV sūktas, mantras to achieve this state and description of this state is given by the Ācārya to the learner. Alongside them, the Āṅgirasa Ṛṣis also contributed. The word Āṅgirasa refers to the Rasa (essence, vitality, or flow) within the body and mind. Without this rasa, the senses fail to function at their peak; the individual becomes disengaged, disinterested, or even paralysed and depressed. To restore this balance, Yoga practices such as Prānayama, Āyurvedic herbs, and specific mantras were prescribed. The Sūktas attributed to Āṅgirasa Ṛṣis focus on mantra, mani (sacred gems) and auṣadhi (herbs) as pathways to restore vitality.[xii] The Atharva Veda thus addresses not only the individual level – ensuring long, healthy and meaningful life – but also the national level. Its vision of education and health extends to the very fabric of society and governance. Two verses from the Atharva Pariśiṣṭa highlight the importance of Atharvan Ṛṣis for kings and nations:[xiii]

यस्य राज्ञो जनपदे अथर्वा शान्तिपरगः ।
निवसत्यपि तद्राज्यं वर्तते निरुपद्रवम्॥

तस्माद्राजा विशेषेण अथर्वाणं जितेन्द्रियम्।
दानसम्मानसत्कारैर्नित्यं समभिपूजयेत् ॥

These verses proclaim that the kingdom where peace-loving Atharvan Ṛṣis reside will prosper without disturbance. Hence, a king should honour and revere the Atharvan Ṛṣis, who, having mastered their senses (jitendriya), ensure the moral and spiritual health of the nation.

Such jitendriya Ṛṣis also served as Ācāryas, and therefore the education they imparted produced learners who were likewise trained in self-mastery, discipline, and inner harmony.

Education in the Atharva Veda

The Atharva Veda contains 726 Sūktas and 5,977 mantras, organised into 20 Kaṇḍa. Many of these are also found in the Ṛg Veda. Notably, the first Kaṇḍa focusses on education and builds an insightful sense of interconnectedness through its Sūktas. This Kaṇḍa is titled Medhā Janana – "the generation of higher intelligence." In modern educational terms, it corresponds to the idea of learning outcomes, where the outcome is Medhā, or higher intelligence in the learner.

The text then addresses the crucial question: How is Medhā generated? Here, the Atharva Veda offers a remarkably holistic vision of education. It emphasises:

- The intent of education in both teacher and learner
- The pedagogy of teaching and learning
- The character and qualities of teacher and student
- The foundational content with which learning begins
- The outcomes of Medhā at both individual and collective levels

In short, the Why, How, and What of education are seamlessly woven into these Sūktas, making the Atharva Veda one of the earliest texts to articulate a comprehensive educational philosophy.

Why Medhā and not just any intelligence?

Medhā is not just IQ or even EQ in today's language; it goes far beyond both. Plants and animals also have intelligence. However, human beings are unique because they have the capability to transcend survival-based intelligence. Medhā is that higher faculty of mind which enables grasping, understanding, retention, and application of knowledge.[xiv] This is also known as Dhāraṇavatī Buddhi – an intelligence sustained in memory and usable across diverse life situations.

What makes Medhā different from other forms of intelligence is that it is not produced merely by external instruction. It emerges within the individual as a process of deep learning from the Heart. Medhā is wisdom and insight that arise by Divine Grace and through expanded Consciousness.[xv] In ancient Indian education, the Heart was central. It was regarded as the gateway to deeper knowledge - knowledge that expands consciousness and enables higher living. Modern education, especially in the West, is only beginning to rediscover the role of the Heart and Higher entities in cultivating intelligence.

Medhā is received by Daiva (Divine Grace). It is considered an 'utsphoṭa' – a spontaneous emergence within, activated by Higher Devatās. In the Upanayana ritual, before formal learning begins with the Guru, a three-day Medhā-invoking process is performed. Multiple Devatās are invoked so that Medhā arises in the learner. While Maa Sarasvatī is naturally invoked, many other cosmic energies are also called upon to awaken Medhā in the Heart.

Medhā is not meant merely for academic success or employment. Its purpose is to expand the narrow, ego-centred identity of the self into the Universal Self – experiencing the Oneness and Interconnectedness with all existence. For individuals and nations alike, this self-transcendence is essential. It shapes both a worldview and a self-view necessary not only for human evolution and peaceful coexistence, but also for deep ecological balance. Medhā represents sāttvic buddhi – a mind illuminated by clarity and goodness. Sattva inspires selflessness and fosters social harmony. By contrast, the crises humanity faces today – the 4Es: Ethical, Economic, Emotional, and Environmental – are rooted in a limited intellect dominated by survivalist instincts and disconnected from Nature. Wars for power are the outcome of such a narrow intellect. Medhā buddhi, on the other hand, cultivates inclusivity, harmony, and peace. Pandit Satavalekar ji, in his commentary on the Medhā Janana Sūktas, highlights two key terms: Ekatā (unity) and Saṅgathana (organisation).

Pandit ji further explains that aspiration or self-actualisation, in Maslow's terms, is an innate human need. But when guided by Medhā and Divine aid, aspiration becomes inclusive and compassionate, rather than trampling others for selfish gain. Lyle Spencer, a modern expert on competencies, notes that Achievement Motivation contains seeds of self-destruction unless infused with Dharma. This is true for individuals, organisations, societies, and Nations.

How is Medhā cultivated through education?

The pedagogy of Medhā janana is inseparable from the intent of both teacher and learner. This paper examines Kaṇḍa 1, Sūkta 1, Mantras 1-4. This single Sūkta already reveals multiple shades of pedagogy, along with the prerequisites for its practice. Pedagogy, in this context, arises not just from teaching methods, but from intent: "Why am I teaching? How do I wish to learn?" These questions are embedded within the Sūkta. Here, the teacher is called Vācaspati and Vasospati.

ये त्रि॒षप्ताः प॑रि॒यन्ति॒ विश्वा॑ रू॒पाणि॒ बिभ्र॑तः । वा॒चस्पति॒र्बला तेषां॑ त॒न्वो
अ॒द्य द॑धातु मे ॥ १ ॥
पुन॒रेहि॑ वाचस्पते दे॒वेन॒ मन॑सा स॒ह । वसो॑ष्पते॒ निर॑मय॒ मय्ये॒वास्तु
मयि॑ श्रु॒तम् ॥२॥

इ॒हैवाभि वि त॑नू॒भे आ॒र्त्नी॑ इ॒व ज्यया॑ । वा॒चस्पति॒र्नि य॑च्छतु॒ मय्ये॒वास्तु॒ मयि॑ श्रु॒तम् ॥३॥
उप॑हूतो वा॒चस्पति॒रुपा॒स्मान्वा॒चस्पति॑र्ह्वयताम् । सं श्रु॒तेन॑ गमेमहि मा श्रु॒तेन॒ वि रा॑धिषि ॥४॥

Pre-Pedagogy: Competency of the Ācārya and the Intent of the Ācārya – Devena Manasā

First and foremost, the words used to describe the teacher in this Sūkta need to be understood with great care. Who is teaching—the very Being of the Ācārya—is central to how pedagogy evolves. The teacher is described as Vācaspati and Vasospati. In the Atharva Veda (AV), each mantra has its own Ṛṣi and Devatā. For the *Medhā Janana Mantra*, the Ṛṣi is Atharva, and the Devatā is Vācaspati. The same term – Vācaspati – is also used for the Ācārya.

The meaning of Vācaspati is *"one who is master of Vacas (Vāṇī, speech)."* But here, Vāṇī refers not to everyday speech (Vaikharī) but to a much deeper, higher dimension of language. As Devata or Ācārya, Vācaspati is one who is endowed with Para Vāṇī, the highest level of communication. *Para*, literally meaning "beyond," arises from Sat-Cit-Ānanda – Truth, Consciousness, and Bliss. Such a Vāṇī awakens Medhā (meta-intelligence) in the learner. Such a Vāṇī awakens Medhā (meta-intelligence) in the learner.

This is possible only when the Ācārya is deeply rooted in spiritual practice and teaches with Devena Manasā – a pure, elevated intent aligned with higher aspirations. In the Bhagavad Gītā, Chapter 16, the contrast between Daivī (divine) and Āsurī (demonic) natures is described vividly. Teaching with Devena Manasā requires Daivi qualities – Śubha Saṅkalpa (benevolent intent), universal welfare, and wellbeing of all beings. In contrast, Āsurī-nature teachers create division, territories, greed, and selfishness. The contemporary "4E" crisis – ethics, economics, emotions, and ecology – can be traced back to the dominance of Āsurī tendencies in education. Thus, the paradigm shift to Devena Manasā in pedagogy is critical for humanity's survival and flourishing. Modern management expert Lyle Spencer, who also has engaged with Indian wisdom, affirmed in personal correspondence with the author that achievement motivation carries within it the own seeds of destruction if it is not balanced with Dharma. When guided by Āsurī Sampat (as described in the Gītā), achievement motivation leads to imbalance. But when directed by Daivī Sampat, grounded in Dharma, it nurtures holistic growth.

The other word used for Ācārya in this mantra is Vasospati. Pandit Satavalekar interprets this as *Vasvoka pati* – one who can teach not only theory but also practical, experiential wisdom.[xvi] The *Wisdom Library* a also records another interpretation: Vasospati as the God of Prosperity or Wealth. Since Vasu also means "cows," one can intuitively imagine a learning space enriched by abundance – not merely material wealth, but the wealth of expanded consciousness, higher awareness, and inner prosperity.[xvii]

Satvalekar ji also points out another variation in the *Atharva Veda Pippalāda Saṃhitā,* where the term is Asoṣpati instead of Vasospati. *Asu* means Prāna. Thus, Asoṣpati refers to one who has mastered Prāṇa. In this interpretation, the Ācārya must be a yogi who practices Prāṇāyāma and Indriya-jaya (mastery over senses), cultivating a refined yogic state. AV contains many mantras to invoke and sustain such states.

Only a yogi – speaking from Para Vāṇī and who has conquered Prāṇa – can invoke Devatās in teaching. This invocation of Devatās was once an integral part of pedagogy in ancient Bhārata, now entirely absent in modern education. When Devatās are invoked, learners naturally awaken Daivī Sampat. Without such higher aspiration, education risks generating only Āsurī Sampat, perpetuating division and imbalance in society.

Kaṇḍa 3, Sūkta 8 contains two particularly relevant mantras here. The Ṛṣis understood human psychology deeply: the innate drive to grow, expand, and become better is universal. Yet, left unchecked, this drive can reduce itself to mere materialistic expansion. Thus, the need to invoke higher energies is emphasized.

हुवे सोमं सवितारं नमोभिः विश्वानादित्यां अहमुत्तरत्वे । (३/८/३)

In this mantra, Soma (Moon), Savitā (Sun), and all the Ādityas of the cosmos are invoked to guide for the seeker towards Uttaratva – higher states of existence. Uttaratva is not just growth but an ascent into better, expanded being. This connects directly with modern constructs such as achievement motivation, self-actualisation, and self-transcendence (Maslow). The Ṛṣis caution that Āsurī growth leads to the 4E crisis, hence higher guidance is indispensable.

इह इत् असाथ, न परो गमाथ । (मं. ४)

Mantra 4 warns: "Follow only this path, not any other." The Ṛṣi recognizes the pull of evolutionary instincts and survival-driven impulses that can lead us astray. The insistence is clear: follow the Devatā path.

When followed, this path unifies the learner's mānas, actions, and saṅkalpa (resolve). It fosters unity and harmony, as expressed in Mantra 5:

वः मनांसि सं वः व्रतानि सं,
वः आकूतीः सम् । (मं. ५)

Pedagogy – Playful and Joyful (Ni-rāmaya)

Teaching pedagogy has to be playful and joy-centred. Mantra 2 of this sūkta offers a profound insight into the nature of learning. The learner requests the Ācārya: "Teach me in a joyful way." Only in recent times has modern educational psychology begun to recognise this approach. When learning is connected with the Heart – not just the cognitive or brain functions – when the whole person is involved and engaged, true joyful learning becomes possible. The Atharva Veda mantras often work like codes. In this case, the single word *Ni-rāmaya* contains the essence of an entire pedagogy. Modern neuroscience now confirms that such joy-centred learning fosters long-term retention. Yet the AV ṛṣi did not expand on this "code", which is why, when searching for ancient Indian pedagogical insights, one might easily overlook this mantra. However, the entire play of life is revealed in this one word. When the Ācārya is a Vācaspati (master of speech), an expert communicator drawing from Para-vāṇī (transcendental speech), and teaches with Devena Manasā (a pure and divine intent) aimed at transmitting knowledge and awakening Medhā (meta-intelligence), then there is no stress, pressure, or burden of learning – only joyful discovery.

Self-Discipline – Niyama

तद्वाचा श्रस्या विधयैदं पक्षं संस्कर्ते ! मनसैव ग्रहा संस्करोति ॥ (Aitareya Br. ५।३३)[xviii]
The earlier three Vedas purify the vāṇī, or speech, of an individual – making it su-saṃskṛta (refined). However, in the Atharva Veda, it is the

mānas (mind) of an individual that is purified and madesu-saṃskṛta. A purified mind (śuddha mānas) leads to mastery over the senses (indriya-jaya). Mantra 3 in the sūkta speaks of *ni-yacchatu* – self-restraint. The learner is requesting the Ācārya not only to live with self-discipline himself but also to guide the students in embodying the same. The relationship between Ācārya and learner is described through the metaphor of a bow. The string is tied between the two ends of the bow, and only when it is well-strung can the arrow be shot. Here, the two ends and the string represent the Ācārya and the learner; the bow symbolises Knowledge, and the arrow signifies the outcome of Knowledge. Without self-discipline, the saṃskāra (refinement) of the mind is not possible. Equally essential is the discipline of svādhyāya (self-study) and manana (contemplation), which allow Knowledge to settle deep within the learner. This mantra also expresses the student's desirefor long-lasting Knowledge – "May the Knowledge be retained by me." Knowledge, in this sense, is not meant merely for examinations or jobs, but for living a meaningful and integrated life. Today, organisations are struggling with a knowing-doing Gap. Self-discipline bridges this gap, transforming Knowledge into Action.

Self-discipline leads to Self-Mastery. Unfortunately, this crucial dimension is what many modern education campuses lack.

Learner-Centred; Question-Centred Pedagogy

The pedagogy described here is learner-centric. As stated in Mantra 4, it is the learner who asks questions to the Ācārya, and the Ācārya who responds to them. Unfortunately, in modern times, we tend to celebrate this pedagogy as a Western innovation, forgetting that it was originally one of our profound contributions to humanity and educational psychology.

The ability to ask meaningful questions arises only when the learner has engaged in pre-thinking and reflection – Manana – on the subject. Asking questions is both an art and a science. This pedagogy makes the learner self-responsible for knowledge rather than a passive receiver of information. What questions to ask, in what sequence, how to connect diverse strands of information, and how to integrate knowledge holistically requires deep readiness on the part of the learner. Learning through questioning cultivates proactivity in the learner. Ultimately, in this pedagogy, knowledge is co-created by the Ācārya and the learner together a dynamic question-answer dialogue.

What is the content that creates such Medhā? What knowledge is the learner truly seeking?

The first mantra of this Sūkta clearly specifies the nature of knowledge that the learner seeks. The learner is not here merely for job-oriented or utilitarian knowledge. The learner carries a deep inquisitiveness, a thirst to know Cosmology – the knowledge of the Universe. It is this knowledge of the Cosmos that leads to self-knowledge and meta-knowledge within the learner. Such was the readiness of learners even in the times of the Atharva Veda (AV).

Triśaptam ($3 \times 7 = 21$): there are 21 Padārthas or Tattvas that constitute the Cosmos. The Ācārya is invoked: *Teach us these Padārthas so that this knowledge may be sustained within us*. Of these, three are the energies of Sattva, Rajas, and Tamas. Seven are the Pañca Mahābhūtas, the Tanmātras, and Ahaṃkāra – each of which is composed of the three Guṇas. Together, these 21 Tattvas create both the Cosmos and the human being. Once I know this meta-knowledge, all other forms of knowledge begin to manifest within me. This is what generates Meta-Intelligence – Medhā – within the learner. As Yamuna Harshvardhan writes about the ancient Indian knowledge system: "Nurturing the student's mind to look with awe at the magnitude of creation helped to churn the cells of creativity in the mind. These were ways to divert one's mind from single-pointed fears, overly centred around the individual, to the magnificence and unfathomable qualities of creation of which the individual is an integral part."[xix]

The knowledge of Triguṇa and Pañca Mahābhūta enables the learner to understand one's own Svabhāva (nature) and Svadharma (duty).

This is not merely theoretical physics or anatomy; it is an expansion of self-understanding and an awakening to the interconnectedness of all existence within the Cosmos. Such knowledge helps the learner evolve beyond a xenophobic life that leads to Āsurī Sampad (demonic tendencies), and instead facilitates self-transcendence towards Daivī Sampat (divine qualities).

Modern Applications of Atharva Veda

Only with one Sūkta of Kaṇḍa 1, and just four Mantras, we can open up numerous avenues for research and application in modern education. The competence of the teacher or Ācārya, the intention (mānas) of the Ācārya, the outcome of developing Meta-Intelligence (Medhā), playful methodologies, joyful learning, learner-centred and question-centred pedagogy, and the initiation into meta-knowledge – all these are powerful guiding orientations for modern educators.

The author has been using the framework of Pañca Mahābhūtas combined with Triguṇa to train Ācāryas who gain deeper self-knowledge and are able to identify their own strengths as teachers. The next step is to extend this application towards understanding learners and mapping their unique learning needs. Another paper is currently being written in this direction. In the West, personality theories based on the works of Carl Jung, particularly the MBTI, are widely used in educational psychology and faculty development programs. However, employing Pañca Mahābhūtas in the context of education psychology opens up a vast, unexplored field of research for us as Bhāratīyas.

Medhā-janana (the awakening of Medhā) lies at the heart of meta-knowledge. As Sri Aurobindo says: *"Our first necessity, if India is to survive and do her appointed work in the world, is that the youth of India should learn to think - to think on all subjects, to think independently, fruitfully, going to the heart of things, not stopped by their surface..."*[xx]

www.ingramcontent.com/pod-product-compliance
Lightning Source LLC
Chambersburg PA
CBHW032105090426
42743CB00007B/239
* 9 7 8 1 9 7 0 4 5 2 0 2 0 *